To Nett,
With love

Ian.
April 1971.

IN MY WAY

IN MY WAY

by

GEORGE BROWN

The Political Memoirs of
Lord George-Brown

LONDON
VICTOR GOLLANCZ LTD
1971

ISBN 0 575 00696 x

Printed in Great Britain by
The Camelot Press Ltd., London and Southampton

FOR SOPHIE AND THE FAMILY
who have made it possible
and suffered so much because of it

Contents

Illustrations

Acknowledgements

THIS BOOK REALLY grew out of an idea of Mr Bill Greig, the well-known political writer. When I went into the Government he quite voluntarily ended his career with the *Mirror* Group of newspapers and from then on served with me for no salary and indeed, I am ashamed to say, no reward at the end of the day. He thought that some attempt should be made to put down on paper the tremendous experiences I had lived through. To Bill I am most grateful.

And next to J. R. L. Anderson, one of the redoubtables of the old school of correspondents and specialist writers. Through all the relevant times, John was one of the respected and authoritative industrial correspondents, working for the old *Manchester Guardian*, later becoming Assistant Editor of the *Guardian*. As Bill pushed the idea on me, so did John push its fulfilment. Without his knowledge, experience, enthusiasm, determination and what he could teach me of his craft, the book would never have been finished. I owe him an enormous debt.

Then to those who have done the grindingly hard work: John's wife, Helen, and Janet Marsh who have typed and typed and typed; Jean Elliott who joined me as my political secretary after twenty years in the Foreign Office and not only shared the typing but has also done most of the research. They have all been marvellous.

Outside this small circle I owe also lots of thanks to people who have read and suggested corrections to my original manuscript. Some, especially those in the Public Service, would prefer, I have no doubt, not to be mentioned, but if they read this they will know that I am acknowledging what they did. Some, like Fred Catherwood, Director-General of the National Economic Development Council, I can appropriately name and thank.

None of these people or institutions bears any responsibility for the final outcome. The opinions, emphasis and deductions I make are mine alone – as, of course, are any errors which, despite all efforts, have still crept in. But errors can be of two kinds, as I discovered after the excerpts from this book had appeared in the *Sunday Times*. There is the error of fact when one ascribes an actual event, for example, to the wrong hour on the wrong day. Such errors I have tried to put right. But there are events which people variously interpret, showing that facts are not always facts; facts are not always absolutes. They depend so much, like beauty on the eye of the beholder, on one's involvement in the event. For this reason I have not changed those passages which were so violently attacked by one or two former members of the Diplomatic Service. They were not challenging the facts but my interpretation of them. They are entitled to their own but I cannot re-write mine. In the same way I have not changed my references to the United Nations Secretary General's decision which I think precipitated the Six Day War. Again, he was not challenging a fact. He saw it from a different angle. I have, however, included as an Appendix a letter from Dr Kissinger which bears upon my views on the recent British Ambassador in Washington. Again, this is two people looking at the same fact from different angles.

For permission to reproduce in this book the following photographs and illustrations, I am most grateful to: Associated Press Ltd, 15a, 15b, 17b, 19b; Camera Press Ltd, 8b; Central Press Photos Ltd, 9a; *Daily Express*, 13a; *Daily Herald*, 9b; *Daily Mail*, 20b; *Daily Telegraph*, 18a; Datali-Nohra, 16a; *Evening Standard* (Vicky cartoons), 8a, 11a; Fox Photos Ltd, 14, 24; Keystone Press Agency Ltd, 11b, 12a; Northcliffe Newspapers Ltd, 5a; Press Association Ltd, 10; Raymonds, Photographers of Derby, 6a and b, 7a and b, 13b, 22a and b, 23a; Sport and General Press Agency, 5b; Angela Thorne, the portrait painter, 4; Topix, 16b, 18b, 19a, 20a; United Nations, Frontispiece; United Press International Ltd, 17a, 21a, 21b, 23b.

I am also grateful to the *Daily Mirror*, the *Derby Evening Telegraph* and the *Sunday Times* for assistance with the photographs.

Finally, I am most grateful to Shapiro, Bernstein & Co Ltd, 38 Soho Square, London W1, for allowing me to reproduce several lines from the song 'My Way' which is an English lyric version of the original French song, 'Comme d'Habitude', lyrics by Paul Anka.

GEORGE-BROWN

Introduction

THE PROBLEM ABOUT writing a book is where to start, so why don't we start at the end. The title of this book is unashamedly cribbed from the song, 'My Way', so superbly sung by Frank Sinatra, and the opening lines of that song are:

And now the end is here and so I face the final curtain.
My friend, I'll say it clear, I'll state my case of which I'm certain.
I've lived a life that's full. I travelled each and every highway,
And more, much more than this, I did it my way.

A little bit later it has what is for me an even more meaningful verse:

Yes, there were times, I'm sure you knew,
When I bit off more than I could chew,
But through it all, when there was doubt,
I ate it up and spat it out.
I faced it all and I stood tall and did it my way.

And when I became Baron George-Brown (after one of the most hilarious exchanges of correspondence, which one of these days I hope will see the light of day, with a gentleman who signs himself as Garter Principal King of Arms) I felt just as though that song had summed up my full career. However, since then much has happened, and I remain somewhere near the centre of affairs. I should like to comment on some of the things that are happening.

First, there is the acceleration of Britain's movement towards Europe. It is not possible even now to know where we shall stand by the time this book is published, but everything encourages me to believe, as things are at the moment, that the negotiations will be

over by the middle of 1971; and that there should be no real obstacle
in our way to enlarging the European Community by the beginning
of 1972. I have written about Britain and the rest of Europe elsewhere in this book. I want here to state as clearly as I can how much
I believe that in every political sense Europe's future, as well as our
own, depends upon our succeeding in joining, and as I think there-
after leading, the community of Europe. It was one of the sadnesses
of my relations with that great man President de Gaulle, who died
while I was writing this book, that I failed to persuade him how
important this was for France and for Europe as a whole. As I have
recalled in a later chapter, he saw this as a conflict and not, as it
really is, as a complement.

We shall change the whole situation in the world if we succeed
in making Britain an integral part of Europe. The *economic* arguments are balanced. The *political* arguments are wholly on our
side. One of our problems is that we cannot speak loudly enough
about it before we join, in case by speaking loudly we spoil our
chances of joining.

The world is indivisible and another reason for the importance
I give to integrating Europe is the influence we might then be able
to exert in the Middle East. The situation there has been terribly,
tragically affected by the death of my great friend President Nasser.
Nobody is irreplaceable, otherwise the world would not have lasted
as long as it has, and we would not be here. But I think President
Nasser's loss will be felt heavily. He had an authority which could
have seen a solution to the situation created after the Six-Day
War on the basis of what I like to regard as my Resolution 242 of
the United Nations. He could have seen that through, simply
because of his stature and authority. On the other hand, his actual
loss seems to have concentrated some people's minds, and it is just
possible that the recognition of the need for an intelligent (meaning
a negotiated) solution, which could have been obstructed while he
lived because of other people's attitude to him, may now, in one
of those odd ways which affect human beings, be brought nearer by
his death. I refer in Chapter 12 to the division between the young
'hawks' in Israel and others. One of the interesting developments is
that since his death some, even of these, have taken up the 'dovish'
position which they had opposed so much while he lived, and the
talks are now to be resumed. Despite the noises which everyone feels
compelled to make, it looks again as though the chance to negotiate
a way out of this problem exists. If President Nasser's death can

hasten the solution which escaped him in life, it is a tragic reflection upon the extent to which we allow human and personal prejudices to get in the way.

As I write these words, we are in the middle of what looks like one of the most anarchical situations in British domestic history. We have known times when working men and women, and their trade unions and organizations, people from whom I have sprung and with whom I have spent my life, have found the going hard. We have known times when we have found the going a little easier and, to be frank, I have never known a time when most of us have found the going as good as it is at the end of 1970. Yet I don't think I have ever known a situation as involved, as difficult, as confused and as dangerous as the one we are creating now. This is not the conflict I was brought up on, between extremists and moderates. This is a business between those who believe in democracy and order and control, and those who simply want to destroy what exists.

It is absurd that people should go on strike rather than receive an increase of £2 or £3 a week. With £2 or £3 in one's hand one is better off than before and can then proceed to negotiate, to arbitrate or do whatever one can to improve one's position. I repeat therefore – the present attitude is absurd. But what is much more worrying is the effect on our whole democracy. So far, we have been the one country in the world which has been able to say that in almost any situation since the seventeenth century, democratic processes have prevailed. We can elect the wrong government, regret it, repent and pay for our mistake. But what we have never considered doing in my lifetime except possibly just after the First World War, is to try to get rid of an elected government by force. As I write these words I have no way of knowing what the outcome will be. I can only hope that my Party, my people, the trade unions whom I know better than I know anybody else, will resist the attempt by some extremists to lead them into thinking that they can destroy a government of which they disapprove (but which many of them, and possibly even more, their wives, helped to elect) by industrial action; because, if one government can be destroyed by them this way, any other government can obviously be destroyed in the same way by anybody else. And then the British democratic system has gone for ever.

There is much we need to do in the field of industrial relations.

So much of our management doesn't even now begin to understand, even in our best industrial complexes, the importance of consultation. It still mixes up *consultation* with *information*. It still seems to think that if you tell people something is to happen, that is consulting them. It isn't. And people are entitled to be told more, to be involved more, and to feel that they can affect the decisions. This, of course, is not to say that the decision-making process should be muddled. At the end of the day management must take the final responsibility. In any field of life, whether it be a field-marshal deciding on his military objectives, a prime minister deciding on a political issue, or a managing director deciding on the line his company should take, at the end of the day it is his decision, and he must be, and must be seen to be, responsible for it. But that doesn't mean that he shouldn't discuss the whole spectrum of possibilities with other people first. In British industry we do not do this. If we did, I am quite sure we would not have the madness that we are living through at the moment. I am certain that our industrial atmosphere would be a jolly sight better if companies would tell people the situation, the propositions, the possibilities, and the costs of doing this or doing that.

This brings me to think about the situation of the Labour Party. I have said I am worried about where the country is going. I am not at all sure that people who become disillusioned with Mr Heath's Conservative Government, as pretty well everybody I talk to seems to be, will necessarily turn back to the Labour Party as I would wish them to do, *unless* the Labour Party itself makes up its own mind about what it wants to do. I have written in this book about why I think we lost the election. This leads me to say that I think the way the Labour Party is currently conducting its Opposition to the Government is just about as stupid as the way it ran the election. I have no very great regard for Mr Heath's Government, or the members of it. I think they are a collection of lightweights.

But, having said that, the problems would be the same whatever the government. They would still be there if Labour were returned to power. We need to have an answer to them; we have to re-think our attitude to some traditional positions. For example, the taxation system on which I was brought up in the era of Philip Snowden, and to which Labour still seems so irrationally attached, really encourages a man to decide between working or not working. That is to say, if he earns what to us older people looks a magnificent sum, yet pays too much in tax, it annoys him. He isn't so pleased by what he earns as he is annoyed by what he is paying away. I shall never get out of my mind's eye the picture of the fellow in the canteen in one of the nicer factories in my old constituency who showed me his pay chit, and asked me what I thought of it. I said 'Marvellous'; to which he replied, 'No, George, you are looking at the wrong figure. Look at the tax deducted.' I said to him, 'Aren't you lucky to be able to pay that much tax.' He didn't think that at all amusing. So I said, 'What are you going to do about it?' He answered, 'You know what I'll do, George. I shall "holiday".' '"Holiday",' said I 'What's that?' He said 'I won't come in for a week, and then your bloody Chancellor will give me a rebate, and I've got it back.'

We shouldn't give a man a choice between working and not working. What we want to do is to give him a choice between spending his money on the things he likes, or saving. For example, I like to run a bigger car than I really need. This is my decision, and I could not complain if big cars were taxed more heavily than little ones. It is my choice. But this means a considerable re-think on behalf of the Labour Party about its whole traditional approach. And if we are to return to power we have to show people that we have thought again. Taxation is one area. There are many others.

One of these obviously is our relationship with, and our attitude to, the trade unions. It has always been said that the great strength of the British Labour Movement is its special relationship with, special dependence upon, the British trade unions. And of course pretty well all our money comes from that source. I wonder whether this is necessarily the right way for us to continue; whether we shouldn't now consider ourselves as a much more broadly-based party, raise our finances in other ways, and not rely upon, or depend upon, this special close attachment to trade unions who can, let us face it, be led by people who have no special attachment to the Labour Party, or can even be actively hostile to it.

As I think about all this it strengthens my conviction that the Labour Party ought to be the natural government party in Britain. Its instincts are right, its beliefs are right, but it ought in the seventies to be differently based. It needs a great deal of thought as to what this involves. At the moment I fear that the Labour Movement is giving in too much to the 'big boys', the fellows with the large card votes which are not always based upon the democratic decisions of those whose votes they are casting. Stalin is alleged once to have said to Churchill, 'How many divisions has the Pope?', as though

B

that were the only basis on which to take into account the views of millions of people throughout the world. I fear only too much that we are falling into the same trap.

And so, as I finish my book and send it away, I do it with tremendous worries in my mind. I said at the opening of this introduction that I would begin at the end of the book, but because I cannot get away from the great issues which are evolving, and from my feeling that I, too, must take a hand, it seems wrong to begin at the end. I seem to get more and more like that monarch Charles II, quoted by Macaulay, who said he realized that he had been an unconscionable time dying but he hoped that people would excuse it. I think I shall be around for quite a bit yet, and therefore this book had better begin, after all, at the beginning.

December 1970

IN MY WAY

I

Political
Apprenticeship

To BEGIN THEN at the beginning. On 2 September 1914, just one month after the declaration of war, I was born in I Block, Peabody Buildings, Duke Street, Lambeth, from which we moved when I was six months old to Peabody Square, Blackfriars Road, Southwark. This Peabody was a nineteenth-century American philanthropist who made a great deal of money out of the grocery trade and gave £500,000 to improve the housing of the London poor. In the setting of their time his Peabody Buildings were a great improvement on the hovels they replaced, but their time was a good while ago, and by today's standards the tenement that was my boyhood home would not be considered up to much in the condition it was then. We had just two rooms, with no internal washing facilities. There was a communal sink on a landing, and one of my earliest recollections is of seeing the light shining over Big Ben from the landing when I went out to wash. That light seemed part of our lives then; it was a regular landmark, as it has continued to be for me ever since.

We were not poor in the sense that some London families knew poverty. Except for a time when he was unemployed after being dismissed from a job for his part in the General Strike of 1926, my father was in regular work, and although his wages would seem a pittance now, they kept us from being hungry, and my mother was a wonderful manager.

My father's side of the family is of Irish extraction. My grandfather came over from Cork, I believe at a very early age, and settled in south-east London. He was a butcher by trade, though he never had his own shop. My memory of him is slight, but I recall him as an enormous man and fond of his pleasures. I was very much afraid of him, although he was always kindly to children. My father was born in London. In his younger days he had worked in a warehouse at the Docks and become a member of the Dock, Wharf and Riverside Workers Union, but at some time before the First World War he had learned to drive a motor-car and went to Pascall's, the sweet firm which was then in Blackfriars, as chauffeur to one of the Pascalls. He joined the Army Service Corps in 1915 and became an army driver, acting as chauffeur to a number of generals and other high-ranking officers. He also learned to drive heavy lorries, and when he came out of the army he got a job with Lyons, driving one of their lorries to deliver cakes and bread to their shops. I have the happiest memories of driving round with him on Sundays and getting cakes and chocolate buns at every shop where the manageress took a fancy to me.

My mother came of a family of asphalters. Their name was Mason. Her mother (*née* Baker) was a Scotswoman from Edinburgh. She went on living at Peabody Buildings, Lambeth, after we moved to Southwark. She was wonderfully good to us. With her own family grown up I think she thought only of her grandchildren, and she wanted more than anything else in the world to see us do well.

One of my earliest recollections is of the weekly visit I used to pay to Wood's Eel and Pie Shop in The Cut to buy the pies which were accompanied by something I have only ever had in an eel-pie shop, a rather wonderfully distinctive parsley gravy which to this day I enjoy as much as the pies. In those days the pies were made on the premises. Of course you can still get factory-made pies, but they are nothing like the pies of my boyhood. In later years, long after I was grown up, one of the little pleasures I could give to my grandmother, which she enjoyed right to her death, was again once a week to visit her in the evening with the girl I subsequently married in order to take the same dish to her. It is perhaps just worth recalling, since it is not all that long ago, that the cost of these delicious pies was (if I remember rightly) twopence.

I went to the elementary school at Gray Street, Blackfriars (it's not there any more – it was bombed in the war), and on pie days I'd first run home from school to collect an enamel dish for the pie and an enamel jug for the 'liquor', or gravy, and then run back to The Cut to get them. Then I'd run home again, as quickly as I could, to keep the dish and jug hot.

The Cut leads into Lower Marsh which takes one very near to the famous Lambeth Walk. Thursday was killing day at the butcher's in Lower Marsh, and I was always sent there then to get fresh calves' liver. This again – all these years later – reminds me of one of my favourite dishes. We had very little money, but my mother saw to it that we ate well.

I couldn't have been much more than four when I went to school. There was less bureaucracy about the schools' starting-age then, and you went to school when your parents thought you should, and when they could get you in. The Gray Street elementary school was very good for me, and I loved going there. It was a splendid school, and did a lot of pioneer educational work in London. One of its earlier pupils had been Harry Gosling, the great leader of the Lightermen, who joined up with Bevin in the amalgamations that formed the Transport and General Workers Union. Harry Gosling came once to a prize-day at the Gray Street school and I remember feeling half mesmerized to see him sitting there.

Irish politics figured large in my early childhood, for there were many Irish people where we lived, and I began to feel myself Irish. The stories of the troubles in Ireland made a deep impression on me. I can remember vividly being taken by my mother and stood on an orange box to watch the funeral procession for Lord Mayor Terence MacSwiney of Cork who had died on hunger strike in Brixton Prison in 1919.

My father was a keen trade unionist and as soon as he got his job at Lyons after the war he began forming a branch of the Transport Workers Union there. He became secretary of the branch and for all practical purposes he was the union organizer there. Then came the General Strike. My father brought all the Lyons drivers out, then on the instructions of the T.U.C. he took them back, then he brought them out again. This was because the General Council of the T.U.C. couldn't make up its mind how it wanted to fight the strike, and, indeed, whether it wanted to win or not. But to me it was all wildly exciting and I helped to overturn trams driven by blacklegs at the Elephant and Castle.

At the end of the strike my father lost his job and he found it hard to get another. When he did manage to get work driving a newspaper van for the *Evening Standard* he was pushed out because he belonged to the Transport Workers and not the Paperworkers Union. And the Paperworkers were not going to have a Transport Worker driving a newspaper van, however honourable his record as a trade unionist.

That was the only time when we knew grinding poverty. We came under the old Poor Law system of out-relief, and every Friday I had to go to the workhouse with a little sack to collect our allotment of bread and treacle. I was bitterly ashamed and bitterly angry. I was twelve then and had gone on from Gray Street to the West Square Central School, and I had what was locally regarded as a rather famous school cap. But I used to take it off when I went to the workhouse because I was ashamed to be seen there wearing it. This made me really want to change society. I swore then that I would do everything I could to see that people didn't have to take bags to the workhouse for scraps of food. We were also given tickets or vouchers which could be exchanged at a butcher's shop for little bits of meat. That, too, was a shaming process.

Another event that happened at this time was that my mother had a haemorrhage and was very ill. I didn't know then that it was a haemorrhage, and if I had known I shouldn't have understood what a haemorrhage was. All I did know was that she seemed desperately ill and that at 3 o'clock one morning I was sent to persuade the doctor to come to her. He did come. We had a big old-fashioned bed with brass knobs on it, and the doctor made us lift one end of the bed to try to stop the haemorrhage. Then he said that my mother must go to hospital, to what was then called the Champion Hill Infirmary and has since been renamed Dulwich Hospital.

The problem was how to get her there. You could only get an ambulance if you could prove need, and some body of officials – the old Poor Law Guardians, I suppose – had to accept that you were sufficiently in need for an ambulance to be sent. They were not sympathetic to the family of a man who had recently received Poor Law relief because he became out of work having taken part in the General Strike. It was well into the next day before we could persuade anybody to send an ambulance for my mother. At last we did so and she went to hospital. Mercifully she survived.

That incident of my mother's illness is the only other event of my childhood that I remember with blinding anger. With the experience of going with my sack to the workhouse it determined my conviction that society had *got* to be changed, and that I was going to do everything I could to change it. In one of my speeches in the 1970 election campaign I said that I would rather 200 scrimshankers got something they weren't entitled to than that one person in genuine need should have to beg pleadingly with officialdom. Those incidents of my childhood explain my feelings about this.

Apart from those two incidents, my childhood was in no sense bitter. Rather, it was a happy childhood, with a wonderful spirit of equality among the people of our neighbourhood. It is hard to put this into words – it was simply that everyone accepted everyone else as being a person in his own right. One man might own a pawnbroker's shop and another take in a jacket to be pawned, but neither felt that the other was in any way superior. There were pawnbrokers and there were people who pawned things, just as there was the man who kept the eel-and-pie shop and the people who bought his eels and pies. Their children all went to school together, some had more money than others, but nobody felt that he was 'better' than anybody else. The feelings about human equality that I have had since were not intellectually thought out – they grew naturally from my own childhood in Southwark. It was a good community to grow up in.

After being out of work for eight or nine months my father got a job driving a van for a local firm. It was nothing like as well paid as his job with Lyons, but the firm was quite nice to work for and it transformed life for all of us that he should be in work again. A little later he succeeded in getting a much better job, driving a big refrigerated meat-truck for a large meat combine. This again changed all our lives considerably. Not only was the job better paid, but it took my father all over the country, and sometimes he would take me with him. I got to know what different parts of England looked like, and met all sorts and kinds of different people.

The job also enabled my father to get back to his trade union work. He became a union official again and soon after that he was elected to the Executive of the Transport Workers Union, on which he continued to sit for very many years. He had much to do with Ernest Bevin. He was always close to Bevin, but there was also a good deal of conflict between them, a relationship that was to be both a help and a nuisance to me later on.

Because of my father's trade union work I met Bevin, Arthur Deakin, Harold Clay and many other trade union leaders in my boyhood. I remember going to hear Ben Tillett when I was eight or nine and being much impressed by the famous story he told to illustrate the stupidities of our people. We behaved, he said, just like potatoes in a sack; it didn't matter which way you put them in, the little ones all went through to the bottom and the big ones ended up on top.

School meant an enormous amount to me. The West Square Central School, to which I went on from the Gray Street elementary school, was one of the first of its kind in London, a sort of early experiment in comprehensive education. The headmaster, who was quite old and retired about a year after I got there, was a man called Samuel, who had made a great name for himself and for the West Square school. We had a whole series of masters, who all seemed to be outstanding men. One of the best, who had a profound influence on me, was John Evans, who became my form master. He was an absolutely brilliant man, no more than twenty-three or twenty-four then, who not only taught us school subjects but made us think about life. He lived to the full himself, qualifying as a barrister in his spare time from teaching, and going on to take a doctorate. Perhaps he was interested in too many things for the good of his own career, for he was never given his due in the educational world and did not get a headmastership until after the Second World War. But he was a wonderful teacher and wonderfully good to those he taught. I owe much to him.

Charlie Chaplin had lived close by the school and may well have been an earlier pupil there. Among my own contemporaries was Oscar Grasso, who later became famous as leader of Victor Sylvester's orchestra. Oscar was my rival for being top of the form – sometimes he would be top, sometimes I would be. He had one advantage over me, for he was quite good at drawing and I was hopeless at it. History and English were always my best subjects. But the school was keen on art and we had a notable art master in a man called Harold Thornton who fought hard to establish the importance of drawing in the curriculum. When it came to examinations he would give me 5 marks out of 100 for drawing, which meant that I had to do extremely well in other subjects to come top. Thornton was a great friend of John Evans, and he could never understand why Evans thought so highly of me when I was so useless in his art class.

Many years later, when I was Minister of Works, the Ministry was allotted some money to spend on pictures for British embassies and other government departments. One day I was brought a selection of pictures which the officials concerned were recommending that we should buy. Among them was a beautiful etching signed Harold Thornton. I'm happy to say that we bought the picture, and I insisted that it should stay in the Ministry of Works and hang in the Minister's own room. It lived over my desk as long as I was at the Ministry.

I left school when I was fifteen. I could have stayed until sixteen and the school put great pressure on me to stay, but I wanted to start earning my own living. My parents had done a lot for me and I felt it was time for me to ease their burden a bit. For about two years after I left school I went to evening classes at an L.C.C. institute near the Elephant and Castle. I acquired a great many quite useless certificates for this and that, but I became too immersed in political activities to have time for going on with this sort of formal schooling. I turned instead to what the W.E.A. and the National Council of Labour Colleges had to offer. This was a great deal. There were not only regular classes with distinguished lecturers, but also the opportunity to attend week-long courses in this country – I remember with particular pride one which took place at Balliol, Oxford (the pride comes from the studies one was enabled to do there, not so much from the fact that it put me on a par with some of my colleagues in a much later Labour Cabinet, although I used to take a lot of malicious joy in referring to my Balliol days without emphasizing that they lasted precisely a week!). In addition to these, there were also courses abroad; and one which I attended a little later, and which gave me a marvellous grounding, was held for two weeks at the International Labour Organization offices in Geneva.

I cannot leave my schooldays without discussing the other major influence in my life—the Church. I was still at the Gray Street school in Blackfriars when I first met that remarkable man Father J. R. Sankey, who was the priest at St Andrew's-by-the-Wardrobe, just across the river from us. He came to the school one day to ask if any of us would like to be choirboys at his church, and I was one of those who said, 'Yes, I would.'

Father Sankey was a relative of Lord Sankey, the judge who was chairman of the Sankey Commission on the coal industry after the First World War, and who first put up the case for nationalizing the mines. Father Sankey was a devoted priest, what would now be called very High Church, and his deep sense of social responsibility put him in line with the great Christian Socialist thinkers of the nineteenth century, to whom the Labour movement owes so much. From the age of nine until I was about sixteen John Sankey had an enormous influence on me. When my voice broke and I had to leave the choir, I stayed on at St Andrew's as an altar server and later as a thurifer, the acolyte who carries the incense, and I got – and get – a deep satisfaction from the beautiful ritual of the Church. I learned to be a catholic – *not* a Roman Catholic, but a catholic in the true and original sense of belonging to 'one catholic and apostolic church'.

I had long discussions with Father Sankey, about God, about people, about social justice. I remember his saying to me once in a fit of exasperation, 'Well, I may not have stopped you wandering, but I have taught you where to return.' That phrase of his has stayed with me all my life. 'Wandering', as John Sankey used the word, could mean doing wrong or making mistakes – what is important is to know how to get back. That gives you, I suppose, what is called a conscience. It teaches you how important the Sacrament is. It makes you think at the end of each day what you have done with the day, and how far you have departed from what ought to be your standards of living. It makes you understand that the catholic concept of religion accepts that you are going to make mistakes, even to do wicked things, but that it enables you sometimes to identify wickedness and avoid it, and at least to make amends if you have not avoided doing something wrong. It makes you more tolerant of other people because it helps you to understand them by knowing that you share their weaknesses. I don't pretend to the sloppy thinking that faith necessarily makes you *like* people more – the Commandment to love thy neighbour doesn't imply that you have got to *like* him. What it does mean is that you must accept him as a human being like yourself, feel a sense of responsibility towards him, and try to exercise endless patience.

Faith helps you to realize that if successes come to you they don't come because of your own innate qualities, but because whatever qualities you may have are being used for some purpose. Faith gives you a basis for living for tomorrow as well as for today. I felt this particularly when I was in office, knowing that however ghastly and bloody today had turned out to be it could not weaken your faith for tomorrow. It makes you see yourself as a servant of what is happening rather than the creator of what is happening. It makes you less big-headed, and if I can use the phrase without seeming priggish, it gives you humility.

The Church of England is sometimes said cynically to represent the Conservative Party at prayer. That is not true. The late Morgan Phillips, when he was Secretary of the Labour Party, once declared that Labour 'owes more to Methodism than to Marx'. It was a brilliant turn of speech, but it is only half-true. The Labour movement owes an immense debt to both the Anglican and Roman Catholic churches. Newman, Manning, Kingsley, Keble, William Morris, George Lansbury and many, many others all bear witness to this.

I am deeply grateful for my years with Father Sankey at St Andrew's. They gave me a faith that nothing can take away, or weaken.

I got my first job through an organization that was set up to find jobs for promising boys from schools like West Square, Southwark. My first job as a 'promising' boy was in the purchasing ledger department of a firm in Cheapside. It was a firm of merchants and general factors of a kind that scarcely exists nowadays, when so many manufacturers deal direct with retailers, but it had been of great importance in the old City of London – one of the partners had been Lord Mayor of London. My first job lasted only a year. I had the bright idea of pursuading my fellow ledger-clerks to join the union, and when the firm started cutting down staff because of the depression I was duly cut down.

I went back to the agency for promising boys, and they sent me along with some other promising characters to John Lewis, the Oxford Street store, which required a young man in the fur skin department to match skins and so forth. I wasn't considered sufficiently promising to be given that job, but I was given a job in the basement of John Lewis. Part of the time I spent shoving trucks around, and the rest in beating fur skins with canes to stop moths getting at them. I never became very good at this, because to be a good anti-moth beater of furs you have to beat with a certain rhythm, rather like playing a drum in a jazz band; I never got the rhythm as well as other people did. But I beat well enough to get by for a time.

The John Lewis Partnership had then (and still has) a journal called the *Gazette* in which old John Spedan Lewis used to urge people to write anything they liked about things affecting the store, anonymously if they wished. Continuing to have bright ideas, I wrote a letter to the *Gazette* saying that it was an absolute disgrace for us to take customers' furs into cold storage for the summer when not only did we have no cold store, but had a great steam-pipe running through the place where the furs were put, thus requiring constant beating to keep out moths.

The letter didn't get published, and in spite of the fact that I'd taken the precaution of exercising my right to be anonymous, people soon came to the conclusion that the letter must have been written by me. The result was (*a*) that John Spedan Lewis came down, created merry murder, and ordered a proper cold store to be built;

and (*b*) that the buyer of the department decided that it would be better if I wasn't seen around in the cold store.

This buyer was a remarkable old man who was really very good to me, and who had a considerable influence on my life. Instead of sacking me he promoted me to the job in the skin-room which I'd failed to get when I first came to John Lewis. The more promising youngster who had got that job originally had moved up to become a junior salesman.

The skin-room job was much more interesting than moth-beating. Learning to match skins, and going to warehouses in the City to buy them was fascinating. I learned a great deal about the fur trade, and the knowledge has stayed with me ever since. As well as learning on my trips to the City I could make a penny or two as well. You used to get your fare to go to the City and if you chose to walk you didn't have to tell anybody about it.

We had by this time become a family of four children, two boys and two girls, and emancipated ourselves from Peabody Square by being moved to an L.C.C. housing estate at Streatham. I had my first experience of being able to have a proper bathroom in our own house and of not using a communal lavatory. We had a nice-sounding address, too, which didn't say L.C.C. estate but Mountearl Gardens, Streatham. It sounded proper middle-class professional, and I remember my delight at the thought that I wouldn't have to put Peabody Square on any more application forms.

John Lewis was a good firm to work for. After I'd got to know about furs and matching skins I was promoted to be a salesman in the department. I was still not eighteen and I spent the next four or five years as a salesman. It was a fascinating period of my life, and I earned more money, relatively speaking, than I ever earned again until I became a Cabinet Minister. I got precious little salary, but a most rewarding commission of 5 per cent on sales. If you could only sell a ten bob stole, that wasn't worth much, but when you sold a mink coat for hundreds of pounds you could have quite a bonanza. There were thin times when you fell back on your basic salary, and the firm had a custom that its employees should have three weeks' holiday instead of two, but the third one was not paid for. But on the whole I did quite well and earned what in my eyes then – indeed to most people's eyes – was a handsome living.

Among those whom I served personally were actresses like Hermione Gingold, Anona Winn and Annie Ahlers, and other great characters like Margot Asquith. Margot Asquith was a terrific

With his parents

With his wife, Sophie,
on their wedding day, 1937

personality. She would never deal with anybody else, and I had the pleasure of selling her furs and taking in her furs for repair or renovation. She was the most impossible woman I have ever met – she could be more engagingly rude, I think, than anyone else in the world, with the possible exception of myself. Poor Annie Ahlers unknowingly did me a bad turn. She was a most beautiful Viennese actress who died after falling from a hotel window. Shortly before her death she had come to the fur department with a friend and I sold her a white ermine coat, a mink coat, and a number of other things. After her death the lot were sent back. I'd already drawn commission on the sales and I had to refund it all, which meant going without much pay for several weeks.

The General Manager under whom I was then working was a man called Cdr Fitzroy, the son of a Speaker of the House of Commons. He obviously thought well of me, for we got to the stage of discussing for how long I should have to mark time before I could be made a departmental manager and a buyer. Things turned out differently. Outside the store I had an immensely active political life and I was speaking night after night at meetings all over London. One evening I went to speak in the Portobello Road, and as luck would have it my pitch was just outside a shop belonging to a lady to whom I had been selling furs. She heard me denouncing the rich and the wickedness of society in general, and she recognized me. She didn't say anything to me, but next morning I was sent for by the nice old buyer who had promoted me from moth-beating and told that he had an irate customer on his hands who said that she would never buy another fur from John Lewis if she had to meet the likes of me. He gave me a great ticking off, and said that if he ever heard any more about my revolutionary ravings it would be the end – selling furs and preaching Socialism in his view did not mix.

Feeling very indignant about this criticism of what I did in my own time I went to see the General Manager, Cdr Fitzroy, and another General Manager who had now joined him. This second man was an ex-Naval officer who later became, ironically enough, a well-known Communist. They discussed my case and gave me very wise advice. Nobody, they said, wanted to victimize me, but I'd have to make up my own mind what I wanted to do in life. Cdr Fitzroy added, 'If you want to go into politics, do it properly. And if you do go into politics I hope it will be along the lines of Herbert Morrison, because my father [the then Speaker] has told me what a wonderful man he is, and not along the lines of some of these other

c

people.' I'm not sure if he knew then about the ex-Naval officer's political leanings, but I rather suspect that he did.

I didn't want to give up either my trade union work or my political work, but it seemed pretty obvious that if things went on as they were I was heading for trouble. So I looked around to see what I could do, and having reached the mature age of twenty-two I applied to the Transport Workers Union to be appointed a full-time officer. I had to go up for an examination and an interview. I regret to say that I did a lot of irregular cramming for the exam before I went up – my father and his pals just tried to make sure that I knew what questions I was going to be asked. My father, of course, did not sit on the examining body, but one of his pals did. In spite of all this I wasn't appointed. At the interview I met Mr Bevin, and Mr Bevin made it plain that he didn't want whippersnappers acting for his great union – it was a job, he said, for men, not boys.

Having said all this and made sure that I was not appointed for the job for which I had applied, which I think now was very sensible of him, Bevin acted like the really big man he was. I was told to go to see the area secretary in London, who was a great East End dockers' leader and a friend of my father, and his assistant, who was chairman of the London Labour Party and who knew of my political work. These two gentlemen cast an eye over me, and sent me to see the chief clerk to prove that I really had got my certificate in short-hand. I had the certificate all right, but alas, I had been so busy selling furs that I couldn't write shorthand any more. Anyway, they didn't send me away, but gave me a job in the ledger room, so I was almost back where I'd started when I left school.

My job was to enter members' contributions in the ledgers according to a very old-fashioned system we had in those days, and at the end of each quarter I had to total up contributions to see how much each member was in arrears. I don't know whether the members or the union won on my calculations, but it was a highly amusing time.

I did two years in that ledger room, getting more and more involved in political activities all the time. This was the period of the Spanish Civil War, and one of my contributions was to take part in organizing an illegal cache of arms to be smuggled out to the comrades who were fighting in the International Brigade. We collected money in the office to buy the arms (how good they were as weapons, I just don't know), and all went well until the police got wind of the exercise and it was nipped in the bud.

Our area office was at Finsbury Park, and from it we covered the whole of London and the south-east. Through doing the ledgers I got to know all kinds of trade union officers, organizers, branch secretaries and so on, and after two years I again applied for a vacancy as a district organizer. This time I got the job, and I became the union's first district organizer for general and miscellaneous trades in Hertfordshire, Bedfordshire and Buckinghamshire, working from Watford. My senior colleague in Watford, who looked after busmen, gave me a wonderful piece of advice on the day I arrived. He talked to me in a fatherly way and added, 'If you ever get into difficulties come and tell me all about it and I'll help you further into them.' It sounded an odd thing to say, but what he meant was, 'You won't get any help from anybody, brother. You'll just find your own way in and your own way out.' That, in fact, is how things did work out.

So I started organizing agricultural workers, brickyard workers, building trade workers, even canal boatmen, all sorts of people whose livelihood lay in the countryside and smallish towns of my area. When I was twenty-four I was brought back to London temporarily to replace an officer in the East End who had had a breakdown. I kept my office at Watford and had to carry on with all my own work there as well as looking after the London job. It was then that I had my first strike. It was in a rag-picking firm, and although it ended in failure as far as getting what we wanted was concerned, we kept it going for some twenty weeks. The chairman of the branch then was a great and gallant man called the Rev. Hugh Lister. He was a bit eccentric, but a wonderful character. When the war came he wouldn't go in as a padre but joined up as a soldier and was killed as a captain in the Welsh Guards. He taught me a great deal.

Our strike collapsed largely because of the Munich crisis. There was a sudden outburst of patriotic fervour and we all went and dug trenches and filled sandbags to make air-raid shelters in Victoria Park. We had a meeting in the park and decided to call off the strike – naturally nobody admitted it, but I think we were all glad of an excuse to wind it up.

My father was a trade unionist first and foremost, and although he always voted Labour at elections he was never an individual member of the Party and he was not much concerned with Labour Party affairs between elections. I shared all his trade union interests, but I was always greatly interested in Labour Party politics as well. I found my way to the Labour committee rooms in Southwark when I was seven or eight. Here occurred one of the first of those incidents – or God-ordained events – that have marked so much of my life.

Why I first went to the committee rooms I do not know. What I do remember is that I met there a bulky figure who was the be-all and end-all of Labour politics in the borough called Len Styles. Len was the agent for Haden Guest, as he was to be later for George Isaacs, and he was obviously not very pleased to have a youngster like me getting in his way. He tried to fob me off by giving me a little Labour pamphlet that we were selling for twopence. I did not take it and this, I suppose, made him take a scrap more notice of me and I persuaded him to let me make myself useful by running errands and delivering leaflets. The meeting was a wonderful one for me because Len Styles, when he was not being king-pin of the Labour Party in Southwark, was one of the greatest authorities on Dickens and Shakespeare, both of whom had been so deeply involved in Southwark's history. It was Len who gave me my love for Dickens and Shakespeare, helping me to understand their real meaning. Later I learned that Len and my mother had been school-mates in what was originally the Lant Street School, which Dickens himself attended. It is now known as the Charles Dickens School.

In one of these early Elections I was sent to distribute leaflets in a big block of flats called Library Mansions just off Blackfriars Road for George Isaacs. The reason for my being sent out with the leaflets there was that it was considered a very tough area. A grown-up going round with leaflets might have got into trouble, but it was felt (rightly) that they would leave a boy alone.

I have written already of my schoolmaster, Dr John Evans. He was then a Liberal in politics, but he didn't try to make any of us agree with him – what he did do was to encourage us to be interested in politics generally, to understand what they were all about. We held political debates in class, and had tremendous arguments. At seventeen, after we had gone to live at Streatham, I became vice-president of the Streatham Constituency Labour Party, and I was also a member of the National Advisory Committee of the Labour League of Youth. I got myself elected to the National Advisory Committee through a speech at the annual conference of the League of Youth fiercely denouncing the representative of the Party's National Executive who came to tell us that we couldn't have a member on the Executive. (This still comes up year by year, and the demand is always rejected; there is still no League of Youth member on the National Executive.)

It was a vintage period for the Advisory Committee, and I served with Ted Willis, Alice Bacon, Maurice Webb, Will Griffiths and a number of other outstanding people. Maurice Webb was editor of the *Nation*, the League of Youth paper, and I became a member of the editorial board which directed it.

Round about this time a group of young Socialists, supported and largely financed by Stafford Cripps, had set out to bring back to life the old *Clarion* newspaper. In association with this venture they had a van which used to go round the Home Counties on propaganda tours rather like the old *Clarion* scouts on their bicycles. The group also acquired a large house called Geddings at Hoddesdon which became known as the Clarion Youth Hostel. We used not only to spend week-ends there, but had many of our schools and conferences there. It was here that I first met a remarkable woman called Deborah Levene and her sister, Sophie. We all met again shortly afterwards at a by-election in North Kensington. One of the moving spirits in the whole enterprise was a man called Maurice Hackett, and he and I were to become brothers-in-law in due course through our marriages to these two sisters. I'd brought a group of young people from South London to work in the election and Deborah Levene brought a contingent from East London, including her sister. We all took part in an election meeting, and after the meeting Sophie bought me fish and chips at a shop in Shepherd's Bush. I was then eighteen. I think we decided then that we were going to get married, and in 1937, when I was twenty-two, we did.

Sophie, Deborah and their younger sister Bella were the daughters of two great East London characters, Sol and Kate Levene. Sol Levene, J.P., was a stalwart worker for the Labour Party all his life and a founder member of the Mile End Labour Party. In 1919, when Labour captured Stepney Borough Council, the question arose of who should be Mayor. This was the period when Labour captured for the first time many local authorities and was therefore very short of experienced people to take the offices. It was common then to go outside the Councillors for the Mayor. This they did at Stepney by approaching a certain Major Attlee, a social worker at Toynbee Hall. Sol Levene was one of a Labour Party deputation of three who interviewed Major Attlee to see if he would make a suitable Labour Mayor of Stepney! They recommended him for the job and Attlee duly became Mayor – the youngest Stepney had had.

When Sophie and I got married, my salary from the union was £3 15s. a week. We decided to buy a house. It had to be convenient for the area office of the union at Finsbury Park, and it had to be cheap enough for us to buy. The only place where we could find one that we thought we could afford was at Barnet. The deposit required was £25. It was a tiny house, but we were very happy there, and there our first daughter, Frieda, was born. When I got the job of district organizer at Watford in February 1938 my salary went up to £5 10s. a week, plus £1 a week allowance for expenses. Barnet was quite convenient for Watford, so we went on living there. When war came I thought that it would be wiser to move a bit farther out of London, so we sold the Barnet house and went to live at Potters Bar. The only thing that had ever happened at Potters Bar before we took up residence was that a Zeppelin had been brought down there in the First World War. What happened to us was that all the bombs and doodlebugs that couldn't quite reach Barnet came down in Potters Bar, including our house and garden. That move was not one of my brightest achievements.

The war changed my work profoundly. My area of quiet country-side became dotted with factories making aircraft and all sorts of war materials. I became involved with De Havillands, and with a number of important war industries round Welwyn Garden City, Watford, Luton and elsewhere. Agriculture also took on a new importance, and in addition to serving on various industrial com-mittees and trade boards, I became a member of the War Agricul-tural Executive.

In the early stages of the war, trade union officials in my category were reserved, but after the fall of France we were taken off the totally reserved list and allowed to volunteer if we were under a certain age. Like so many of us at that time I'd had my earlier period of pacifism, and as soon as this happened I decided to volunteer for the Royal Air Force. I went to the R.A.F. recruiting centre in Edgware where I had my medical examination and was asked what branch of the R.A.F. I wanted to join. I said that I wanted to fly. I was given a card and a number and told to await instructions to go to Cardington, where I should have to undergo tests to see if I were suitable for air crew.

Before my joining instructions came I got a letter summoning me back to Edgware. There I was seen by the same man who had recruited me into the R.A.F. He said, 'Do you know Mr Bevin?' I said, 'Yes.' (Bevin was then Minister of Labour and National Service.) 'Well,' he said, 'an interesting thing has happened. I have been told that you are not to leave your present job.'

So my R.A.F. card was taken away and I was sent back to Watford and told to get on with the war from there.

I was heavily involved in both industry and agriculture throughout the war. I opened a new office in Luton and spent my time
travelling all over my three counties, sorting out problems in
factories and helping farmers and growers to get more food off the
land. This had neither the drama nor the danger of being a pilot in
the R.A.F. but it was my job, and I threw myself into it. They were
totally absorbing years.

Soon after we moved to Barnet I had become secretary of the St
Albans Divisional Labour Party, and in 1938 fought my first election
for the East Barnet Urban District Council, being defeated by the
handsome majority of 2,200. And it was in the capacity of secretary
of the St Albans Party that I first moved on to the national political
stage. In 1939 I attended my first Labour Party Conference as the
constituency delegate.

That was the year in which the great question dominating the
Conference was the expulsion of Sir Stafford Cripps. He had been
expelled by the National Executive for continuing to advocate a
political alliance with Communists and others in a Popular Front
after the executive had held that such an alliance was incompatible
with membership of the Labour Party. Cripps had demanded to
address the Conference, but as he had been expelled from the Party
he could address the Conference only if Standing Orders were
formally suspended to permit him to do so. This required a vote by
the whole Conference.

Although I was there as a constituency delegate for the Party, I
was also an official of the Transport Workers Union and as such I
attended the delegate conference of the Transport Workers delegation. Not only did I go to this meeting, but I exercised my right –
which no one seemed to have thought of before – to speak.

The Transport Workers, on Bevin's recommendation, had decided
to vote against allowing Cripps to speak. I told Mr Bevin that I
thought he was doing a wicked thing in using the union's massive
card vote against giving Cripps a hearing. Mr Bevin thanked me
politely for my advice and told me to keep my mouth shut. However,
I persisted, arguing that while I thought it reasonable enough for
Cripps to be expelled, I felt it monstrous that he should not be
allowed to put his case against expulsion. I also said that I would
cast the St Albans vote in favour of giving him a hearing – St Albans
had a card vote of 1,000 against Mr Bevin's 337,000.

When Monday morning came I found myself sitting three or four
rows from the front, with Mr Bevin sitting massively and impressively

immediately behind me. When we were called upon to vote I duly
held up my little card in favour of giving Cripps a hearing. This
irritated Bevin, for in spite of the Transport Workers' massive vote
we won, and Cripps was allowed to put his case to Conference.

He made a disastrous speech. He was appealing for sympathy,
and one of the things he said was to remind the Conference of his
services to the Mineworkers Union after the Gresford colliery disaster
by acting for the victims and the union without charging a penny.

In the subsequent debate Ralph Morley, the former Member for
Southampton, was the first speaker from the floor calling on the
Conference to support the Executive and reject Cripps's appeal. The
late Hugh Dalton was to be the platform spokesman to wind up
the debate.

The chairman of the Conference that year was George Dallas,
who had been an official of the Transport Workers Union from
before the First World War, and was almost a founder-member of
the St Albans Labour Party. And by a series of coincidences he had
held almost every office in the Union and the Labour Party which
I subsequently held twenty years or so later.

After the proposer had put the motion that Cripps's appeal should
be rejected, I got up and waved my little card at George Dallas.
Whether he saw Bevin sitting behind me and thought that I was a
member of the Transport Workers delegation I don't know, but
anyway he called me and I went up to second the resolution.

It was the first day of my very first Labour Party Conference and
I nearly fell off the rostrum with fright. But I knew what I wanted
to say. I had been all in favour of giving Cripps a hearing, but I still
thought that he ought to be expelled and his speech had made me
angry. I set about him in no uncertain fashion and said that I didn't
see any reason why he should have wanted money for representing
miners after Gresford. I thought that my members in Hertfordshire
were doing quite a lot for him, and some of them had less than 35s.
a week to live on.

My speech was a youthful effort, but it got a great ovation and the
Conference carried the motion without even waiting to hear the
Executive speaker. When it was all over Sir Stafford Cripps was
escorted out, together with Mr Aneurin Bevan and Mr G. R.
Strauss, who were both also expelled on the same motion. Neither
Bevan nor Cripps ever took kindly to me after that. Bevan did relent
in time, but Cripps never spoke to me again. I've even stood in a
toilet with him when we were both Ministers, and he still couldn't

remember my name. He was a great Christian, and certainly had faith and hope, but it never seemed to me he really got the point about charity.

At the end of the session, people rushed up to pat me on the back, and I was ever so proud of myself. As we were going down the stairs Bevin said, 'Well, that was a good speech, George. One of these days I'd like to hear you make a constructive one.'

The events of that 1939 Conference did me a lot of good and I began to be known a bit nationally. Hugh Dalton and Harold Laski were both favourably impressed and took over a lot of my political education. Both, right up to their death, went out of their way to help me along.

As I have already explained, I went on with my trade union work throughout the war. One day towards the end of the war, Laski sent John Strachey to see me. Strachey was going to Dundee to become the Labour candidate for what was then a two-member constituency. Laski had recommended Strachey to have a trade unionist as his fellow-candidate, and suggested that he should have a talk with me. So Strachey got in touch with me and invited me to lunch at his London club. And very impressive it was – it was the first time I'd ever been inside such a place.

But I didn't run in double harness with John Strachey. At that same North Kensington by-election, our Labour candidate had had a much harder task because he'd been opposed by a Communist who succeeded in splitting the Labour vote. And at the spearhead of the Communist candidate's campaign had been John Strachey! When we had lunch together, Strachey suddenly realized that the chap whom Laski had suggested as a running mate was the chap who'd stood on the opposite side of the street in North Kensington shouting against him. Although we came close to each other in later years, it didn't seem then either to him or to me that we could offer the sort of duet to attract the electors of Dundee, so that particular enterprise came to nothing.

Laski and Dalton thought again, and as a result of their thinking George Dallas sent for me. He told me that he had been nursing the Belper constituency in Derbyshire. It had been a Labour seat in 1929 but had been lost in the débâcle of 1931. The former Member had not stood again, and George Dallas had been adopted in his place. He was sure that he could have won Belper had there been an election in 1939, but there wasn't and his wife now felt that he was too old to think of standing after the war. Would I like to take his place?

What nicer thing could be said to anyone! Of course I said that
I'd love to stand for Belper, so very quietly and stealthily I was
paraded there and given letters of introduction to the right people to
make sure that when the selection conference met the right decision
should be made.

All went beautifully until the moment came when I had to ask
the union to nominate me. George Dallas had been a union-
sponsored candidate, and clearly I had to have the union's backing,
too. That brought me to Mr Bevin's attention again. And he thought
that standing for Parliament was the very last thing that I ought to
do.

At this point I had to make the great decision of my life. Bevin
had been Minister of Labour and National Service from the forma-
tion of the Churchill Government in 1940. When the war-time
coalition was dissolved and a Conservative caretaker Government
took over to prepare for the 1945 election, Bevin, of course, left
office with the other Labour members of the coalition. He had
returned briefly to his old job at the head of the Transport Workers
Union. I was convinced that the old man wanted to stop me from
being a candidate for spiteful and malicious reasons. I recalled how
he had refused to give me a job when I first applied for an appointment in the union and I felt that I had got to fight him. So I got
tough and awkward, and I demanded my right to go before the
Executive to appeal for sponsorship. I said that if the Executive
didn't want to sponsor me, well and good; but it was their business
and not his.

I got my way. Bevin was a big man, and he was big enough to
let me go ahead. I went before the Executive, was nominated for
sponsorship, and I won the selection conference at Belper. On 5 July
1945 we had the election, and on 26 July – we had to wait for
Service votes to come in and be counted – the result was declared.
I had become the Member of Parliament for Belper.

Looking back now, I think I certainly misjudged Bevin. He was
a strange man. If he respected you he somehow made you want to
fight him. He didn't give reasons – it was up to you to find out.
Bevin was a great Minister of Labour and a great Foreign Secretary.
But he came in, as it were, at the top. In his heart he had a certain
contempt for Parliament and he always considered trade union work
as vastly more important than being an M.P. He didn't say so,
being Bevin he couldn't say so, but I think that what he was really
doing was trying to tell me to stick to the union. Had I stayed and

not gone into Parliament there was a reasonable chance that even the topmost job, Bevin's own job, could in the end have come my way. I was senior to Frank Cousins as a union official and senior to Jack Jones, who is general secretary now. When the time came for Arthur Deakin to appoint a deputy general secretary, I would clearly have been a candidate for the post, and my chances of being elected to succeed Deakin would have been quite high. I think that this was what Bevin really wanted to tell me.

But he didn't, and I made my own decision. Much as I have enjoyed my political life since, I have often wondered if I was right.

2

Arrival in
Parliament

I took my seat in the House of Commons, in the second row, right at the end, and found myself sitting next to George Isaacs, the very man for whom I'd delivered handbills as a little boy back in the early twenties. We were chatting away, and I said, 'What are you going to do? Are you going into the Government?'

'Oh,' he said, 'I think they'll probably offer me a parliamentary secretaryship at the Ministry of Labour. I'd rather like that.'

George Isaacs was that year's chairman of the T.U.C. The day after our meeting in the House I got a message asking me to ring him. I did, and he said, 'Do you know, George, what they've done? They've gone and made me *Minister* of Labour.'

'Good Lord,' I said. 'What are you going to do?'

'Well,' he said, 'the first thing I've got to do is to find somebody to help me with the parliamentary work. I was wondering whether you would like to become my P.P.S.?'

I scarcely knew what a P.P.S. was, or did. I'd been in the House of Commons for three days, and I'd been a parliamentary candidate for three months. Now I found myself parliamentary private secretary to the Minister of Labour. In the ordinary way I suppose that wouldn't have meant much, but with the ending of the war the Ministry of Labour had the enormous task of unwinding the whole war machine. Among its jobs was that of dealing with the tens of thousands of displaced persons who were then in Britain – people of almost every nationality in Europe who had been caught up in the war and had come to Britain, either to fight in Allied armies, like the Poles, or to work for us in the struggle to defeat Hitler. I was given the job of helping with the resettlement of all these people. The Ministry of Labour had a parliamentary secretary in Ness Edwards, who was the Junior Minister, and although I was only the P.P.S.

(and therefore unpaid), I was given an office at the Ministry and found myself acting as a second Under-Minister. It was a magnificent opportunity, and I took it.

As a P.P.S. I couldn't speak officially for the department in the House, but I did practically a full-time job for the Ministry, and this soon led to another wonderful opportunity.

George Isaacs had been a printer, and in his trade union career he had been on especially close terms with the American printing trade union, which had then (and still has) its headquarters in a lovely part of Tennessee called Happy Valley. One of the first things he had to do as Minister of Labour was to head the British delegation to the annual meeting of the International Labour Organization, which that year was in Canada. He decided to leave Ness Edwards, who was officially the Junior Minister, to hold the fort at the Ministry of Labour and to take me with him to the I.L.O. We went across on the *Queen Mary*, travelling with a couple of thousand G.I. brides. On the way across George Isaacs decided that he, Mrs Isaacs and I should go down to Tennessee to spend a week-end with the American printers while the rest of the delegation went on to Canada. We would go independently to Montreal and meet them there.

We had a marvellous time in Tennessee, and back in New York on the way to Montreal we met more of the leading American trade unionists, among them the great John L. Lewis of the Mine-workers, the Reuther brothers of the Automobile Workers, George Meany, of the American Federation of Labour, Dave Dubinski, of the Ladies Garment Workers Union, and another prominent leader in the tailoring and garment-making trades called Potovski. He had a magnificent head and was a most cultured man, who had come to the United States originally, I think, as an émigré from Russia. He was so touched by what he had heard of our sufferings from clothes rationing in Britain that we'd scarcely got back to our hotel before a messenger arrived to ask about the collar sizes of Mr George Isaacs and Mr George Brown. Then we were presented with an enormous consignment of Arrow shirts. There were far more than we could have worn out in a lifetime. When we rejoined the I.L.O. delegation we handed them round to anyone who could get into them, and so most of the British party had new shirts for the rest of the trip.

I enjoyed that first visit to the United States and Canada enormously. At the I.L.O. conference I was not just a visitor but an

EAST BARNET U.D.C. ELECTION
SATURDAY, APRIL 2nd, 1938
8 a.m. 8 p.m.

ELECTION ADDRESS

OF

GEORGE

BROWN

Labour Candidate

GEORGE BROWN
Trade Union Official Transport and General Workers' Union.
Resides at 29, Lakeside Crescent, East Barnet.
Hon. Secretary, St. Albans Divisional Labour Party.
Has served on National Committees of Labour Party.
A well-known Lecturer in the Labour, Trade Union and Co-operative Movements.

FOR

Lyonsdown Ward

COMMITTEE ROOMS:
47 NETHERLANDS ROAD

One foot on the lower rungs of politics. The war with Hitler was just eighteen months ahead when George Brown stood as Labour Candidate in the East Barnet U.D.C. Election. He lost.

25

GENERAL ELECTION, 1945
BELPER PARLIAMENTARY DIVISION

Polling Day: THURSDAY, JULY 5th, 7 a.m. to 9 p.m.

GEORGE BROWN
THE LABOUR CANDIDATE

ASKS <u>YOU</u> TO

SUPPORT LABOUR'S FIGHT FOR FREEDOM

Election
addresses

Ernest Bevin

Drawing by
Angela Thorne

official member of the British delegation, which meant that I took a full part in the proceedings and served on various committees. I made a number of international friendships there which have enriched my life greatly.

I stayed at the Ministry of Labour until the spring of 1947, and then George Isaacs said to me, 'You'll be hearing from Dalton. I don't know what he is going to suggest, but if it is anything to do with his place, you go there, and don't think that you are being in any way disloyal to me.'

Dalton was then at the Treasury. Shortly after George Isaacs's chat with me, Dalton did send for me. He said, 'I can't offer you a ministerial post here at the moment, but I should very much like you to become my P.P.S. You must know that to be P.P.S. at the Treasury is the stepping-stone to the next vacant job, so you'll have a good chance of being in the Government at the next shuffle.'

My predecessor as Dalton's P.P.S., Hugh Gaitskell, had just gone to the Ministry of Fuel, so the opportunities seemed bright. Dalton had always been good to me since I had first come to his notice at the Labour Party Conference in 1939, and I think he sincerely wanted to give me a helping hand in my new political career. I was grateful to him, and since he had spoken to George Isaacs first, and Isaacs had generously told me to take the chance of advancement, I felt free to accept Dalton's offer.

I served him through a dreadful time at the Treasury when the events that ultimately led to the devaluation of the pound in 1949 were taking shape. That did not come until Dalton had left the Treasury and been replaced by Sir Stafford Cripps, but Dalton had all the strain of fighting for Britain's economic survival since 1945. My brief experience at the Treasury with Dalton showed me how things went wrong. I saw the way the Treasury behaved, saw what I believed to be their collective arrogance and incompetence, and saw how money and their dogma about the balance of payments dominated Treasury thinking more than anything else on earth. In that respect the Treasury had not changed all that much when I next got to know its mind in 1964. When I went as Minister to the Department of Economic Affairs (D.E.A.) then, I remembered vividly the experience of 1947. That is one of the reasons why, as I shall describe later, I fought so hard for the D.E.A.

In 1947 I was merely the P.P.S., but I was close enough to Dalton to see how he suffered under the strain. Just as I was to do nearly twenty years later, so he wanted to encourage economic expansion

D

and to give some hope to ordinary men and women, but he couldn't get his way in the Cabinet. Bevin, who detested him, was his particular bugbear. Dalton used to come back from No. 10 seething with rage about what he called 'the incompetent little Prime Minister' who just sat there doing nothing to influence a decision 'while I had to sit listening to rambling monologues from your friend Ernie Bevin'.

I didn't share Dalton's view on Bevin, but I did begin to wonder about Mr Attlee. Everybody seemed to be talking about Attlee's indifference, and I spent a lot of time in the tea room of the House of Commons (I've learned better since!) listening to, and taking part in, the discussions that went on. At that time Patrick Gordon Walker was Herbert Morrison's P.P.S., and he and I had long discussions about what we regarded as the Attlee problem. Finally we decided that we should have to do something about it, so we determined to organize a '*putsch*' to get rid of Mr Attlee and replace him by Bevin. Bevin was the only possible strong man to take his place as Prime Minister. One lot in the Parliamentary Labour Party wouldn't have Cripps, others wouldn't have Morrison, and nobody would have Dalton. So Bevin was the only man, and we set out to organize a revolt by collecting signatures in the tea room to a resolution demanding the resignation of Mr Attlee and his replacement by Bevin. I was deputed to be the man to go to Bevin to tell him that we'd got all this arranged, so would he please put on his best suit and be ready to go to the Palace at any moment.

At this stage things began to go a bit awry. Instead of going directly to Bevin I went first to his P.P.S., Percy Wells, who had been my union colleague in the Faversham area and was now its Member of Parliament. I said to Percy, 'I want to see Ernie because we think we've got it all fixed up and we propose to tell the Prime Minister that there are enough of us to vote him out. I'd like to see Ernie first just to let him know about it.'

Off Percy went to see Ernie, and off Ernie at once sent him to see the Chief Whip, who then saw the Prime Minister . . . and before I got anywhere near Ernie the fat was in the fire, and the Whips were marching round the House to find out what was in this extraordinary story, and who was behind it.

Then I was sent for by Ernie. He saw me in his room next door to the Prime Minister and wanted to know what it was all about. I told him. He looked at me, said that he had never really trusted me, and added, 'And now you are acting as office boy for that bastard

Dalton! I don't want to see you again.' (Happily for me, this wish was not permanent.)

So my great attempt to make him Prime Minister was not really well received. As I went out of his room he came down the corridor after me and put his great hand on my shoulder. I thought that he was trying to make things up a little, but he gave me another ticking off about organizing revolts and disloyalties, asked me to tell Dr Dalton just what he could do with himself and assured me that he, Bevin, would see to it that Dalton was properly dealt with for organizing such a revolt. Nothing I could say would persuade him that it wasn't poor Dalton who was doing it at all.

I went back to Gordon Walker to report what had happened, and we sat in the tea room feeling very crestfallen indeed. Then came the inevitable summons to the Chief Whip's office. The Chief Whip then was Willy Whiteley, who was a kindly man but a very firm Chief Whip. He gave me a real clobbering, and said that as far as he was concerned it was only my relative youth and inexperience that could save me. A day or two later I received another telephone message: would I please go to see the Prime Minister?

I felt that that was the end of everything. I'd had the Foreign Secretary, I'd had the Chief Whip and now I was going to get it from the Father himself. Well, there was nothing I could do about it. My chances of progressing from P.P.S. at the Treasury to a government job seemed to have receded into an indefinite future, if, indeed, there was to be any future for me in the House of Commons.

I went to Downing Street to receive the biggest surprise of my life. I was duly received by the Prime Minister who proceeded to offer me the job of Under-Secretary of State at the Ministry of Agriculture! So there I was, a full-blown Junior Minister, with barely two years in the House of Commons and one abortive revolt behind me!

I left Dalton and the Treasury to go to the Ministry of Agriculture where Tom Williams, later Lord Williams of Barnburgh, was then Minister. Dalton appointed Douglas Jay to succeed me as his P.P.S.

There was an Autumn Budget in 1947 and it had, of course, to be introduced by Dalton. The tradition in Dalton's day was that before the introduction of a Budget the Chancellor and the P.P.S. had lunch together at No. 11 Downing Street, and then the P.P.S. would accompany the Chancellor to the House, staying by his side to make sure that he was not waylaid. On this occasion, however,

Dalton was stopped on his way to the Chamber by John Carvel, a well-known lobby journalist and the father of Robert Carvel, the present political correspondent of the London *Evening Standard*.

Dalton had known John Carvel for years and he stopped to chat with him for a moment, very misguidedly mentioning one or two of the things that he proposed to do in his Budget. It never occurred to Dalton that there could be any harm in this; he was on his way into the Chamber to make his Budget speech, and it never crossed his mind that any newspaper could print it before he said it.

But it did. A few lines of Budget news got into the Stop Press column of the old London *Star*, not, indeed, before Dalton got up, but before he sat down. That was enough to make Dalton feel that he had to resign as Chancellor. He was by then so broken by his struggles in the Cabinet that I think he would have resigned soon, anyway, but he would not have gone because of what was inevitably described as a Budget scandal. Dalton was undoubtedly indiscreet, but whether the incident was sufficiently scandalous to require the resignation of a Senior Minister I am less sure. Dalton himself felt that it was, and that was that.

The reason I was chosen for the Ministry of Agriculture is rather interesting. When Labour took office in 1945 the senior Ministers, who had mostly served in the Coalition Government during the war, more or less chose themselves. The 1945 election brought in a host of new and unknown young men, but nobody got around to sorting us out and seeing who had experience of what. The junior posts went mostly to people who had been M.P.s before or during the war, or who had reached fairly senior positions in the Labour Party, in their unions or in local government.

Mr Attlee was concerned to keep a balance between the political and the trade union sides of the Labour movement. Tom Williams, the Minister of Agriculture, had been a miner, but he had been an M.P. since 1922, and he had been at the Ministry of Agriculture in the Labour Government of 1924. So although he had been a trade unionist and was one of the miners' groups of M.P.s, he had for long been identified with the political side of the movement. Mr Attlee wanted another trade unionist at the Ministry of Agriculture, so he had appointed Percy Collick as one of the joint under-secretaries there. Collick was a railwayman who had been assistant general secretary of the Associated Society of Locomotive Engineers and Firemen, and he was on the National Executive of the Labour Party. He was a splendid person, but for all his sterling qualities as a trade unionist, he was not outstanding at negotiating agricultural Bills through the House of Commons. When it came to getting the great Agriculture Act of 1947 on the Statute Book it was realized that a more detailed knowledge of agriculture might be helpful in the ministerial team.

Somebody noticed that I was not only a trade unionist but had worked with the agricultural industry throughout the war, had been a member of the Hertfordshire War Agricultural Executive Committee, and had, indeed, a good deal of first-hand agricultural experience. So it was decided to put this to work.

For me, that was another wonderful opportunity, because it meant that instead of sitting night after night with next to nothing to do except to deal with an occasional question, which is the lot of many parliamentary secretaries, I was plunged in at the deep end of some of Labour's major pieces of legislation. I went through all the debates, learned how to handle committees, and acquired a great amount of invaluable parliamentary experience.

Those years of Labour Government were bedevilled by rows with a group of 'left-wingers' in the Parliamentary Party, already beginning to be called 'Bevanites'. They were always an odd mixture, and although they took their name from Aneurin Bevan and it flattered him to be regarded as their leader, he didn't really share the views of most of his followers: indeed Aneurin would probably have been about the first man sent to Siberia if the rest of them had ever had their way.

The Bevanite row in the Labour Party was partly endemic in the philosophical differences between theoretical Socialism and the approach of those of us who were in the Labour movement to secure practical reforms; and partly it was concerned with personalities. Aneurin Bevan was no Marxist, though he tended to be surrounded by theorists and the natural descendants of the I.W.W. – the International Workers of the World, or the 'wobblies', as they were called in America. Despite all the evidence to the contrary, and even if they themselves were not Communists, they still believed that pretty well everything that came out of the Russian Revolution was somehow good. Even when millions of people, including their own friends, suffered from Russian actions, they still believed that the Russians were 'goodies' standing up to the 'baddies' of all the rest of the world. This was not logical reasoning, it was sheer illogical belief.

All these differences came to a head over post-war British policy in

Germany. Ernie Bevin at first had been very much against any question of allowing the Germans arms to share in the defence of Western Europe. Gradually his views changed, partly because he grew to realize what a noble and heroic part many German trade unionists had in fact played in the war, partly because harsh experience of Russian tactics in Greece and elsewhere made him understand the importance of Western defence, and partly because of the enormous cost that would fall on Britain if some degree of German rearmament were not to be permitted.

The 'left-wingers', who, of course, love all their fellow-men far more than horrid 'right-wingers' are supposed to do, could not bring themselves to love their fellow German Social Democrats or their fellow German trade unionists. A tremendous and fearful battle ensued, mostly fought behind the scenes, and when bits of this fighting emerged in public it often seemed to concern quite secondary issues. It was never really clear how much of the 'left-wing' or Bevanite opposition to the Government reflected anti-German emotionalism, how much was theoretical 'Socialism', or how much reflected simply personal political ambitions. The squabbles, however, went on and on, and undoubtedly contributed to the sadly reduced majority with which we won the General Election of 1950.

In October 1950 Sir Stafford Cripps resigned as Chancellor of the Exchequer because of illness, and he was succeeded by Hugh Gaitskell. In the spring of 1951 Mr Attlee had to go into hospital with a duodenal ulcer, and during his absence the Bevanite row finally broke into the open. Ostensibly this was over charges, proposed in Mr Gaitskell's Budget, for false teeth and spectacles supplied under the National Health Service, but this was merely the culmination of endless rows in the Cabinet over Germany and defence policy generally. Aneurin Bevan, Harold Wilson and John Freeman resigned from the Government. Whether Gaitskell was right to force the issue on teeth and specs with his Budget, or whether he would have been allowed to force it if Attlee had not been in hospital, are neither here nor there. But the main issue had to come out at some time and had it been left to fester it might have broken out at a moment that would have been much worse for the Government. Anyway, the resignations created various vacancies requiring a minor reshuffle. I was sent for by Herbert Morrison, who was Acting Prime Minister, and he asked if I would like to leave the Ministry of Agriculture for the Ministry of Works. I thought that he was offering me another under-secretaryship, so I said that I didn't see much point in the change. But Morrison said, 'No, no, I didn't mean that. I meant, would you like to go to the Ministry of Works as Minister?'

I was flabbergasted. I remember that I managed to gasp out, 'Do you mean that I get the title as well?'

Morrison said, 'Yes, of course you will. You will be a Minister of Cabinet rank but outside the Cabinet.'

I left with strict instructions that I was not to say anything about my impending promotion until it was officially announced. This was to allow time for King George VI to be formally consulted.

I felt that I had to get advice from somebody, so I went to my old friend Dr Mont Follick, who was then Labour M.P. for Lough-borough, and who will appear again in these memoirs when I come to write about the Middle East. He was a wealthy eccentric of great kindness of heart – when he died he left, I believe, a quarter of a million pounds to a University to found a Chair in what I used impishly to call 'pidgin English', a bequest, incidentally, which has not yet been carried out. Mont Follick invited me to lunch at Claridge's – which he regarded as his 'club'. I told him that I'd been offered the job of a full-blown Minister of Works and asked whether I should take it. We discussed the pros and cons and decided that it was a reasonable risk!

Until the appointment was announced I was still Under-Secretary at the Ministry of Agriculture, and next day I had to preside at a great meeting of agriculturists in Wisbech. The tomato-growers, horticultural producers and glasshouse-owners were then up in arms over our handling of some of their problems, and I was sent up with a top official in the Ministry to try to sort it all out. I couldn't tell anyone that it was really nothing to do with me any more, and matters were not improved by a telephone call that came for me in the middle of the meeting to say that an aeroplane was being sent to fly me back to London to go to the Palace. Not unnaturally the horticulturists were far from pleased. They had taken the trouble to come from all over the place for this meeting, and here was a pipsqueak of a Junior Minister saying that he had to dash back to London. I still couldn't tell them why – all I could do was to mutter that something important had happened which required my presence in London – they assumed, I suppose, that it had to do with agriculture. They didn't speed my parting very well.

However , I flew back to London, went to the Palace and was sworn in as a Minister and member of the Privy Council. When you become a member of the Privy Council you are sworn in on a little red Testament, and you are permitted to keep this as a memento of the occasion. But there is nothing to distinguish it from any other little red Testament, and if you want an indication that it was actually used for your swearing in you have to go afterwards to the office of the Lord Privy Seal and persuade him to sign the flyleaf. This I did, and there was an amusing sequel thirteen years later. In 1964 I was sworn in again as a Secretary of State – as Minister of Works in 1951 I was merely a Minister of the Crown. Again I was given a little red Testament and thinking that it had been given to me personally I put it in my pocket. But the Clerk to the Privy Council came up to me and said, 'I'm sorry, but I must ask you to give your Testament back. I see from our records that you have had one before!'

At the General Election of 1951 Labour was defeated. I held my seat at Belper, but of course I lost my job as Minister of Works and became an Opposition M.P.

The Bevanite row, which simmered on, contributed to our defeat, but the major figures of the Government, the architects of the great Labour victory in 1945, were also tired. Looking back, I'm not sure that it might not have been better for Labour to have lost the election in 1945 and to have come to power in 1950 – or in 1948 or 1949, when a post-war Conservative Government might well have had to go to the country. Our top men in 1945 had all had five gruelling war years. Moreover, we took office in 1945 with a lot of war-time quarrels unresolved. Aneurin Bevan, for instance, had campaigned viciously in the war-time Parliament against Bevin as Minister of Labour and against Morrison as Home Secretary in the Coalition Government, and he had shown his contempt for Attlee, whom he regarded as a Churchill stooge. It was Bevan who had campaigned most vigorously for the break-up of the war-time Coalition. Of the major Labour figures in the Coalition I think it was only Morrison who really supported him. Ernest Bevin regarded this as a betrayal, forcing Labour out of the Coalition and thereby producing a situation in which (as he saw it in the spring of 1945) the country would probably be left with a Tory Government to deal with the tasks of peace. With all that sort of conflict lying around it was hardly likely that these men would form a very harmonious team when they met around the Cabinet table.

There was disharmony from the start, but that first post-war

Labour Government was a great one because the tremendous personalities in it automatically balanced one another. Ernie Bevin had no personal ambitions to be Prime Minister. He wanted to be Foreign Secretary and he had no designs on anybody except that he was determined that Herbert Morrison should never shove Attlee out. He disliked Cripps and had no time at all for Bevan. Whatever personal ambitions there were in the rest of the team more or less cancelled each other out. Attlee was hoist up on Bevin's shoulders, and as long as Bevin kept him firmly there nothing could break.

By 1951 Bevin had gone, Cripps had gone, Attlee and Morrison were both ageing. Moreover, Morrison had had a disastrous period at the Foreign Office when he succeeded Bevin. In-fighting by the Bevanites hampered the political development of the younger men who succeeded these great figures of the past. Bevanite quarrels also seriously hampered Labour in Opposition. But for the Bevanites and the various splits they brought about, Labour would certainly have won the General Election of 1959. They kept Labour out of office for at least five years.

Aneurin Bevan was a strange man. He had great ability and great ambition. He could do the most contrary things, but you could never call him insincere. He had a burning faith in whatever seemed good to him at the time but, outside politics, had no personal faith at all. I have tried to write of what the Christian faith has meant to me in my approach to the Labour movement in its widest sense: many others in the Party have likewise come to Labour primarily because of religious faith – there is a long history of Christian Socialism in our movement. Others, of whom Ernie Bevin was one, grew up without religious faith, but acquired faith in such qualities as the dignity of man; it was a different sort of faith, but it gave them something that they stood by all their lives. Aneurin, and certainly his friends, seem to have grown up without faith in anything. He was a bigger man than his friends, a law to himself, and he had qualities which set him apart from those who were called (or called themselves) Bevanites. He certainly saw himself as a potential Prime Minister, a greater Lloyd George. He was flattered by all the attention and the publicity he got, but he never commanded that solid backing in the Labour movement which would have been necessary to give him the leadership. His friends, or so-called friends, were not of his stature. They needed their dogma or, for some, a belief in Soviet Communism, as a prop. They did not like admitting that they needed a faith; they wouldn't accept any of the Western faiths; and they were not big enough to invent a faith of their own. That is the difference between the so-called 'Left' and the rest of us. We want the Labour Party to maintain certain beliefs in freedom and personal liberty, and to support them throughout the world. In political terms, if this sometimes means agreeing with the Tories about certain courses of action, so be it. These other chaps are fighting to maintain something long since shown to be flyblown, and in their view the touchstone of political action is whether it is in line with their current dogma.

The contrast between Bevin and Bevan was fascinating. Ernie always wanted to do things; he wasn't much interested in discussion, he wanted to get things done. Aneurin loved discussion, and except on one or two matters, I don't think he really much minded which way the vote went at the end. Ernie hated flattery – he would bawl your head off if you dared to say a kindly word about him in his presence. Aneurin was the most flatterable of men.

You had to have a taste for strong meat to like Ernie. He was a tough and ruthless man. But he had certain broad principles about people, how they should live and how they should be treated, and he stuck to them. He was essentially a practical idealist, and he made up his mind about issues on their merits as he saw them, but always in accordance with his principles. What he didn't have was dogma – he accepted that there could be more than one way of accomplishing a purpose. I think this mainly explains why the 'Left' hated him; they wanted everything decided according to their ideological touchstone.

Aneurin had great charm. Some people are naturally made to be bigots and they deliberately try to turn on charm when it suits them. Aneurin was the other way round; he was naturally made to be charming, and he had deliberately to turn on the bile. He was generous in every sort of way, and naturally kind. Paradoxically, he could also be a bully, but really he only bullied those who let themselves be bullied. If you stood up to him he would smile broadly, and accept that you were not going to let him get away with something. We had tremendous battles – I remember his describing me at one meeting of the Parliamentary Party as 'Arthur Deakin's lackey'. And yet, in spite of everything and our wide divergencies politically, there was a kind of friendship between us which couldn't be denied. I have described how Cripps never forgave me for my speech at the 1939 Party Conference. Aneurin could forgive, and I think he really respected you if you stood up to him. Indeed, his tragedy was that not enough people stood up to him. After fearsome rows at Party meetings in Room 14 at the House of Commons or in the Shadow Cabinet, we would meet in the smoking-room, where Aneurin, like Churchill, had his favourite corner. He never resented the fact that we'd just had a battle.

I don't know what sort of Prime Minister Aneurin would have made, but I could have accepted him as Leader if it hadn't been for his friends. If one could have divorced him from the group of sub-servient acolytes who surrounded him – well, history might have been different. But I suppose that couldn't have happened.

The years in Opposition, from 1951 to 1964, were formative years for me. There were four Conservative Prime Ministers over that period, Churchill, Eden, Macmillan and Alec Douglas-Home. About Churchill I shall not try to say anything. He was a towering figure from the past, and I saw him closely only in the enfeeblement of age. Eden, I had a lot of regard for. But, as Montgomery is alleged to have said about somebody else, 'his tragedy was that he was promoted above his ceiling'. He was not cut out to be the No. 1; he should have remained No. 2. He was right about Hitler, about Mussolini and about Chamberlain, but he always managed to be late in being right, and even when he was right he always seemed to remain in two minds. Yet I think he is a genuinely good man.

I have much less regard for Macmillan. As Prime Minister he always seemed to me to be a man who believed in acting the part of Prime Minister. He was an actor who believed in acting. Now I don't think you can ever have a great actor who does not in some sense believe in the part he is playing. Macmillan was the reverse – he believed in acting, not in the part. This may seem a harsh judgement, but it is what I genuinely feel about him.

Alec Douglas-Home I like as a good guy, but I think he should have remained the 14th Earl of Home. But he *is* a nice guy, and politics has so many of the other kind.

Iain Macleod I respected greatly, and I share the feeling that his death was a sad loss to the nation as well as to his Party. For Maudling I have also a great deal of respect.

Two Conservative politicians from an earlier generation who impressed me greatly were Oliver Stanley and Harry Crookshank. Oliver Stanley seemed to me to be a really great man, and I think he might have made a great Prime Minister if he had not had all his other interests as the scion of a great family. He brought a real sense of integrity to politics. Harry Crookshank was deceptively gentle in speech and appearance, but he could be cruelly incisive. He was a wonderful man in Committee, and I learned a great deal from him.

I had a lot of time for R. A. Butler. He seems to me to be a man who, in a way, destroyed himself, at least in a political sense. I suspect that he is enjoying himself more in academic life than he ever enjoyed Parliament. In politics he wasn't sufficiently dedicated to what he had to do. He was always too apologetic, too given to explaining himself. Yet I think he could have made a very considerable Prime Minister – I can't think that under him the country would have taken a single decision that was morally wrong. He is a pleasant man and a very good man – I mean a *really* good man. But he is not ruthless. He simply did not have what it takes to become Prime Minister.

I can't say that any of the Liberals ever impinged on me at all, either in my period of Opposition or later when we were again in office. But I think that there is a place, and probably a growing one, for a third party in our political system. That third party may not be the Liberals, indeed it probably won't be. It will be more like the Labour Party in the first days of Labour representation in Parliament. Essentially it will be a party that stands for people as individuals as against the mass parties of the Organization Age. Both Labour and Conservative parties are going the same way in becoming more and more authoritarian – I don't mean Communist or Fascist, but simply authoritarian. Neither is paying half enough attention to people as individuals. The two major parties may be the Ins and Outs like the old Whigs and Tories, with five years of one followed by five years of the other, but I think that, if they continue in this way, a growing number of people will get fed up with both and want a third party strong enough either to hold a balance between them or to kick the bottom of whichever of the other two is in power. It is not easy to see how an effective third party can come into being, nor that it would really be desirable. That is why I feel so strongly a need for the Labour Party to recapture its humanity and concern for the individual.

But I'm reflecting, and I must get back to my narrative. When I lost my job as a Minister in 1951 I found things far from easy. I had my pay as an M.P. but in those days it wasn't all that much – with all the expenses he has to meet an M.P.'s pay is not really much even now. In 1951 I had young children, a house with a mortgage and I wasn't at all sure whether I could carry on in Parliament. I had my union job to go back to, and I debated seriously whether it would not be wise to return to it.

One week-end while I was much bothered about all this I was invited down to Cambridgeshire by Harry Walston, whom I'd got to know when I was Under-Secretary at the Ministry of Agriculture.

Harry Walston – he became Lord Walston in 1961 – farmed several thousand acres near Cambridge. I met him for the first time when I addressed a meeting on Labour's agricultural policy. He took part in the discussion after my speech and his contribution, though critical, was tinged with friendliness. He clearly didn't think much of this townie (as he regarded me) coming along to talk of agricultural policy, but some of the things I'd said had made him think that I might not be so bad after all. When the time came for me to reply I picked on him in no uncertain terms.

Out of that came one of my most abiding friendships. Shortly after that meeting Harry Walston invited me to visit his farms and he discovered that I did know something about farming. He had stood as the Liberal candidate for Huntingdon in 1945, but he was sympathetic to Labour and later he joined the Labour Party and subsequently fought a whole series of elections for us. He was very good to me, inviting me to the country with my family, and putting up the children at week-ends. On one of these week-end visits after the election in 1951 I discussed my future with him, and it so happened that a fellow-guest at his house was Cecil King. I talked about the possibility of leaving the House of Commons to return to the union, and King asked, rather directly, if this was because I wanted to, or because I had to. I said that it was quite a bit of the former, but it didn't really matter, because I didn't see how I was going to maintain the family and keep our house and our car on what Parliament was then willing to pay M.P.s.

King then made me what I am convinced was a wholly genuine offer of a retainer to work for the *Mirror*. Our relations soured later, but he said then – though he might deny it like fury now – that he thought it important for me to remain in politics. There have been some pretty wild rumours about the money I am supposed to have had from the *Mirror*, but it wasn't particularly lavish. King offered me £500 a year as a retainer, to be available to give advice, to suggest social topics that the *Mirror* might take up, and I was to be paid separately for any articles that I might write. (Later the retainer was increased to £1,250.) There were no commitments, I was not expected to support the *Mirror* in any way, or to write on any subject I might not want to.

After discussing King's offer with my wife, and with Harry Walston and his wife, I decided in 1953 to accept it. At the time it seemed to me generous, and I am quite certain that it was well-meant. Without it, I do not see how I could have managed to stay in politics.

At first I enjoyed my association with the *Mirror*. I met a great many interesting people, I was paid properly for everything I wrote, and the money was a great help. But there came a period when my views about things and some of the *Mirror*'s views began to clash. There also came a period when Mr King seemed to become more aware of being the nephew of his uncle (Lord Northcliffe). I used regularly to lunch with Mr King alone, always under the picture of his uncle with his forelock falling down, and gradually I saw Mr King steadily looking more like his uncle.

I could not help being caught in the crossfire of some of the *Mirror*'s domestic politics. I was on good terms with Hugh Cudlipp, and at first Cudlipp and Cecil King were very close. Then they began to drift apart.

Mixed up with all this was the dreadfully confused situation that arose over Lord Thomson's bid for Odhams, which would have given him control of the *Daily Herald*. Quite how he came round to the view I don't know, but Hugh Gaitskell was persuaded that it would be best for the Labour Party if Lord Thomson acquired the *Daily Herald*. John Beavan, then editor of the *Daily Herald*, shared the Gaitskell–Thomson view.

On the other hand, I was certain that the *Herald*, which the Labour Party badly needed, would be better off in the hands of Cudlipp and King. This put me rather at loggerheads with Gaitskell, and as I was also having my own disagreements with King, there was a very tangled situation.

The *Mirror* ultimately got control of the *Herald*. It was said at the time that I backed the King bid because of my retainer from the *Mirror*, but that is absolutely untrue. I did not and do not think that the Thomson organization was the right stable for the *Daily Herald*. I did want the *Herald* to stay Labour, and I did then believe that King would do what he said and put in enough money to keep it going. He did in fact keep it going for the seven years he promised, but nobody seemed to be able to make a go of it.

Where I was wrong was over Cudlipp. I thought that Cudlipp

could run the *Daily Herald* as it ought to have been run; and I'm still convinced that a popular Labour newspaper could be run successfully. But they just weren't able to do it. Maybe a younger Cudlipp could have done it; maybe Cudlipp just lost his touch for running newspapers. We have now seen what the Australian Rupert Murdoch has done with the *Sun*. A few years ago we'd have said that just wasn't possible, but it has happened.

The best friend I made at the *Mirror* was 'Cassandra', the late Bill (Sir William) Connor. He was one of the greatest men the world of journalism has ever seen. We used to have tremendous fights – we would argue from El Vino's to the Savoy and back again – but I had infinite affection and infinite respect for him. He was incapable of doing or saying a mean thing.

I made another splendid friend in Bill Greig, then political correspondent for the *Mirror*, though I'd met him before as one of the most distinguished members of the Lobby group of journalists in the House of Commons. Bill Greig couples great ability with humanity and sound judgement, and he is the soul of honour. Later, when I had severed my connection with the *Mirror* and needed someone to help me with Press relations at the D.E.A., Bill Greig at once volunteered to give up his newspaper work to join me. He came with me to the Foreign Office and no one can ever have had a more loyal Press adviser. Throughout our association he has never taken any salary either from me or the Government.

My friendship with Connor was ended only by his death – if death can be said to end friendships which, in the deepest sense, of course, it can't. My friendship with Bill Greig, I am proud to say, goes on unchanged. My association with the rest of the *Mirror* just petered out, and was finally ended, as they say, by mutual consent. Before it turned sour I enjoyed it, and I'm quite sure that Cecil King's original offer sprang from a genuine, decent desire to help, coupled with the realization – for he was a shrewd newspaperman – that the kind of unbiased advice I could give was of real value to a popular newspaper. In any case, I wasn't the only person to whom he gave a retainer: there are people now regarded as the epitome of public propriety who were kept alive when they were struggling by Mr King. And why not? Winston Churchill was kept alive by Lord Beaverbrook. Young men making their way, and politicians out of office, need help if they are to maintain themselves: nobody thinks the worse of an ex-Minister who is given a job in the City, or becomes a part-time member of some company's board. There are always people ready to cry corruption as soon as it becomes known that a politician gets a retainer from anybody, but such criticism often derives from envy as much as anything else. In my own case I can say only that my connection with the *Mirror* never influenced my vote or my judgement in any way at all, any more than it influenced the *Mirror* editorially when it argued that I should stand down from the second ballot in the election for the Leadership of the Labour Party after Gaitskell's death in order to give Harold Wilson a clear run.

My personal experience of journalism has not given me a high regard for modern newspaper men. I can just forgive professionals for writing as they say they have to, but only just. But standards have declined everywhere. Journalists, or at any rate some of them, used to be men of integrity on whom you could rely. If men like Trevor Evans or the late Ian Mackay came up to you and said, 'George, like to have a chat? And of course it's off the record', they meant just that. But there's a new generation of chaps now, and they work in tandem. If they get something off the record that they know they mustn't use they seem quite likely to arrange that somebody else uses it so that they can pick it up, and then they say, 'Well, I'm awfully sorry, George. Of course *I* didn't break your confidence, but as *he'd* got it already I couldn't *not* use it.'

They say to me, 'It's more than my job is worth not to do it.' Well, I've had to do things in my life which have cost me my job, or might have done so, and I don't see why journalists shouldn't sometimes. But the standards of the Press have dropped terribly. Almost everyone seems to be on the make, to want a scoop at all costs, and if it means cheating you, well, you'll just be cheated.

Journalists nowadays don't seem to write their own thinking any more. The old political and industrial correspondents did – they knew what was happening but they didn't betray confidences, for they wrote what they themselves thought about it. That doesn't seem to happen now. Too many of the modern men don't seem to work like that. They just walk around the lobby or the conference, buy drinks for a certain number of chaps, and churn out a few gossip paragraphs. They are not acting as thinkers, or exercising a judgement of their own. They become just eavesdroppers and gossip-writers.

I'm particularly vulnerable to this sort of journalism because I'm given to being slightly uncontrolled. I don't like giving handouts, and this breed of journalists seems quite uninterested in reporting

Hugh Dalton, Chancellor of the Exchequer, 1947

Leaving for Poland with
John Hind, M.P., Roy Mason, M.P. and Hugh Delargy, M.P., 1954

Talking with constituents, May 1955

accurately anything you may actually say. They just follow you round and watch and wait for the break, for the phrase or action which, taken by itself, without regard for anything that went before or came after, is supposed to 'make a story'.

They also refuse to accept that at some point we are all entitled to go off duty, that we all have personal lives. There was an appalling instance of this when I went to New York as Foreign Secretary to attend the new session of the United Nations General Assembly in September 1967. I had a gruelling time, and at the end of a very long day somebody suggested that I might like to go to a party that was being held on board the *Queen Mary*, which was then in New York.

I did what anybody else would do – I was gay and entered into the spirit of the party. One of the people I danced with was the wife of a member of the ship's company.

What happened next was that I was followed round the dance floor by photographers until they could get a picture taken from an angle that made it look as if I was looking down the lady's bosom. That picture was flashed all over the world, and it did me a lot of harm, because it scarcely helped my credibility as Foreign Secretary. But it had nothing to do with my being Foreign Secretary, it had nothing to do with news value, it was simply an effort to get a picture from an angle that could make it look as if I was misbehaving. Much the same sort of thing happened at a subsequent Labour Party Conference.

The journalists and photographers say that they have to do this in order to get on in their profession. All I can say is that when I first knew the journalistic profession it didn't need to do that: it got on by being good at its job. It seems to me that the Press, the journalists, the photographers and everybody in it, has deteriorated enormously. I suppose that this has to do with the fight for circulation, which is the fight for advertising, which in turn is the fight with television. It is a sad reflection on our times.

E

3

Shadow Cabinet:
An Odd Encounter

Soon after the election of 1951 when Labour went into Opposition I was elected to the Shadow Cabinet and became the spokesman on defence. During this period a very curious incident occurred. This was the dinner party which the National Executive Committee of the Labour Party, with the Shadow Cabinet also present, gave to Mr Khrushchev and Mr Bulganin on 23 April 1956. Acres of print have been written about this dinner and my alleged part in it. Here are the facts.

To explain them fully, I must first go back briefly to a visit I had made to Poland in September 1954. That was my first visit to a Communist country, and I went in company with several other members of Parliament, among them Desmond Donnelly, Hugh Delargy, John Hynd, Lewis Silkin, Ian Mikardo and Roy Mason, as officially invited guests of the Polish Government. It had been for me the most depressing, and at the same time one of the most impressive, visits I have ever made. Repression was at its height – even Gomulka was in prison – and the harshness with which people were treated, politically and otherwise, was terrifying. We had travelled across Poland in a locked sleeping-car, we had met English and Scottish wives of Polish ex-Servicemen in the most unhappy circumstances, and we had been followed around late at night by the secret police. We had been given a guided tour of a war-time concentration camp. As our interpreter-guide described the place to us it didn't need much imagination to see him wearing the stormtrooper's uniform that the people who had run the place wore. When we would much have preferred to have left, he insisted that we should see what he called 'the *pièce de résistance*', which turned out to be the gas-oven. We saw a mound of charred remains, and I remember his turning them over with the toe of his shoe and saying, 'Look, these are all charred bones.'

The whole Polish scene was infinitely depressing, redeemed only by the courage and determination of the Polish people themselves. Roy Mason and I went down a coalmine near Krakow and the miners were absolutely delighted to see us. Guards or no guards, they were determined to show us the conditions in which they worked, the kind of food they had to eat, the extent to which they were not Communists. They worked in conditions that would never have been tolerated in British pits and their courage was deeply moving. Everywhere we went people showed the same impressive determination not to be cowed by the régime. We were always meeting Poles who had served with the French or British armies, so there was no great language difficulty. The courage of these individual Poles was wonderful, but the conditions in which they had to live were appalling.

There was one particularly harrowing incident at a railway station. One of our members had been asked by a family in his constituency to try to see their daughter, who was married to a Polish ex-soldier. He had her address and he kept on asking to be taken there. He was always promised that this would be done, but it never was, and finally it became apparent that he was not going to be allowed to see the girl's home. We made quite a demonstration about this, and finally our guards relented to the extent of agreeing to bring her to meet us at a railway station. It was a pitiful interview on the open platform. The poor girl had her babies with her, and she was in such a state that we all had a whip round to try to do something to alleviate her position. What happened afterwards I don't know; perhaps it was a mistake to have insisted on seeing her.

In the train I was sharing a sleeping compartment with Hugh Delargy. He is a left-winger compared with me, but he is also a Roman Catholic, and he was very upset by the conditions in which he had found his Roman Catholic fellows in Poland. Our coach was locked off from the rest of the train, so that we couldn't talk to anybody else on the journey, and next door to Hugh's and my compartment were our two chief guards. Hugh has a magnificent Irish voice (although he was actually born in Manchester), and he suggested that it might be a good thing if we treated our guards to a concert, which, incidentally, would also keep them awake. Throughout the night we made those two Communist interpreters listen to a remarkable repertoire of Irish revolutionary songs. When we got out of the train in the morning we ourselves weren't feeling any too bright, but we had the satisfaction of seeing that our guards looked decidedly the worse for wear.

In Warsaw we had been taken to the bank of the Vistula to see the ever-burning flame which is a memorial to the Russian liberators: and we looked across the Vistula to where the Russian Army had actually stayed put while the Germans murdered the inhabitants of Warsaw. I shall never, as long as I live, forget Hugh Delargy in his best Irish brogue saying very loudly, 'I have never before seen a memorial to an army that didn't come.' Subsequently we visited the ghetto, still then walled, where the massacre took place. It was a miserably depressing visit.

I have described it here because it was still vividly in my mind only a short while later when I saw Khrushchev and Bulganin being lionized in London, and having a considerable success. Bulganin looked the most benign figure one could ever wish to see, with beautiful blue eyes and a very handsome head. Mr Khrushchev, who stayed in power when they dropped Bulganin, scarcely needs description. The Labour Party wanted to give them a dinner, and although some of our left-wingers were wildly excited about it, in fact there was a good deal of touchiness on both sides in making the arrangements. We wanted to take the opportunity to present a list of Democratic Socialists who were imprisoned by Communist régimes in various countries and to ask the Russian leaders to use their influence to get these comrades out. The Soviet Ambassador made a lot of difficulty about this list being presented. Hugh Gaitskell insisted, and finally it was agreed that the list should be handed over at the dinner on condition that Gaitskell made no speech about it. The whole question of speeches was gone into in great detail, and it was finally accepted both by us and the Russian Embassy that there should be only two – a speech of welcome by Alderman Edwin Gooch, of the Agricultural Workers Union, who was that year's chairman of the Labour Party, and a reply by Bulganin.

In the Harcourt Room of the House of Commons the seating was arranged so that the guests sat at a top table with their backs to the Terrace, and the rest of us sat at tables set at right-angles to the top table. I was seated about three down on the inside of one of these tables, right in front of Khrushchev.

When dinner was over and the time for speeches came, a number of our left-wing colleagues were very anxious to demonstrate their friendliness and warmth for the Russian visitors. They felt this the more so because they knew that others of us were very bothered about the things that were going on in Russian-dominated countries. We felt that we were really being too generous and welcoming to these Russians, and allowing them, as it were, to get away with murder. There wasn't supposed to be an opportunity for rival speech-making, for the speeches, as I have said, had been carefully limited to two. These were duly made. Alderman Gooch said his piece, and Mr Bulganin read his reply.

Instead of leaving it at that, some of our colleagues began to thump the table and shout, 'We want Khrushchev', repeating it rather like a football slogan, banging on the table and chanting, 'We – want – Khrush – chev.'

Khrushchev was not averse to being wanted, and when all this was interpreted to him he beamed on everybody, and – to the consternation of the officials on both sides – he got up to make a speech. Quite obviously he hadn't prepared anything and he just went on and on, working himself up as he went along. He delivered a great denunciation of Germany, put in a lot of stuff about the beginning of the war, and followed this with a particularly offensive passage about Britain's role in the war – how we had thrown the bloodthirsty Germans at the throat of the nice Russians, and so on.

In those days I smoked a pipe, and I was sitting there filling my pipe when I felt that his condemnation of Britain was more than I could stand, and I muttered, 'May God forgive you.'

To my astonishment Khrushchev stopped and asked what I had said. I had no intention of responding, and the people round me were most anxious that I shouldn't reply, when Khrushchev went on to say that I was apparently afraid to repeat what I had said. All this was being interpreted back and forth, but I got an impression that Khrushchev really knew more English than he let on, for he seemed able to take up points before they had been interpreted to him.

Anyway, I wasn't going to be told that I was afraid to speak, so I said that I'd gladly repeat my remark, which had been, 'May God forgive you.' And I explained that what I meant was that it was 'you' who signed the treaty with Ribbentrop, not us, and that if 'you' hadn't signed your treaty with Ribbentrop, we wouldn't have been at war for a whole year before you even got started, that a lot of my comrades wouldn't now be dead, and that a lot of brave Poles wouldn't now be dead.

At this, absolute pandemonium broke out. The various members of the Labour Party National Executive, of course, were pretty horrified, and Khrushchev launched into a tremendous tirade against Democratic Socialists, against Britain, and denounced pretty well everybody. In the course of this he got all kinds of people's tempers up. He and I went on having an altercation, whenever one could break in, about releasing prisoners and other things. This not only angered me but it also angered Sam Watson, who was among the gentlest of men but who was passionately concerned about the fate of Socialists in Eastern European countries. After a set-to with Sam Watson, Khrushchev succeeded in rousing Aneurin Bevan, who got up and said that he wanted to put a point to Comrade Khrushchev.

Comrade Khrushchev then rounded on Comrade Bevan in no uncertain terms, and I treasure the picture of Aneurin attempting to advance on the top table, wagging his finger and saying in that Welsh lilt of his, 'But this is ridiculous, Mr Khrushchev, this is ridiculous, Mr Khrushchev.'

It took a devil of a lot to restrain Aneurin and to get him back to his seat, and finally the whole episode more or less collapsed in total disorder. Gaitskell obviously thought it wiser to get the Russians out, and they retired from the room in what I suppose could be called high dudgeon. It was probably the only time in Europe that they had really been talked to seriously. I say 'in Europe', because I learned later that much the same sort of thing had happened when they had met the A.F.L.–C.I.O. trade union leaders at a dinner in Los Angeles. Walter Reuther, apparently, had been provoked into making much the same sort of observation that I did. I knew nothing about this at the time, but learned about it when I met Walter Reuther at an international conference later and we compared notes. But although I knew nothing about the American incident, it is just possible that the Russians thought that the two events were connected, and that there was some deep-laid plot between us.

I don't want to leave an impression that the events of this Khrushchev dinner were all either ludicrous, or bad-tempered, or bitchy. We had, in fact, a serious argument to put to the Russians, and as far as we could, we put it seriously. The wild stories that went round about the dinner put us all in a wrong light, and cloaked the fact that Gaitskell, Sam Watson, Aneurin Bevan and a number of other people as well as me had tried to put serious questions to the

Russians. It was not just a rather boorish evening with the hosts being discourteous to the guests. Khrushchev asked for what he got by the way he spoke to us – and it is just as important that a guest should not be rude to a host as that the host should be courteous to a guest. It was also particularly important at that time that the Russians should be left in no doubt about the feelings of Democratic Socialists throughout the world, especially about what was going on in countries that had not yet thrown off the Stalinist yoke.

The affair had a curious little anticlimax next day. The Speaker gave a lunch to the Russian visitors at the House of Commons and I was among the guests. I decided that the right tactics were to keep myself well away, so when drinks were being handed round before lunch I stayed in a corner with one or two of my own cronies, and didn't go anywhere near where the Russians were being made much of by people who seemed to me a bit over-anxious to mollify their feelings. All went well until after lunch. We were having coffee when who should approach me but Bulganin. He looked closely at me with those lovely blue eyes and said something in Russian which clearly meant something like, 'So you are the naughty fellow from last night!' The interpreter didn't want to interpret anything, but was persuaded to, and I said, 'Oh Yes.' We were perfectly polite and Bulganin invited me to come to Moscow and see Russia for myself. I said that I should be delighted to accept the invitation. At this point Khrushchev noticed the conversation and in typical Khrushchev fashion he barged over and asked the interpreter what was going on. The interpreter told him about the invitation to Moscow. I didn't want to get involved again, so I said that I regretted that I was just about to leave because I had to go to my constituency. I wished him a pleasant journey and said that I looked forward to seeing him in Moscow when I was able to take up Mr Bulganin's invitation.

I held out my hand, but Khrushchev didn't take it. He said very clearly, 'Niet, niet', and moved away. No confirmation of that invitation to Moscow ever arrived.

I don't think that the events of our dinner did any harm, and they may even have done a certain amount of good. There was, I think, some risk of the Russians being carried away by the decent generosity of ordinary people, and by the obsequiousness of some of our left-wingers, into believing that they could say or do just what they liked. We at least made it clear that there were some actions that we were not prepared to tolerate, and that they shouldn't mistake courtesy and hospitality for acceptance of Russian Communism.

The things that Khrushchev said in his speech conveyed a clear warning that it is still wise to remember. He threatened that if we didn't agree with the Russians about how to handle Germany, the Russians would make their own agreement with the Germans, as they had done before. I understand very well Russian feeling about the problem of Germany, but all the understanding in the world can't hide the fact that the Russians regard the whole of Central Europe as the area of their power of decision. Khrushchev made plain that night that if anyone in the Russian orbit sought to be free of Russian domination, he would be stamped on. To anyone who was at that dinner, the events in Czechoslovakia in 1968 can have come as no surprise.

4

Shadow Cabinet: Party Politics

MR ATTLEE'S RETIREMENT left the Labour Party in a gap, as it were, between two political generations. The great figures of the years between the wars, the men who had formed and carried on the Labour Government from 1945–51, were almost all gone from the scene. Herbert Morrison was still active, still full of political ambition, and he made a bid for the Leadership. But Herbert, for all his magnificent qualities, for all his splendid work for Labour, was ageing, and cruel as it was for the Party to appear to throw him aside, the instinct to look for a younger man as Leader was certainly right. Politics is a cruel business. Jim Griffiths commanded deep affection and respect, but in 1955 he was sixty-five. He did not seek the Leadership, and his election as Deputy Leader was clearly understood as a tribute to the Old Guard, and a means of maintaining continuity while the Party sorted itself out.

In different circumstances Aneurin Bevan might have succeeded to the Leadership. He could fill meetings in the country as hardly any other man could, and he himself considered that he had almost a right to the Leadership. But Aneurin suffered from his friends, and from his own temperament: the solid core of the party, particularly on the trade union side, was in no mood to go Bevanite. Hugh Gaitskell, who was the only one of his generation to have held really great office as Chancellor, was the obvious choice. Aneurin always held that Gaitskell was forced on the Party by the machine. To the extent that most responsible officials in the Labour Party and the unions – the professionals – preferred Gaitskell to him, he was right, but that is simply to contrast political realism with wishful thinking. As I've said before, without his friends Aneurin might well have become Leader of the Labour Party. With his friends, he was impossible.

But Aneurin's feeling that Gaitskell had been rather foisted on the Party had substance in another sense. Hugh was elected by the Parliamentary Party as the Leader always is, but he owed his support to the backing he was given by the old hard core of the great unions, then controlled by men like Arthur Deakin of the Transport Workers, Tom Williamson of the General Workers, Sam Watson and Will Lawther of the Mineworkers. Gaitskell was not elected to the National Executive of the Labour Party by the vote of the constituency parties, of the rank and file members. He was projected forward by Arthur Deakin and his colleagues, using the block vote of the unions to put him on the National Executive as Treasurer. Somehow our movement will put up with things like that, but it never forgets them. It was the source of much of the continuing hostility to Gaitskell from the Bevanites, and later reflected on me when the time came to choose between me and Harold Wilson.

Gaitskell's election, like Attlee's before him, reflected a division in the Party that is as old as Labour itself. It is presented sometimes as a division between trade unionists and intellectuals, but it is much more complex than that. It is more nearly a division between practical reformers and theoretical Socialists, between those whose approach to politics is fundamentally pragmatic, and those whose approach is essentially doctrinaire. Deakin, Williamson, Lawther and most of the trade union leaders of their generation were practical idealists in the mould of Ernie Bevin. They supported Gaitskell as Bevin in his time had supported Attlee, not to keep out intellectuals – Gaitskell himself, with his background of Winchester and Oxford, was an intellectual of no mean calibre – but to keep out theorists who, in their view, were dangerous to the Party. The common division between Right and Left is quite misleading in this context. I am usually described as on the right wing of the Labour Party, and yet in much of my social thinking I am far to the Left of many who are called left-wingers. When I was in the Cabinet, for instance, I resisted postponement of raising the school-leaving age against men who consider themselves among the keepers of Labour's left-wing conscience, and I fought battle after battle for reforms on the economic front, lost by the surrender of left-wing colleagues to orthodox Treasury thinking. But I shall come to all this later. Here I am concerned with the structure of the Party in the Gaitskell era.

Hugh Gaitskell saw his task as to lead Labour away from the

Talking with constituents, May 1955

A game of dominoes at Belper Labour Club,
February 1968

Cartoon by Vicky, 1962

With Hugh Gaitskell

cloth-capped image of the past, to modernize and refashion the
Party as an instrument of reform and humane Government to appeal
to all sections of society. He neither succeeded nor altogether
failed – he did not live long enough to show what might have happened to Labour in office under his leadership. By all the portents he
ought to have won the General Election of 1959: the country was
sick of the Tories and ready for a Labour Government. Labour lost
that election because of the squabbles and in-fighting of the so-
called Left, much of it shadow-boxing masking a vicious play of
personal ambitions. Many of the causes at issue were not the real
issues. The famous clash over Clause IV in the Labour Party's
constitution is a case in point.

Gaitskell's approach to this had nothing at all to do with any
desire to weaken or to water down Labour's Socialism. His point
was simply that Party thinking should be brought up to date. In
his speech at the Blackpool Labour Party Conference in November
1959 he said:

'I do think that we should clear our minds on these fundamental
issues and then try to express in the most simple and comprehensive
fashion what we stand for in the world today.

'The only official document which embodies such an attempt is the
Party Constitution written over 40 [1918] years ago. It seems to me
that this needs to be brought up to date. For instance, can we really be
satisfied today with a statement of fundamentals which makes no mention at all of colonial freedom, race relations, disarmament, full
employment or planning? The only specific reference to our objectives
at home is the well-known phrase:

'"To secure for the workers by hand or by brain the full fruits of
their industry and the most equitable distribution thereof that may
be possible, upon the basis of the common ownership of the means
of production, distribution, and exchange. . . ."

'. . . I hope, then, that the Executive will during the next few months
try to work out and state the fundamental principles of British Democratic Socialism as we see and as we feel it today, in 1959, not 1918,
and I hope that in due course another Conference will endorse what
they propose.'

Gaitskell, quite reasonably, felt that this bit of old-fashioned dogma
was part of Labour's out-of-date image, and that far from attracting
adherents to the Party it probably put off many people who would
otherwise vote Labour. I didn't think it really mattered a damn, one
way or the other. But the proposal to amend Clause IV at once
aroused all the hostility of those who were really opposed to Gaitskell

on defence and all the other matters on which a practical approach to the problems of government contrasted with a doctrinaire approach.

The ostensible dispute over Clause IV ended almost in a farce. I thought I saw a way of patching up the differences over Clause IV. I wrote an addition to the traditional Clause IV which I likened in the arguments then to adding the New Testament to the Old Testament. But no amendment was put formally to the Party and so none was ever written into the Party's constitution. Instead the Executive presented its statement to the next Conference, and its statement on Labour's aims was accepted as 'a valuable expression of the aims of the Labour Party in the second half of the twentieth century'.

It was an unhappy quarrel and it did nobody any good. The shadow-boxing over Clause IV did not matter: the vicious dispute between the doctrinaires and the realists did. That was not settled then, and has not been settled yet. It has done Labour incalculable harm.

In 1959 Jim Griffiths stood down as Deputy Leader and was replaced by Aneurin Bevan. In 1960 Harold Wilson made a bid for the leadership. There were therefore two elections: one in which Wilson stood against Gaitskell for the leadership; and the other in which I was nominated to stand against Fred Lee and Jim Callaghan to succeed Aneurin Bevan as Deputy Leader. Gaitskell defeated Wilson by 166 votes to 81. The figures in the election for the deputy leadership were:

Brown	118
Lee	73
Callaghan	55

This did not give me the clear majority needed for victory in the first ballot, so that there had to be a second ballot. In this Callaghan stood down and the voting was:

Brown	146
Lee	83

In some ways Gaitskell and I made a strange partnership, but I think that we each gave the Labour Party something it needed. I won't say that my relations with Hugh were always harmonious. We had our differences – I describe one, over Britain's approach to the Common Market, in some detail in a later chapter (see pages 217-19). But I could work with Hugh and he could work with me. If it doesn't sound too priggish to say so, we both put an ideal of service to the nation and the Party above everything else. Neither of us ever intrigued against the other; Hugh had no fear that I would ever try to do him down, and he let me go about things in my own way. It was by no means an easy relationship, but it worked and it paved the way to Labour's victory in 1964.

Gaitskell's death in 1963 came unexpectedly. He was only fifty-seven and the sudden illness from which he died came out of the blue. During his illness I took over, and acted as Leader of the Party. On the night of his death I was in Herbert Morrison's house. I went from there to broadcast a tribute to Hugh Gaitskell. Moved and saddened as I was, as I came away from that broadcast I could not help reflecting on my own position. Morrison, a politician to his fingertips, had discussed it with me even while we talked of Hugh's death. He said that the election for the leadership that would now have to take place had come too soon for me: that I hadn't really had time to establish myself as Deputy Leader, and that I should meet a good deal of opposition. He also said that Labour would never elect someone with a working class background to the leadership. Perhaps he was thinking back bitterly on his own experiences, but that, at any rate, was his view.

For myself, I was not even sure whether to stand for the leadership. I had not been long in the job as Deputy, and I was by no means clear in my own mind whether I ought to put myself forward. Then I thought that *not* to stand would be a rather cowardly form of dodging responsibility. I had been Acting Leader during Gaitskell's illness, the Party had trusted me to do the job, and it would be wrong to turn round now and say I didn't want it. My friends all said that of course I must stand for the election. So I did.

It was not a nice election. The Left was pretty solidly against me, and in my own union Frank Cousins had been consolidating his position against the legacy which the old Bevin–Deakin hierarchy had left behind, and I suffered in the process. I discouraged active campaigning on my behalf, but that didn't prevent a bitter campaign from being waged against me. A complicating factor was Jim Callaghan's decision to be a candidate for the leadership. Some of my friends thought at first that this would help me; that Callaghan, who was less identified with anti-Left policies than I was, would take votes from Harold Wilson, thus improving my own position. It did not turn out like that. In the event Wilson came top of the poll with 115 votes; I was second with 88, Callaghan third with 41.

Since there was no absolute majority there had to be a second ballot to decide between Wilson and me. A lot of people now put pressure on me to stand down so that Harold Wilson could be returned unopposed, and the *Mirror* was kind enough to publish an editorial counselling me to take this course. I felt differently. I was now determined to fight. I considered that a victory for Wilson would in the long run be disastrous for Labour (and the events of the General Election of 1970 have not exactly changed that view). Belatedly, I and my friends tried to whip up support, but it was a hopeless effort because, unknown to us, Wilson's allies had brought a good many of the trade unionists, on whom I thought I could rely, into the Wilson camp. So the decision went against me. In the second ballot I got 103 votes, Wilson 144.

Then it fell to me as Acting Chairman of the Parliamentary Party, as it had fallen to Herbert Morrison earlier, to announce my own defeat. All was done with proper propriety and I made the appropriate speech of congratulations and all that. But a campaign of denigration against me was already under way: I read next morning that I was alleged to have declined to shake hands with Wilson, which was totally untrue. What I did say at the meeting, having congratulated him, was that I would need a little time to consider my own position, to decide whether to continue as Deputy or not. I think that annoyed some people because they had expected me to say that of course I was carrying on, so that there could be an enormous whoop of joy and everybody would seem happy. But I didn't feel like that. I was not sure that I wanted to work under Wilson, by no means sure even that I *could* work with him. I needed time to think. So that night I wrote a letter to the Chief Whip, Herbert Bowden, telling him that I was going to Scotland for a few days' holiday, giving him an address where I could be got hold of, and indicating that whatever my final decision on this issue I should like to concentrate in the Shadow Cabinet on Foreign Affairs.

There was no secret about my trip to Scotland. All sorts of people knew where I was, and my wife and I went about quite openly. Harold Wilson spoke to me on the telephone, and so did the Chief Whip and a number of other colleagues. But because I had not told any newspapers where I was going, and had asked my colleagues not to tell the Press, the newspapers invented a silly story that I was sulking in my tent somewhere and would not tell anybody where I was. This was utterly ridiculous. I was staying at a private house in Scotland and the local Press knew where I was and came to see me. But nothing would put the other papers off, and they continued to make it look as if I'd gone into hiding. I had intended to go away for a week, but before the week was up my friends in London telephoned to say that they thought I'd better come back, because my absence was being made to look odd. So I did return to London, and made it known officially that I had decided to carry on in the post of Deputy Leader.

I didn't have a very agreeable start. The first thing I learned on my return was that the various posts in the Shadow Cabinet had already been allotted, and that without any further discussion of my own wishes the Foreign Affairs portfolio had been given to Gordon Walker. This in itself was an unpleasant little incident, because before I went away I had discussed with Gordon Walker what I was thinking of doing and had said that I was going to ask to be allowed to do Foreign Affairs. He gave me no indication then that he was interested in the job himself.

So things got off to a rather shaky, or at least rather disagreeable, start. But a General Election – the 1964 election – was looming up and we all put on our best faces and did our best. I began to concentrate on Home Policy for the election and soon became absorbed in the economic discussions which led to the establishment of the Department of Economic Affairs, and which I describe in more detail in my chapters on the D.E.A.

The election for the leadership after Gaitskell's death seems to me to mark another turning-point in Labour history. Real power in the Labour Party has always derived from the trade unions. The unions created the Labour Party and they saved it after 1931. Led by Bevin, trade union realists saw the need for standing up to aggressors and brought in Attlee to replace the pacifist leadership of Lansbury. Attlee was kept in power by Bevin after 1945. Deakin succeeded Bevin, and Gaitskell succeeded Attlee in the traditional pattern of power. Then two things happened – or rather two simultaneous processes working through society and the unions began to make themselves felt.

The first, and easiest to describe, was simply a reaction to the exercise of power by Bevin and Deakin. Both were violently anti-Communist. The word 'Communist' has little meaning nowadays, but in the Bevin–Deakin era it stood for all fellow-travelling supporters of the Soviet line, for the minority in the 1920s who wanted the T.U.C. to affiliate to the Red International of Labour Unions, for supporters of the pre-war Comintern and post-war Cominform.

Bevin and Deakin used their power to crack down on anyone who, in their view, seemed to threaten the Social Democratic Unity of the Labour movement. Both sought to secure successors to themselves in men who were cast in their own mould. Bevin succeeded. Deakin's chosen successor, A. E. 'Jock' Tiffin, died within six months. This unexpectedly opened the way for Frank Cousins, who was sore because he had been, or thought he had been, a victim of Arthur Deakin's use of personal influence and power, which had kept him out of posts in the union which were his proper due, because Arthur had intervened.

Nobody could accuse Bevin or Deakin of not having understood the meaning of power and how to use it, nor Frank Cousins for that matter. But there was a major difference between them. Bevin and Deakin had spent a large part of their lives in positions of great national prominence. By contrast, Cousins, and even more his successors, were relatively inexperienced men when they reached the top. They are all able men. That they have left-wing sympathies is neither here nor there, but they hadn't the long experience of power that their predecessors had.

This seems to me to manifest itself in various ways, among them the attitude to sponsored candidates and M.P.s. The trade unions who sponsor candidates have always been in the difficulty that if they try to take any action against a Member of Parliament whose views have changed, or who supports policies they do not like, they run the risk of being convicted of contempt of Parliament. This is not just a theoretical risk. In 1944 the case of Mr W. A. Robinson, then M.P. for St Helens, was actually referred to the Committee of Privileges.

Mr Robinson had been an official of the (then) National Union of Distributive and Allied Workers. The union made him an allowance of £200 a year as a contribution towards his expenses as an M.P., and also gave him a postal allowance and secretarial assistance. For various reasons the union became dissatisfied with Mr Robinson, and asked him to resign from Parliament. He refused, whereupon the union sent him a letter intimating that the Executive Council had decided to discontinue his allowances. This prompted questions in the House and the Speaker ruled that it should go to the Committee of Privileges.

The then chairman and acting secretary of the union were called to the House and claimed that their differences with Mr Robinson were related to constituency matters and 'were not directed against his votes or speeches or his actions in relation to the business of the House'. According to the report of the Committee of Privileges, they disclaimed 'the slightest intention to affront Parliament', and added that 'if they had inadvertently done so they desired to express the fullest apology'.

The Committee, satisfied that whatever may have been the complaints against Mr Robinson they did not relate to his conduct as an M.P., accepted the union's disclaimer and found that there had been no breach of privilege. They added, however:

> Your Committee do not think that there is any general rule which can be stated, but every case of this or a similar kind must be considered in the light of the particular circumstances.

Since the Robinson case the unions have generally considered that they can't do anything about a sponsored M.P. during the lifetime of a Parliament, but of course there is no law which tells a union whom it may or may not sponsor for the next Parliament. The problem for the unions is that when a Parliament ends there is only three weeks before a new Parliament is elected, and in practice there is no time to get together a new list of sponsored candidates. Nor, in practice, can they ring up, say, the Belper Labour Party the day after Parliament has ended and say, 'Well, George Brown won't be receiving any money from us as a sponsored candidate if you run him again, so if you want our money you'd better pick another member off our list' – although, incidentally, in the 1970 election the T.G.W.U. in fact did something barely distinguishable from this. However, as there isn't in practice time for a local party to adopt a new candidate, and as it is Labour practice that a sitting Member must be reselected unless the National Executive has given special permission for a local party to consider someone else, the sitting candidate is almost sure of being readmitted.

There is pretty nearly a 'parson's freehold' for candidates in a good many seats, and although this may have theoretical disadvantages, it tends to prevent small groups of dedicated minorities from throwing out an M.P. who may be doing a very loyal and decent job and whose sole offence is that he or she refused to toe some minority line.

I used to have fearful rows with Bevin and Deakin, but neither of them, however much they disagreed with me, ever attempted to discipline me for what I was doing. They accepted the constitutional position that an M.P. is a representative and not a delegate. You are elected to Parliament to exercise your own judgement on behalf of your constituents as you think fit, and that, constitutionally, is that. Cousins also understood this, and to his eternal credit, despite our really deep ideological disagreements, he always resisted attempts by the union's Executive to call me to account.

By the time of Gaitskell's death the political tradition left by Bevin and Deakin was well on the way towards being reversed. Cousins and his friends were firmly in the saddle, and, as I have just said, although this did not yet affect my position as an M.P., it did affect me in the election for the leadership. I was still an official of the Transport Workers Union seconded for parliamentary duties, I had been chairman of the trade union group of M.P.s, and under the old dispensation I could have expected an almost solid trade union vote. I got a loyal personal vote—144 to 103 is not exactly a walk-over – but the trade union vote was split because many of my former colleagues had been persuaded to go over to Wilson. I am not saying that the kind of trade union solidarity that Bevin, Deakin and the men of their generation stood for was necessarily always a good thing. It gave the Party stability and continuity, and since those who exercised great power included men of really great stature, the Party was usually safe in their hands. But as democrats I think we must recognize that this is basically an unhealthy situation and inevitably there was a reaction. The events after Gaitskell's death marked the end of an era.

Since then things have moved faster and farther. Frank Cousins naturally sought to get men who agreed with his way of thinking on the union's list of sponsored candidates, but he stood out against attempting to penalize anybody who was already on it. After his retirement the union's Executive decided to wind up the existing list and to offer existing members the opportunity of being nominated for a new list. In order to be nominated a member must be vetted both by his Regional Committee and the National Executive, and submit to questioning about his adherence or non-adherence to the policy decisions laid down by the union's biennial conference.

This seems to me to come about as near to a breach of parliamentary privilege as you can get. In my own case it no longer matters, for on my defeat at Belper in 1970 I decided that after forty years in national politics I had done about as much as anyone should be asked to do on this kind of level and with this degree of intensity. I decided, therefore, not to stand for the Commons or for the National Executive again. I accepted a life peerage just to keep

me in Parliament. However, others in this position who might have
wished to continue a career in the House of Commons could have
been removed from the sponsored list. And if they were, as I had
been, a full-time official of their union, unpaid of course, but
retaining all their rights under the superannuation fund, this could
have affected them seriously in other ways. Once struck off the list,
there would be no basis in the rule-book for such a person remaining
an employee of the union and he would therefore lose such benefits
as he might otherwise be entitled to. That would seem a heavy
penalty for an M.P., let us say, backing the bringing about of an
incomes policy, or the Government policy supporting the Americans
in Vietnam, or any other unpopular thing you like on which an
M.P. is supposed to exercise an independent judgement. It seems to
me to come very close to putting outside pressure on an M.P.

That is one process of change which, as I have said, can be described fairly easily. It reflects the problems that arise if the unions,
or even one or two powerful trade unions, are no longer willing to
accept the limitations of conforming to the rules of parliamentary
democracy.

The other change, at once more fundamental and far-reaching, is
the change in society of which the unions form a part. Trade unions
took to sponsoring candidates in the days when the majority of
working men and women were so inarticulate, and so liable to be
victimized, that they needed a special sort of candidate to speak for
them. Before M.P.s were paid, no one without a private income, or
some profession or business which provided both an income and
spare time, could contemplate standing for Parliament. Trade union
sponsorship helped materially to enfranchise working men.

The typical worker nowadays is a highly articulate person, miles
and miles removed from the typical under-privileged worker of
even twenty-five years ago. Five years from now that will be even
more true, and the pace of change here is accelerating. My children
are workers and my children's children will still be workers, but any
idea that they are going to have an outlook similar to that of my
lorry-driver father is nonsense. They will make their political views
heard all right, but it will only be through the Labour Party if the
Labour Party adapts itself to representing them and people like
them in contemporary terms.

The assumption that working men and women will always vote
Labour has never been wholly true and it is becoming less and less
valid. The whole idea of trade unions having their own tied members

in Parliament is out of date, and I think it is bound to wither away. The lists of trade union sponsored candidates nowadays contain some fairly surprising people—solicitors, barristers, economists and the like. They may all be very worthy men, but their links with some of the unions that sponsor them are, to say the least, tenuous. If to obtain sponsorship they have to submit to political questioning, perhaps even to give undertakings to support this or that political line, a dangerous situation will arise. Suppose, for example, you have given an undertaking to oppose an incomes policy, and suppose a Labour Government decides to introduce such a policy. Do you honour your undertaking and ignore the Whips, or do you ignore your undertaking and support the Government? If this issue is forced by unwise trade union executives in demanding assurances from M.P.s and striking them off sponsored lists if the assurances are not given, it will invite a head-on clash with Parliament that will be very damaging and disrupting to the Labour Party. No doubt it is anomalous for an M.P. sponsored by a trade union to vote against a policy adopted by a delegate conference of that union, but this is a case where it is better to let sleeping dogs lie, knowing that in due course they will peacefully pass away. If you insist on stirring up the dog you risk getting involved in a dangerous dog-fight.

Social changes which have reduced the need of union sponsored candidates have also changed the unions themselves. Bevin, whose picture looks down on me as I write, left school at eleven and rose to greatness in and through his trade union work. An Ernie Bevin born today would almost certainly go to a university and become an economist, a statistician or a businessman. His qualities might be equally great, but they would not be expressed in trade unionism. The hard school of the past gave the unions their greatest men. I am not in favour of going back to the past, and I am in favour of making it possible for every boy and girl who wants to, to go to a university. But I am also in favour of facing facts, and these social changes are facts to be faced in political thinking. It is futile to pretend that trade unions today are the same institutions as they were in my boyhood, or even ten years ago. Their approach to politics still reflects too much of the past. It is never easy to adjust one's ideas to social change; for a great political party rooted in the past perhaps it is impossible to do so quickly. But failure to adjust in time means death. There is a really urgent need for hard, fresh thinking on the aims and objects as well as on the structure of the Labour Party.

No one can look back on life, as I am now trying to do, without feeling saddened by the possibilities of might-have-beens. One is brought, too, to a proper sense of humility by the consequences of death in human affairs. Hugh Gaitskell's sudden death had consequences on the Labour Party – and on my own life – that have not yet been worked out. Another man whose untoward death was a grievous loss to the Party was Hector McNeil. Had he lived he would certainly have held great office, and he would have been a tower of lovable strength to all of us.

Hector McNeil was a man of great ability but with a certain earthiness about him which made him easy to like and to get on with. He had been to a university and could hold his own with any academics, but he had also been a Glasgow journalist and had experienced life in a tough school. He became Minister of State to Ernie Bevin at the Foreign Office, worked closely with Bevin and got on well with him. Then he became Secretary of State for Scotland, and then he died. He was an exceedingly unpushing man, and although he was an admirable Secretary of State for Scotland, his abilities would certainly have brought him back into a wider field. Had he lived in the Gaitskell period he would have been a very important member of the leadership team and would have had great influence on the Party.

Another potential Leader was Alf Robens. Alf, happily, is still alive and flourishing. He has been an outstanding chairman of the National Coal Board, but I have always thought it a tragedy that he left party political life when he did.

His loss to the Party was, I suppose, another part of the price that we paid for the Bevanite squabbling that lost us the General Election in 1959. Alf Robens, who had been an official of the Union of Distributive and Allied Workers, entered Parliament in 1945. He rose quickly to office, becoming Parliamentary Secretary to the Ministry of Fuel and Power in 1947, and Minister of Labour in 1951. Eight years in the wilderness must have seemed killing to a man of his ability and ambition, and when we lost the election in 1959 it must have seemed the last straw. In 1960 he accepted the job of Deputy Chairman of the National Coal Board, with reversion to the chairmanship at the beginning of 1961. Had he remained in Parliament at the time of the election for the Deputy Leader in 1960, there isn't much doubt that he would have stood for that, in which case it is very unlikely that I would have been nominated. Certainly in that case, had he still been in Parliament in 1963, it is again quite unlikely that I would have opposed him for the leadership. Even if I had, it is probable that he would have defeated me. Had he done so, I would willingly have served under him. Had things gone the other way, I think we could have worked equally happily together. Had Robens stayed in the Parliamentary Party there is little chance that Harold Wilson would ever have been Prime Minister.

But these are might-have-beens. They are interesting, if saddening, to reflect on now, but I did not have much time to think of them in 1963. I threw myself into the work of preparing for the 1964 election and to the economic planning that was to bear fruit in the setting up of the Department of Economic Affairs, as I shall describe in the next chapter.

5

Government:
Creation of the D.E.A.

THE STORY OF the D.E.A. (the Department of Economic Affairs) is the record of a social revolution that failed. The D.E.A. was meant to be – and it might have been – the greatest contribution of the Labour Party to the recasting of the machinery of government to meet the needs of the twentieth century. Its setting up was also the opening campaign of a major social revolution; its consequences – had it succeeded – more far reaching than anything else attempted by Labour since 1945. It envisaged a wholly novel form of national social accountancy to replace the orthodox financial accountancy by which the Treasury has always dominated British life.

The revolution failed – partly because it was betrayed by some of those who were pledged to see it through, and partly because, as I shall show, fundamental changes in other policies were not carried out. Whether it was a total failure, or whether, as with some other great revolutions in human affairs, apparent failure at one point in time will become ultimate triumph when once-revolutionary ideas are taken up again and seem so obvious that they must be carried out, history will show. Here I can only set out the simple record of what happened.

In 1963 I was chairman of the Home Policy Committee of the Labour Party, and we began to concert our planning for the General Election that would have to come in 1964. At Transport House we were already thinking of all kinds of ways of re-styling the Government.

Economic thinking was very much a part of this, and at that stage there was a considerable body of opinion which held that economic policy in Britain was too much subordinated to the financial considerations of the Treasury. We were all (at least, most of us who were concerned with Labour Party policy) expansionists at heart, and we thought that the economy was being held back, that unemployment was being kept high, that all sorts of barriers were being erected to keep down industrial activity, by reason of the orthodox financial policy of the Treasury. Out of this kind of thinking grew the idea that it would be better to have an economic department, which (as I always saw it) would be superior to the Treasury in determining the country's economic priorities.

Looking back, it seems that my own thinking may have gone farther ahead than that of the Prime Minister and some of my other colleagues, and it is possible that I made assumptions in my mind which the others did not, in fact, share. But at that time I believed that we were all agreed on the necessity of having a major government department to deal with economic affairs in ways which would not be subservient to the Treasury.

With the approval, or at any rate with the knowledge of, the then Conservative Ministers, I began to discuss things informally with senior Civil Servants – not only to help us, but also because of the obvious value to them in making their contingency plans against the possible return of a new Government. I tried to work out how a Department of Economic Affairs, such as I envisaged, might be established and staffed, what its relationships with the Treasury should be, what should be the lines of communication, and so on.

I had discussions not only with Civil Servants, but with economists, newspaper writers, trade unionists and industrialists, local authority people, and with all kinds of academics from the universities. We formed a large collection of overlapping study groups, and gradually our ideas emerged and clarified, though they were never, as it were, put together on one piece of paper. I think it is a pity that we didn't produce a 'blueprint' setting out precisely what we were trying to achieve. That would have been a valuable exercise in itself, and a useful source of reference when some of our ideas were questioned later. But everybody was always so busy that things just didn't get done in that way.

To do such things you need an elaborate secretariat, and the problem in the Labour Party always has been – and still is – that we run our administrative and research departments on the most ridiculous shoestring. In those vital days I, as Deputy Leader of the Party, Chairman of the Home Policy Committee and heaven knows what else, had to work in a tiny office in the House of Commons with just one secretary for all attempts at co-ordinating policy, plus my constituency work, plus my parliamentary work. The wonder is that anything got done at all.

Finally, we took our whole collection of ideas to a meeting at the St Ermin's Hotel, at which the Leader, Harold Wilson, and I were both present, together with all the other people concerned with policy-making and strategy for the coming election. Our meeting was followed by a dinner, from which those of us who were M.P.s had to go to a division in the Commons. Harold Wilson and I travelled together in a taxi, and it was on that ride to the House that we decided firmly to set up a Department of Economic Affairs, and that I should head it. That is the origin of the much-told story that the D.E.A. was born in a taxi – true, but not by any means the whole truth. From then on the establishment of the D.E.A. became a settled part of the official Labour policy.

One of the great problems was who was to be the Civil Service head of the new department, its Permanent Secretary, and here I probably made a grave misjudgement.

Among the people with whom I discussed the question was Sir William Armstrong, then Joint Permanent Secretary to the Treasury. I spent some time with Sir William, going over with him the potential work of the new department, and discussing the personalities to be reckoned with in making it work. What I failed to consider was whether Sir William might have been interested in heading the D.E.A. himself.

I never asked him about this, but I have the feeling now that had I pressed him to consider moving to the D.E.A. he might well have done so. If this had happened, events almost surely would have turned out very differently; and to say this is no reflection on the man who actually took on the job. Had I been even more conscious than I was of the battle that would have to be fought between the entrenched Treasury and our new department which was going to usurp some of its functions, the appointment of Sir William as the head of the D.E.A. might have resulted in that battle's being won before it started.

But I didn't ask Sir William, and instead considered all the other names that he and other people had suggested. In the end the decision was settled by a fortuitous meeting whilst visiting New York. I saw walking towards me along Fifth Avenue our then recently appointed Economic Minister to Washington, Sir Eric Roll. He was one of those whose names we were considering, and I thought, 'Given his experience, here is the very man for the D.E.A.!'

We talked there and then, and later in London. With all the

G

appropriate proprieties observed towards the then-Conservative Government, Sir Eric became very much involved in our planning. Sir Donald MacDougall, who had been Economic Director of the National Economic Development Council since 1962, had already agreed to join us as Director-General. Anthony Crosland had come to be accepted as the probable Deputy Minister, and our discussions began to take more formal shape.

Then came the election of October 1964. I was re-elected for Belper, and left Derbyshire quite early on the morning after polling day thinking that we had won handsomely. We all gathered at Transport House to give a send-off to Harold Wilson on his expected summons to the Palace. Suddenly we found ourselves enduring an absolute cliff-hanger, and it was not, I think, until about 4 o'clock in the afternoon that it became apparent that we had won by the slenderest of majorities.

When the awaited summons came from the Queen, Harold Wilson and I had a quick word together. He asked me to hold the fort at Transport House while he went to the Palace, and said that as soon as he got to Downing Street he would telephone me, so that I should be the first one across, as it were. He did this, and I went to No. 10 to be appointed First Secretary of State as well as Secretary of State for Economic Affairs.

The title of First Secretary then was meant to indicate what it said. There is no provision in our constitutional system for a Deputy Prime Minister, and the First Secretaryship was a convenient way of indicating who was in fact deputy to the premier. The title had been used before (by R. A. Butler, at one stage), and it was conferred again after I left the Government, but not in its original sense. For the rest of the Labour Government it came to be associated with economic affairs, but with my departure from the Government it ceased to signify the Deputy Prime Minister.

Having been duly commissioned, I went home to my flat, which is about the size of three hen boxes, and started telephoning all over the place. Sir Eric Roll, Sir Donald MacDougall, Tony Crosland and a number of others came round, and we spent most of the night working out just what we were going to do. Next morning we went to the old Ministry of Defence building in Great George Street and opened shop.

Many people—Tommy Balogh among them, and he was one of our keenest supporters – had advised me not to go there. The place had its own entrance in front of the building, but it is also approached at the other end from the Treasury. Tommy Balogh warned me strongly against allowing myself to be installed at the backside of the Treasury, observing, 'That's exactly where you will end up.' How right he was!

Nevertheless, it was convenient, it didn't involve moving people out, and we went there. In its odd little way I think that, too, was probably a mistake, but at the time I wanted chiefly to get on with things and an unoccupied building saved many complications. Unoccupied it certainly was! When we got in there was only one office with a table, a chair and a telephone, and that was the Secretary of State's room. The rest of the building was of empty rooms and corridors. We had our first departmental meetings with me sitting in the chair and everybody else squatting on the floor or sitting on the desk!

A lot of people helped us to get straight. Ian Hudson, a splendid fellow whom I had known since I was P.P.S. to the Minister of Labour in 1945, came as Establishment Officer to find staff for us, and David Hopkins, another man who was absolutely first-class, went to work to find tables and chairs and to get the telephones put in. This may all sound rather simple stuff, but at the time we were in the middle of an appalling economic crisis, we had discovered the £800 million deficit, Ministers were constantly being called to Cabinet meetings, and everybody in the whole government machine was at something like panic-stations. There had to be an immediate decision – and I mean in a matter of days – whether to devalue, or whether to try to hold the parity of sterling. There were endless agonizing arguments about this, and in the middle of it all I, as the Minister in charge of economic affairs, was trying to get a telephone or two installed so that the senior Civil Servants could work in their own offices instead of in mine.

That appalling economic crisis which we took over had an impact on our future at the D.E.A. because it meant that we simply couldn't give as much attention as we should have given to establishing the relationship between the department and the Treasury in formal minutes. We did manage to draft something that I called a 'Concordat', but it never got itself formally accepted between Jim Callaghan, the Prime Minister and myself. This had an unhappy bearing on the never-ending disputes that came later between the two departments at every level – at Civil Service level, among our various advisers, and, of course, at ministerial level between Jim Callaghan as Chancellor and myself.

Once the heady first days had gone and the novelty had worn off, the Treasury began to reassert itself, and with its absolutely superb mastery of the government machine gradually either filched things back or – more to the point – made it rather difficult for us to effect the grand design we had in mind so that a coherent and continuous economic policy could emerge.

But our immediate task was the economic crisis. The Economic Ministers and leading Civil Servants assembled for the famous meeting at Chequers at which we had to make up our minds whether to devalue or to seek some form of substantial American aid in order to hold sterling. We decided then not to devalue. Many would argue now that this was a mistake, but I agreed with the decision at the time. It looked as if with American help we could build up the economy within a reasonably short period of time. This done, I was determined that our first priority at the D.E.A. should be to produce an economic National Plan, and this was masterminded by Donald MacDougall, assisted by John Jukes, who had come to us from the Atomic Energy Commission as his No. 2, and a whole group of other experts who had come in and were now Civil Servants. Tommy Balogh had not joined the department, but had become the Prime Minister's economic adviser at No. 10. This was another problem akin to that with the Treasury: there was yet another separate economic advisory body in the Cabinet Office. In fact, there were too many of us advising and counter-advising one another.

Anyway, we had created our Planning Department at the D.E.A. and put it to work on the task of producing a long-term plan for the economic expansion of Britain over a period of years, with consideration of all the policies that would be needed to support it. We also created a Regional Department, and in the most unlikely of places we found an admirable man to head it. He was Arthur Peterson, who had been chairman of the Prison Commission since 1960, and he turned out to be an absolute winner. His job was to assemble a team of regional experts to create economic and physical planning machinery to cover the whole country, and he did it brilliantly. At the same time came the establishment of the Prices and Incomes Department, which became the most argued-about (but not necessarily the most successful) part of the D.E.A.'s work.

I got with the job of bringing in outside industrial advisers, some to join the Civil Service team, some without actual posts in the department. The Industrial Advisers' Department itself was established originally under Fred Catherwood, managing director of a subsidiary company of Tube Investments, who later became the director-general of the National Economic Development Council (or 'Neddy'), which already existed, but which we in the D.E.A. now took under our wing. I became its chairman and we greatly changed its functions. Starting with this we went on to increase rapidly the number of the 'little Neddies', the bodies which would, industry by industry, take charge of reconstruction and modernization to fit in with the National Plan and attached to them one or other of the Industrial Advisers.

Here began an argument – still unsettled – about how much one should pay in the public service for these outstanding men, whose salaries in private business were very much higher than anything in the Civil Service. I took the view then, and hold it still, that the salaries paid in private enterprise, particularly in these days of high taxation, are in many cases pretty ridiculous. Such salaries are more a matter of prestige than of reward for work. Over a certain level they do not much affect a man's 'take-home' pay, although they may be of additional value to the individual in helping to determine his pension and so his standard of living in later life. There should, however, be other ways of securing pensions for senior men than paying huge nominal salaries, most of which go in tax.

Whatever may be the merits or demerits in the argument for very high salaries (and I know that others hold strongly that they are justified), the fact remained that I didn't see how we could run a campaign for a prices, productivity and incomes policy – which involved trying to limit increases in people's incomes to whatever might be covered by increases in productivity and to holding down prices – while at the same time dishing out vast salaries to the people who were coming in to run this policy. That led to protracted negotiations between me and the leading industrialists from whom I wanted to get the men I needed, to persuade them to pay the difference between whatever we could pay in the department and what they were getting formerly.

At that stage, and for quite a long time afterwards, the relationship between leading industrialists and the Labour Government was exceedingly close and good. I found an official flat in Carlton Gardens, and there started a system of highly detailed discussions at monthly dinners to which leading industrialists came with Fred Catherwood and other senior people of the department.

Frank Kearton (Lord Kearton) of Courtaulds, George Cole

(Lord Cole) of Unilever, (Sir) Siegmund Warburg and John Berkin of Shell became part of the continuing core of our group and were joined by others from time to time. This unpublicized body of industrial advisers had an enormous influence on the apparatus we set up.

One outcome of these discussions was that I became convinced of the need for a wholly new body to assist in shaping industry into a structure suitable for carrying on the job of a vast, planned expansion. This led to the establishment in January 1966 of the Industrial Reorganization Corporation (I.R.C.), which started on its job although the legislation it required and which provided authority for the large sum of public money (up to £150 million) did not take effect until December of that year. It was given the job of finding and bringing together companies that ought to merge to form units of a size, strength and efficiency to match competition from the Continent and the United States.

Its first chairman was Frank Kearton, who did an absolutely fantastic job there while still having his own job as chairman of Courtaulds. How he managed to find time for both has always puzzled me – it goes to prove the old saying that if you want to get something done, ask a really busy man to do it. As the full-timer at the head of the I.R.C. we brought in Ronnie Grierson, a partner in the merchant bank of S. G. Warburg, who worked devotedly at his job, and refused to take any salary.

Two urgent immediate tasks faced the I.R.C.: to work out an order of priorities, so as to concentrate on industries where its efforts could have the biggest and earliest impact; and to win the confidence of industrialists. Both tasks were accomplished in a manner which I think reflects the highest credit on Kearton, Grierson and their colleagues.

Initial hostility to the corporation as a body set up to impose theoretical ideas on practical men soon changed. As soon as they realized what the I.R.C. was really trying to do, and that its members and staff were practical men themselves, many businessmen who recognized the need for structural change in their industries welcomed the help that an independent agency could give. Indeed, it was not long before the I.R.C. began to receive approaches from companies and their financial advisers.

I think that few would now question that the I.R.C. was one of the greatest successes of the 1964 Labour Government, although the Tories have since set out to destroy it on narrow doctrinaire grounds.

We got things right – we insisted on the Corporation's independence of government control, but at the same time secured a sensible working relationship between the officers of the I.R.C., ourselves at the D.E.A., the Ministry of Technology, the Board of Trade, and all the other departments whose work was touched upon. And we succeeded in this without ever infringing the confidentiality which was fundamental to the I.R.C.'s relationship with industry.

Another appointment I look back on with particular pleasure was that of Aubrey Jones to the Prices and Incomes Board. Finding the right man for this job bristled with difficulties. He had to be someone not obviously committed to some past line of policy, but also sufficiently a national figure to command respect, sufficiently detached for his judgements to have a fair chance of voluntary acceptance.

Both the Treasury and the Cabinet Office maintain lists of people considered suitable as members of commissions and so on. I grew to know these lists. They contained mostly the same names, and I came to call them 'the lists of the good and great'. The people on them may have been volcanoes once, but, with every respect for their past achievements, by the time they got on the list they tended to be extinct, or at best rather weary, volcanoes. I wanted active ones.

I drew up my own short-list of 'possibles' and constantly rewrote it. I considered various leading figures in the Labour movement and in industry, but there was always something that left a doubt in my mind about the man's suitability for this particularly tricky job.

One name which stayed on all my lists was that of Aubrey Jones. He was not at all an obvious candidate. He was a Conservative M.P. and had been a Minister in Conservative Governments. He was also an industrialist, among other things a director of Guest, Keen and Nettlefolds and chairman of Staveley Industries. But I knew him to have a great deal of sympathy for and interest in the whole idea of trying to bring some sort of order into our wage bargaining, to introduce some reasonable relationship between what happened to incomes, what happened to prices, and what happened to productivity.

I was warned by many people of the storm that might ensue if I appointed a Conservative M.P. to this very vital post. But I couldn't see anybody else with as much chance of doing the job with the authority and success that I felt that Aubrey could bring to it. So I carried on. In 1965 he came, and as things turned out the row over his appointment was never as fierce as people had forecast. Because he was so good, and with his colleagues tried so hard to be scrupulously fair, and because most of their reports stood up to criticism, he established the board's position astonishingly well.

All this was preliminary to what I saw as our main object of getting a National Plan for the economic strategy of Britain worked out and carried out. Our National Plan – the first attempt at economic planning on such a scale that has ever been made in Britain – was related to every other aspect of policy.

Our incomes policy was only part of this – much of the later criticism of it derives from a complete misunderstanding of what we were trying to do. Perhaps we failed here to get our intentions understood as widely as they should have been; perhaps the failure was not so much ours as that the concept of planning on such a scale was something so new that people gave up trying to understand it.

But there was also, I think, a good deal of quite deliberate misrepresentation. We were never out to limit incomes just for the sake of limiting them. The incomes policy was integral to the plan as a whole, and I believe now, as firmly as I did then, that if the plan had been carried out every man, woman and child in Britain would be both more secure and better off.

The plan of course had to be presented to Parliament, but it seemed to me futile to offer it there unless a wide measure of agreement among the people who had to carry it out had been obtained beforehand. In August 1965, the work was sufficiently advanced to be put formally before the N.E.D.C. If the employers, trade unions and all the nationalized industries represented there agreed to accept the plan, then, I felt, it could be carried out. If not, then we should have to start again.

On 4 August 1965, the day before that crucial meeting of the N.E.D.C., I suddenly got wind of a story that the industrialists were about to go cold on the proposals. They were reported to be having a last-minute debate to reach a decision before morning.

I picked up the telephone and asked one of my secretaries to get hold of A – one of the leading industrialists – for me. He wasn't in his office, and nobody in his office seemed to know where he was. So we telephoned his wife, and she didn't know.

Then we started on B and C . . . working our way through every single member of the group who had represented what was then called the Federation of British Industry in our discussions. Not one of them was in London, and nobody seemed to have any idea where they were – it was as if the entire group of leading British industrialists had been packed into a spaceship and put in permanent orbit round the moon!

Then began some hours of the most extraordinary detective work. Sir Donald MacDougall, our director-general, and everybody in my private office at the D.E.A. all took part – telephoning everywhere to try to break through this ring of secrecy. I am afraid we got up to some rather questionable tricks to try to persuade some typist somewhere to drop a word that might help us.

In the end, Pat Kelly, one of my secretaries, rang one of the industrialists for the umpteenth time, and was put through to the man's wife. She, not realizing what was going on, said she thought that her husband had gone out of London to attend some dinner. She wasn't sure exactly where, but she believed it was in Buckinghamshire, near Aylesbury – it might be a place called Whitchurch.

There the finger pointed straight at Frank Kearton. It was then near 9 o'clock at night, and we'd been on the job without a bite to eat since 2 o'clock in the afternoon. I rang him up, and discovered that actually the meeting was at Sunningdale. There 'the conspirators' all were, tucking into cold chicken and ham.

I told Frank that I was on my way down. He said that the meeting was over. I said, 'Never mind that. *Don't let anybody go.* I'm on my way down – now – to see you all.'

With the precious document, the only copy that was supposed to exist, under my arm (I didn't have time even to put it in a briefcase) we got out the official car and Sir Donald and I set forth. When we got to Sunningdale – it couldn't have been earlier than half-past ten – there they all were, sitting around. I'd never seen such a collection of obviously 'guilty' characters, though they were decent enough to give us something to eat and drink.

We weighed into the group as well as into the food, and somewhere around 2 o'clock in the morning I got an agreement out of them that they would not torpedo the show but would, in fact, go along with it.

The government car we were using then was a magnificent old hearse of questionable age, and coming home the old thing broke down. It was then about 3 a.m. The chauffeur and Donald MacDougall went off to find either a police car or a telephone box, leaving me by the roadside with my precious bundle that was so secret that nobody else could be trusted with it. As I was standing there a very tiny car came by, driven by a young man, with a girl as passenger. They drove past, then stopped, and backed to where

I was standing. The young man said, 'Aren't you George Brown?' I said, 'Yes.'

He then said, 'Do you want a lift?' and I said, 'Not half.'

'Where do you want to go?' said he. 'To Great George Street, to the Ministry,' I replied.

This excellent young man and his girl-friend were only going as far as Chiswick, but quite uncomplainingly they took me and my precious document all the way back to Westminster. Meanwhile Sir Donald was still running up the road. Eventually he stopped a police car and got back to the Ministry as fast as he could, worried stiff about what had happened to the document, to say nothing of the Minister. The old hearse was put away wherever the government transport pool puts old hearses and I got a new official car.

As well as the F.B.I., which dealt mainly with economic matters, there was then also the British Employers' Confederation, which was concerned with labour affairs (they subsequently merged, together with the National Association of British Manufacturers, into the Confederation of British Industry). The F.B.I. was directed by Sir Norman Kipping; the Confederation by Sir George Pollock. Much of the behind-the-scenes negotiations on the National Plan and most certainly on the prices and incomes policy were carried out with these two men, and with George Woodcock, who was then general secretary of the T.U.C. We owed them all very much.

There was a rather similar drama with them over prices and incomes policy. I learned by chance that Pollock and Kipping and Woodcock had all met for lunch at the Westbury Hotel and I had a sort of instinct that this meeting boded no good for our agreement. So I went round to the hotel and invited myself to join them for coffee. I knew that if I let them walk out of the room without a renewed assurance of agreement, there was a real risk of their breaking off discussions, and that then we'd never get our proposals implemented.

We argued for hours. We tried it with brandy, we tried it with tea, we stormed, we insulted each other, we broke up, we broke off, but somehow the serious discussion was kept going and, largely due to the ability of George Pollock, the policy was miraculously saved.

There was a third excitement of a similar kind when with Fred Jones, who had been the responsible man on the prices and incomes policy in the department and an absolute tower of strength, I set off at about 8 o'clock one morning for Brighton to meet the General

Council of the T.U.C. and explain to them all the arguments and reasons that really lay behind it and to seek their full approval for it.

It turned out to be the most incredible birthday (my fifty-first) that I have ever had. The discussions went on until well after midnight. In the end, with much assistance from George Woodcock and others, but above all, I remember, from Victor Feather, who was then George Woodcock's assistant, we got the General Council's acceptance.

George Woodcock was in favour of the policy, but he is a most up-and-down fellow: even in his most enthusiastic moments he sounds rather like an undertaker. One day he would be 'for' it, but the next day you would find that while he was still 'for' it, he now saw all the snags and the impossibilities.

He was always sure that I was in too much of a hurry – that if only one would do things in a fairly leisurely way over the next fifty years, then one could bring it about. He professed to be well aware that you had to make 'shoddy, shabby compromises' (his phrase). It was only naïve fools like me who thought that you might do something rather better.

George Woodcock, an intensely sincere man himself, didn't have much faith that many of the others meant all they were saying. He was continually warning me that while people might well sign the Declaration of Intent, I needn't have any illusions about their living up to it afterwards. At the time I thought that this was pessimistic. But it must be confessed that subsequent events have largely confirmed his judgement.

One of the other aspects of our operation which has had less attention than it really deserves, but was equally vital to the whole plan and has worked astonishingly well, was our establishment of a totally different approach to regional policy from that pursued by our predecessors. This involved not only the establishment of the planning councils and the planning boards, but also the working out of policies for stopping – or at least discouraging – the build-up in the 'golden triangle', as we say, of London, Birmingham and the south-east. Instead, we sought to move, but without powers of actual direction, commercial and industrial development to the hitherto underprivileged regions. One of the first steps in this direction was the order banning office building in London and tightly controlling it elsewhere in the south. That was followed by very substantial grants being made available for plant and machinery in the

development areas, another very successful idea which the Tories
are now destroying on narrow doctrinaire grounds. We also made
vigorous attempts to get government administrative offices and the
like away into Wales, the north-east, Scotland and so on. It has been
one of the great means of spreading our industrial activity over the
whole country and has been an enormous boon to the areas which
have special difficulties.

Simultaneously, we built up our regional machinery for getting
economic planning carried out. We worked out what we felt should
be the effective regions of England and Wales, which were not the
same as the existing administrative regions, and we decided to
establish a Planning Council for every region. I wanted these councils to be not only consultative bodies, but also embryos of something that could become a new form of regional government. This
was all anticipating the Maud Report on Local Government, but
I was quite sure even then that local government would have to be
reorganized and take on a new character.

I refused to have nominations or appointments from the existing
local authorities for the new regional planning councils because
I'd seen what happened when this sort of thing was done in the past –
it would have been the Treasury's lists of the good and the great all
over again. Also I didn't want the new councils to *represent* local
authorities – I wanted them to have a character of their own. I did
agree to accept short-lists of recommendations from local government associations, but insisted on retaining the right to decide who
should be appointed, so that the appointments would be mine and
not theirs. We worked out elaborate formulas which varied for each
council – so many local government people, so many industrialists,
so many trade unionists, and so many totally non-representative
people.

These councils were formally called Regional Economic Planning
Councils. We wanted them to be called simply Planning Councils,
and the 'Economic' was put in to appease the local government
people, who feared that their functions might be confused with
physical planning, which was in local government hands. I always
thought that the two forms of planning went together, but I reckoned
that by agreeing to have the word 'Economic' in their title we could
leave enough ambiguity in the situation for our scheme to go ahead
without too much fuss. My hope was that, as time went on, the
connection between planning for the economic development of an
area and planning for its physical development would become so

obvious that the two would naturally fuse. And whatever way these bodies are fitted into a reorganized structure of local government after Maud, this is what will ultimately happen.

Finding all the appointments for these local councils was a weary business, all the detailed work of which was undertaken by Bill Rodgers, then the Parliamentary Under-Secretary of State, but it was an important job, and I gave it a lot of attention. After a great struggle, I managed to get approval to pay the chairman of each council the magnificent fee of £750 a year. The rest were unpaid. I persuaded my colleagues to set up, alongside the Planning Councils, something that I called the Planning Board. This consisted of Civil Servants from all the Ministries concerned, serving under the Chief Regional Officer of the D.E.A. The Planning Board was intended to be, as it were, the executive arm of the Economic Planning Councils, and to be responsible for seeing that planning policy was carried out in each particular area.

This whole machine worked, as may be imagined, sometimes well, sometimes less well. It was cumbersome and ill-defined, but it had to be if one was to make a start at all. This is an area in which, if you sit down and wait for the ideal arrangement, you will never get anything moving. We accepted all the disabilities in order to get our ideas off the ground.

It think it would be said now that most of the Economic Planning Councils have done extremely good work, and are unlikely to be dropped. Part of the problem in setting them up was to make sure that the work they put in and the advice they gave was in fact used in Whitehall. This was a struggle, because not all departments were as pleased with the idea as we ourselves were. You get jealousies among Ministers as you do among other people, and some Ministers saw our scheme as that of a great overbearing Secretary of State trying to collar all their jobs. We had a good deal of friction and difficulty at all levels, but somehow things worked out.

6

Government:
Decline of the D.E.A.

THE GENERAL ELECTION in March 1966 eased our burden by giving the Government a substantial majority in the House, but it didn't solve the monetary crisis. That went on and on, and we got into successive difficulties. Repeated doses of vast deflation were forced upon us – which was simply the old Treasury remedy still being applied in order to maintain the fiction that the pound was worth X number of dollars. In retrospect, the decision not to devalue in 1964 began to look wrong.

I started to feel that the Prime Minister had never really intended to allow the D.E.A. the degree of freedom from Treasury control which was imperative if our ideas were to be carried out. Our National Plan (as we at the D.E.A. saw it) would break the ancient Treasury tradition of making economic policy and industrial activity subject to all the inhibitions of orthodox monetary control.

Although we tried to hide it, and tried even harder never to confess it, the D.E.A. and the Treasury were running two diametrically opposed policies. We were vigorously stirring things up to try to get the whole economy running ahead; the Treasury was constantly damping things down. If there were to be any validity in the establishment of the D.E.A., it had to be laid down that the D.E.A. was the senior economic Ministry, and that the Treasury would have to take on something of the style of a Continental Ministry of Finance. The Prime Minister never did this.

I may have been wrong, or partly wrong, in assuming that we all had meant more or less the same thing when we had decided to set up the D.E.A.

I may have misunderstood the degree of the Prime Minister's acceptance of the ideas of the various working parties which led to the setting up of the D.E.A., but however he may have changed his

H

mind later, at the time I felt sure that he was with us. I do think though that he came to believe that a state of competitive existence between the D.E.A. and the Treasury would keep everybody on their toes: in fact, all this internecine warring achieved was to make everyone work many times as hard and quarrel far more often than was necessary to secure an outcome that was practically no improvement on what had happened before.

Throughout most of 1965, I had gone along with those who thought that devaluation could be avoided. This was a very difficult subject to discuss because it was absolutely essential that nobody should know that it was being discussed; and indeed, only now can even part of the story be told. The Prime Minister and the Chancellor were not unnaturally always terrified lest talking, or even thinking, about devaluation should alert the world to what was going on and give our friends the 'Gnomes' the opportunity which would force that result.

I had accepted the deflationary shackles that were periodically clamped on the country: budgets, mini-budgets, credit squeezes and all the rest. However, I came more and more to the view that these restrictive policies which were being forced on us were not really in the country's interests. I took some time to be convinced, but I was persuaded by my advisers, and by such friends outside as I dared to consult, that the case for devaluation was overwhelming and inevitable.

This was not only my view, it was shared by almost all the Government's economic advisers and not only those in the D.E.A.

I therefore got my own people, working with the utmost discretion, to set out the extent of devaluation which they considered necessary, and the various economic measures that in their view should accompany it. The original note I still have. It was never typed, it was never put into a file, and therefore escaped destruction.

But this exercise convinced me that we had a viable economic proposition to make; not just the emotional one of devaluation, but a set of economic measures, only one of which was devaluation and which, taken together, formed a sure base on which to rebuild Britain's economy. I then risked all the fury that might ensue by putting the issue to my colleagues.

That was in June 1966. We also had before us proposals for yet another round of cuts and squeezes and that brought matters to a head. I, and one or two Ministers with whom I had quietly discussed things, insisted on not being stopped from raising the alternative policy of devaluation.

This resulted in long discussions, and finally it emerged that there was a minority of us – substantial, but still a minority – in favour of devaluation and the accompanying measures as an alternative to yet more cuts. Those who took this view were not only those widely assumed to be of this mind, but included, as I remember, others generally thought to be a good deal more to the 'Left' on most political issues.

The point I must make here is that we were not, as we were sometimes called, 'devaluers' *per se* – we accepted the necessity of devaluation as one of a series of positive measures to put the country on its feet once and for all. Collectively we formed, I think one might say, the most distinguished part of the Cabinet, but we were not the largest part. Therefore, especially as we did not have the Prime Minister on our side, we were unable to get this policy put into effect.

I argued as strongly as I could that however many times we set back the economy with another round of pointless deflation, we should come back to the need to face devaluation; that one day we should have to devalue, perhaps too late and with a weakened economy (as in fact we did a year later); and that it would be wiser to devalue now.

When it became obvious that this view was not going to prevail, and that a majority of the Cabinet was going to accept the cuts, freezes and squeezes that became known as the July measures, I said that in that case I should leave the Government. I felt – and said – that I could not continue to make a nonsense of myself and of my department's policy by agreeing to do further harm to the economic life of the country. When the Prime Minister and the Chancellor went to the House to announce the new economic misery, I rather ostentatiously did not go and sit on the front bench.

I had not publicly announced my intention of resigning and I spent the afternoon in the department, discussing the situation with various people, both Ministers and Civil Servants. There were some (as there always are in such situations) who cried, 'Don't resign' – if those people had their way, no Government would ever be seriously questioned. But there were a number of others – some very distinguished men among them – who said that I ought to go. One of them observed, 'If you don't go you will have lost your credibility for ever, and you will pay a very heavy price.'

That night I told the Prime Minister that I was going to resign. However, a tremendous pressure then emerged against my resignation.

About 100 M.P.s signed a letter which was hurriedly brought round to me, urging me not to go. I had meetings with the Prime Minister, the then Chief Whip (John Silkin) and the then Leader of the House (Herbert Bowden), and at all of them I was pressed not to go.

It was not a question of what harm I might do to myself or even to the Government, although the latter was obviously in our minds. The most telling argument put to me was that if I resigned I should have to say why I had resigned, and if I said that the Government was seriously split on whether or not to devalue, there would at once be a most devastating run on our Reserves.

I think that this argument was probably exaggerated, but in the circumstances of the time it was a very, very telling one. So about midnight I stood on the steps of No. 10 Downing Street with Mr Bowden (now Lord Aylestone) and informed the assembled multitude of journalists that there had been a disagreement – on what I did not specify – but that I had decided not to resign but to stay at my post to assist in carrying out the policies that the Government had decided upon.

One of those policies was to put through the Bill on a statutory prices and incomes policy which I had not favoured but which, by staying, I should have to force through the House, which I did. Mr Frank Cousins, who had been general secretary of the T.G.W.U. and who had joined the Wilson Government as Minister of Technology, resigned over this Bill and led the Labour opposition to it; but for me, having undertaken to stay, there was no honourable course open but to assume responsibility for the Bill.

It was a difficult time. As soon as we set up the Standing Committee to deal with the Bill, it was apparent that we were going to have trouble with our own people. Frank Cousins was leading the Labour opposition to us, and, of course, the Tories were opposed to the Bill. It was clear that unless we took absolutely unheard of steps we should never get the Bill through Committee – and we couldn't afford to have it in Committee for long, because we had said that this legislation was urgently necessary.

At an early meeting I moved that we should sit without a break until we finished the Bill. This turned out to be impracticable, but the committee did stick to a gruelling timetable, which included two all-night sittings. Although people were very much on the look-out for opportunities to accuse the Government of unfairness, Harold Lever (the Chairman) never gave the slightest grounds either to the

Tories or to Frank Cousins and the Labour opposition for claiming that he was unfair or behaving in any way improperly. With scrupulous fairness he saw that we got on with the job, the Government got its majority and the Bill went through unscathed. By then everybody was thoroughly exhausted, and the Bill went through its report stage and Third Reading pretty easily.

The proceedings in that committee so impressed everyone who took part that, although we had our turbulent times, we became a particularly friendly little group. Two Conservatives, Sir Tatton Brinton, the Member for Kidderminster, and Mr K. Lewis, the Member for Rutland and Stamford, organized the printing of the whole proceedings of the committee in a beautiful leather-bound volume, inscribed in gold and presented jointly by the whole committee to the chairman. The rest of us purchased copies for ourselves as a record of the unstinting work that we had gone through – Government and Opposition alike – to deal with the Bill.

That leather-bound book enclosing the proceedings of the Standing Committee on the Prices and Incomes Bill also closed my time at the D.E.A. The Bill passed its third reading on 10 August 1966, and once it was on the Statute Book, for all practical purposes my period at the department was at an end. It was widely known that I had offered my resignation earlier. Many people guessed why – even if they did not dare say so. I had carried out the most unpopular task of all as the price of the Government not doing what I thought should have been done, and really, therefore, what good I could do at the department became very limited. I would never seem credible to anybody in the economic field since they all knew how much all of this went against my thinking. It was therefore sensible that I should leave the department, and indeed, that very day, the Prime Minister offered me the Foreign Office. The D.E.A. itself effectively came to an end when I left. Although it lingered on for a bit under other Ministers in various reshuffles, it was never again of much significance in Whitehall. When the Prime Minister finally killed it and divided its remaining functions among his own secretariat and other Departments, there wasn't much left to kill.

Morale in the department was still high when I left, but there was a good deal of feeling that they had been sold down the river and that D.E.A. policies were impossible in the atmosphere of industrial deflation that we then had. Everybody in the department knew how hard I had fought for those policies and realized, I think, that having been defeated I should have let them down more by staying at the D.E.A. than by going.

In personal terms we had become the closest-knit department in Whitehall: the friendships that were formed and the feelings involved in all the work that we had tried to do had brought us together in an atmosphere I have never met in any other department I have served in. This quite remarkable spirit still survives. Even after this lapse of time, those who were colleagues then, regardless of where they are serving today, still come together periodically and recall the excitements and struggles they then shared.

Although everybody tried hard to summon up enthusiasm anew, there was inevitably a changed atmosphere with my departure. Various top men began to return to their old departments in the Civil Service, the level of outside people began to crumble and the whole thing took on an air of a Ministry that had not only lost its Minister but had really lost itself.

But although the department was ultimately axed, its work wasn't. Hardly any of our innovations at the D.E.A. disappeared. The Ministry of Labour became the Department of Employment and Productivity and took over all that side of the D.E.A.'s work; other sections went to the Ministry of Technology. The I.R.C., the regional bodies, the prices and incomes machinery, all lived on.

To that extent I think it is fair to claim that the D.E.A. really succeeded far better than anybody thought. Success does not depend upon a particular ministerial title – what counts is whether things get done that were not done before, and whether those things take root and grow. Pretty well everything we did took root and is still growing.

We made a good many mistakes. I'm pretty sure that one of them was to allow myself as Secretary of State for Economic Affairs to become over-immersed in the working out of prices and incomes policy. That meant that the whole job was turned in on itself, as it were; that prices and incomes policy, instead of being just one of the parts of the National Plan, seemed to become the central core of economic policy. But in fact the major central theme of the D.E.A. was economic expansion. Only in that way, for example, could we provide the massive resources needed for the kind of social revolution we aimed to bring about in Britain at the same time.

However, because of this concentration on prices and incomes policy, we ended by appearing to involve ourselves in a number of major contradictions. We were trying to persuade people to restrain wage demands and to hold down prices at the very time when the rest of the Government, as a matter of deliberate policy, was forcing up prices. We were trying to hold down fares when the Government was determined to force them up to save the subsidies. We were urging one policy for prices and incomes when all the Government's other actions were encouraging people to do exactly the opposite.

In a belated attempt to put the balance right, I persuaded the Prime Minister and the Cabinet to pass over the detailed work of implementing policy on prices and incomes to the Minister of Labour, but I fear that it was too late. There were some who saw the danger before I did, and who warned me that in getting myself identified as the Prices and Incomes 'King' I was losing the chance of being identified as the general Economic Minister. I saw this too late: those who saw it before I did are to be applauded.

We were, perhaps, too intent on our own vision at the D.E.A. We knew, of course, precisely what we were trying to do; I doubt if the outside world understood. For example, we saw most clearly how much the achievement of everything depended upon a rate of growth of the order of 4 per cent per annum which we thought to be practicable and within the country's capacity. The whole point of the National Plan was to identify the areas where there were weaknesses in the existing situation and where we should concentrate our resources. In that way individual industries and sectors could see clearly what they had to do to enable this overall national result to be achieved. At the same time, we provided for the distribution of the increased wealth this would produce so that the continuous refurbishing of our industrial structure, the level of social expenditure and of private consumption could all be matched.

One of the assumptions we made was that the plan would take priority and other policies pursued by the Government would be made to fit its provisions. In the event this was not done, as I have shown, and as a result the 4 per cent growth-rate was made impossible of achievement. I still believe there was not all that much wrong with the plan – it was our failure to adhere to it.

So orthodox financial control won, and our basic social reformation failed. I believe the central cause of that was the failure clearly to establish what D.E.A.'s functions in the Government were to be. Too many people had vested interests in our department *not* succeeding. Putting it in rather crude political terms, our success meant a tremendous threat to half a dozen old-established departments. Not only the Treasury, but also Labour, the Board of Trade, Local

Government, and the Scottish and Welsh Departments felt themselves threatened.

More serious still, this threat was also felt at No. 10. What came to be referred to as the 'strained relations' between the Prime Minister and myself was not due to any move on my part to oust him in any way. I fear that he has never quite believed this, but it is, in fact, true. I have never made any attempt to supplant him.

I think what really happened, though I did not see it clearly at the time, was that in its early days the D.E.A. was so much in the public eye, and the Minister at the head of it appeared such a powerful figure, that if we had succeeded it would not only have been the Treasury that was down-graded – No. 10 and the Cabinet Office would also have felt the same way. Apparently this was discussed most seriously by various officials at the time, although I did not learn of it till later.

Personalities also influenced our failure. We should not, I think, have failed under Clement Attlee. He was not himself an innovator, and his temperament was such that he did not need to feel that he had a finger in everybody else's pie.

Above all, he had a team containing three or four men of roughly equal stature in the Cabinet and in the country. Attlee didn't actually have to balance Ernest Bevin against Herbert Morrison – they balanced themselves. He didn't have to balance either against Sir Stafford Cripps – the team was self-balancing.

Our set-up in 1964/6 was utterly different. Because of Labour's long period in Opposition after the Attlee Government, almost all the leaders had been removed either by death or retirement. Things have changed now, of course, but in 1964 we were, broadly speaking, an untried team, with only a few of us with any real ministerial experience.

Therefore if someone had wanted to attempt a *coup* against the Prime Minister, he could have feared it might succeed. As a result, whether I wanted it or not, I was put in the position of a Minister who appeared to be amassing great power through his department, and who also had a strong position in the Party and in the country.

I was too busy in those days to bother about such things, but I've discovered since that there were plenty of people to put nagging doubts into the Prime Minister's mind. A lot of talk went on, among some Ministers and Civil Servants, about ways and means of thwarting what seemed dangers to them all that might emerge from the D.E.A. One who never took this view, I am quite certain, was the then Joint Head of the Treasury, to whom I have referred earlier.

It is a pity also that Anthony Crosland left the D.E.A. for the Department of Education and Science as early as he did. He began by being my Minister of State, and he is a man of great integrity as well as an economist of repute and an exceptionally able administrator. If Patrick Gordon Walker had done us the favour of holding Leyton and thereby remained Foreign Secretary, there would have been no shuffle just then and the ministerial set-up at the D.E.A. would not have been disturbed. A whole range of jobs which in the end I had to do myself would have been done and supervised by Crosland, and I should have had more time to be a politician as well as a Departmental Minister. Although Austen Albu, who succeeded Crosland, did an excellent job, it was a different one because he is cast in a different mould.

I should have known more about what was going on behind my back, both in the ranks of the Government and in the Civil Service. So things might have been different, but it is not much use to reflect on political might-have-beens. It is far more important to consider what we did achieve, and the D.E.A.'s achievement was substantial. Some Government, some day, will re-create a department on the lines of the D.E.A. and limit the out-dated authority of the Treasury. When that happens – and it is bound to happen – the thinking that went into the D.E.A. will be acclaimed.

I must let one incident suffice to illustrate the range of what we tried to do, the experiment that led to the creation of what afterwards became known as Upper Clyde Shipbuilders. I learned through our regional office that a certain shipyard (Fairfields) on the Upper Clyde was in danger of being closed down, with the loss of several thousand jobs. This was of limited concern to me, in the first instance, because other Departments were dealing with the matter, but I was able to intervene because of our regional set-up.

It happened that in Scotland Iain Stewart, a leading industrialist with new and imaginative ideas about management and industrial relations, was himself ready to do battle, and from then on he and I worked closely together. I asked for an examination of what could be done to help, and I took the matter to the Cabinet. That led to a considerable battle, indeed to a series of battles, first with the Chancellor, who had made some money available to the yard a bit earlier and had now decided to put his foot down, and then with the Board of Trade and a number of other Departments. But the

more involved I became the more passionately I felt the disastrous
effect of putting thousands of men out of work and so wasting the
skills that should – and could – be used to benefit the whole
community.

Bit by bit new ideas emerged, and then we did something that as
far as I know has never been done before in Britain – we got the
unions together and asked them if they were prepared not only to
accept the new ideas, but also to invest some of their own money in
the yard. The Boilermakers, often accused of being troublemakers in
the area, proved splendidly co-operative, and the Electrical Trades
Union, led by Les Cannon, showed a bold and imaginative readiness
to help. In the end we got several unions to subscribe tens of
thousands of pounds apiece, to become shareholders in a new company to run the yard and to be represented on the board.

I went round various industrialists and wealthy men and persuaded them to put up private money. Having got all these promises
I was able to go to the Cabinet and ask the Government to provide
the rest of what was needed. I learned afterwards that there was a
good deal of backbiting about this, and that some other Ministers
felt that too much credit was going to flow to me instead of to the
Government as a whole. However, the Secretary of State for Scotland, William Ross, was unaffected by all this, and he saw that the
saving of the yard for Scotland was a much bigger thing than to start
arguing about who was going to get the credit for it.

After all manner of last-minute crises I thought that we had finally
got everything pinned up with absolutely cast-iron undertakings.
However, we ran into new difficulties with the unions over money
and various of the private interests suddenly wholly or partially
withdrew. I was furious because I felt that they were going back on
solemn undertakings and could in every case well afford to accept
any risk involved.

I was determined to go on. I went up to Scotland, got Iain
Stewart and another industrialist friend of mine to invite more local
people to a discussion, and again we got promises of money. I went
back to London thinking that we were safe again, and then a telephone call told me that one of our new supporters had decided to
withdraw. I went along to a colleague who might prefer to be name-
less and poured out my cup of woe. He listened to me and then said
quietly, 'Go ahead. Tell them that you have got the money. Put
it down to A. N. Other. If all else fails I'll be the A. N. Other.'

He was as good as his word. He found a new source of wholly

reputable private finance, and he was not, in fact, required to take up the option he had promised, although I know that he would have done so without question. That is how Upper Clyde Ship-builders came into being with Iain Stewart as its Chairman. It changed the whole basis of management, it changed work-practices and began to break down demarcation agreements. It was an experiment in a new form of capitalism, part-unions, part-employers, part-Government, part-private shareholders. It was, of course, hated by all the other shipyards, who saw the prospect of Fairfields' earnings going up to their detriment as cherished traditional practices were changed. But we saw it as a wonderful proving-ground for new industrial relations in shipbuilding.

Now, it seems, it is all in danger of destruction. After I left the D.E.A. few were willing to fight for the experiment on the Clyde, and other shipbuilders did everything they could to hamper it. Another failure? No, I don't think so. Whatever happens to this particular experiment, the seed of something really important has been planted on the Clyde. And I shall always be proud of the D.E.A.'s part in helping to plant it.

7

Government:
Foreign Secretary

I LEFT THE D.E.A. late on the Wednesday after the Third Reading of the Prices and Incomes Bill, and having been sworn in at the Palace on the Thursday, I arrived at the Foreign Office at 9.30 a.m. on Friday, 12 August 1966. The Thursday's newspapers had made much of what no doubt they thought was a very clever head-line, 'Brown of the F.O.' – which referred to a then currently popular film called *Carlton-Browne of the F.O.*

As it happened, this couldn't have been a more prescient introduction because my arrival was a piece of almost pure farce which deserved to be enacted by Sir Laurence Olivier and possibly put to music by Sir Arthur Sullivan. Because of my past associations with Ernest Bevin, I knew that there was an inconspicuous door opening on to St James's Park which he had used some twenty years earlier. As I had now become Her Majesty's Principal Secretary of State for Foreign Affairs, it did not occur to me that I should go in by any other door. So I parked my car outside and went in.

Two messengers greeted me and did not seem particularly surprised to see me. They ushered me into the lift – incidentally, a marvellous piece of ancient engineering, which had been specially slowed down for Ernest Bevin because of his heart condition and which no engineer had subsequently been able to speed up. And so, as I thought at the time very appropriately, I was hoisted slowly and majestically up to the Secretary of State's floor, and deposited right outside my own office, which I entered. What I did not know was that, while I sat there taking in my surroundings, faced by a ridiculous portrait of that ineffective monarch George III – which I shortly afterwards replaced with a picture of Palmerston – my Principal Private Secretary and all kinds of other senior Foreign Office officials were downstairs at the main door with the assembled

Press and Lord knows how many photographers waiting for my arrival.

After a short interval a very impressive but worried Principal Private Secretary, Mr Murray MacLehose, now our Ambassador in Copenhagen, and soon to be Governor in Hong Kong, arrived. He was to become one of those in the Office on whom I leaned most heavily. In my view he was one of the wisest of the middle generation in the Foreign Office and tremendously able, hard-working and sympathetic to the new world in which we were operating. He was ever after always referred to as my 'gloomy Scot', but there was never any question of our trust of each other and my respect for his advice.

He 'suggested', in the way which the Foreign Office has, that it would be rather 'nice' if I went out again and came in through the proper door.

It was an odd introduction to an odd building and a service which I was to find, with all its impressive qualities, nevertheless greatly different from the Home Departments I had known.

The building in fact is downright inconvenient, ugly and shabby inside. People literally still work in what must have been once upon a time intended to be cupboards and in corridors. Quite senior officials interview foreign diplomats in the most incredible little cubby-holes. One of the ironies of the thing was that, some fifteen years earlier as the Minister of Works, I was actually involved in events which I thought had arranged that the Foreign Office should be moved across the Park and across the Mall to Carlton House Terrace, where a new building could be erected on what is after all a most appropriate site, the processional route from Westminster to the Palace. However, in the meantime everybody had intervened – the Fine Arts Commission, the preservationists, the traditionalists, the people who thought the façade looking on to St James's Park must be retained – and so the Foreign Office stayed put, and inevitably the building has its impact on the people who work there.

The Foreign Office brought home to me more directly, I think, than any other Ministry I served in, the exciting but also the frightening responsibility of power. You make judgements which are going to affect the lives perhaps of whole generations of people, and often you have to make your own decisions by relying on other men's judgement. And therefore I saw the first priorities as being to acquaint myself with those areas of the world where our national or alliance interests were especially and urgently involved; and, since

With Sam Watson, at Labour Party Conference,
Scarborough, 1963

With Gerry Reynolds, M.P.

Handing in nomination papers,
Matlock, Derbyshire, October 1964

to achieve this I would need to be very carefully briefed, I wanted to be in a position where I could judge whether the background and thinking of the people who were briefing me really fitted with my own outlook.

As a newcomer to the Foreign Office I had my partiality for areas of the world, either because I had visited them or because they had come up during my Labour Party days or during my D.E.A. days. These areas I could reckon to know fairly well, and also to know many of the characters involved. Among these were the Middle East, all the territories concerned with NATO and, of course, the continent of Europe, with which I felt our destinies in the end were so bound. To a lesser extent, I knew Latin America and East Africa.

But obviously there were vast areas of the world of tremendous importance to us and to our allies which I hardly knew at all and on which I had to be very fully briefed. The Foreign Office is equipped to give the best of information, the best of briefing on any international issue one cares to mention. But what bothered me, made as I am, was the thought that it was they who were deciding the areas I should be briefed about, and I quickly became aware that, unless I was very determined, I would inevitably become the purveyor of views already formed in the Office.

So I quickly decided to change the system by which the Foreign Secretary was informed and so in theory enabled to assess for himself the issues and the value of the courses of action being put before him, in a way that brought me face to face with those who were advising me. I shall return to this later.

At the same time the reliance one could place on advice from the men on the spot – both at home and our Heads of Mission abroad – raised the whole question of who they were and how good they were. Some of them of course I knew and, like everybody running a business, you tend to be pretty sure of the views of the men you have met and have liked; rather doubtful about the men you have met and have not liked; and very uncertain about the views of the men you have never met at all.

Quite early on, therefore, I began to consider how to ensure that the people in at any rate the more important posts should be the people whose qualities fitted them to be in that particular place and, so far as one could arrange it, at that particular moment. From my previous experience, I had already formed the view that somehow we had got the chief men in the wrong places. That they were the

I

best men I was prepared to believe, but they weren't where they should be. This view was confirmed when I came into the Office.

And so, to simplify the choice of their successors – already knowing when they would become due for replacement – I had prepared for me a list of the posts becoming vacant and the candidates in terms of age, experience and qualities. We could then marry men and their abilities to particular posts.

It was in this way that I arranged that Sir Denis Greenhill should be the next Permanent Under-Secretary. He was not by any means the obvious candidate. Indeed, there were a number of other more senior candidates. But on every kind of basis it seemed to me that he had the qualities that that post required. And I hope he will not find it embarrassing if I confess to being rather proud of him!

A different kind of example of this was the case of Sir Con O'Neill.

Sir Con had retired from the Service on two previous occasions and was now back in the Office as a Deputy Under-Secretary. He liked Germany very much and he really did want to finish his diplomatic service in Bonn. I had no animosity against him at all, but in the course of fairly close association with him – not only in discussions in the Office but during missions on which he accompanied me abroad – I came to the conclusion that he was better fitted to serve at home in the Foreign Office than he was to become our man in Bonn. This implied no criticism of his qualities, but rather an attempt to assess where those qualities would be best employed. I was at the same time thinking about the direction that political developments in Germany might take, and here again I thought a different person from Sir Con might be more effective in that post. The upshot was that when this was made known to him he chose to resign for the third time, and despite what was said in some newspapers afterwards, this was done in a very civilized fashion – there was no row between us; he had his back to my fireplace and a glass of sherry in his hand and simply said that, if he couldn't go to Bonn, he just wouldn't stay in the Service. The interesting footnote to all this is that he has since entered the Service for the fourth time and is now doing the very kind of job that I invited him to stay in London to do while Sir Roger Jackling went to Bonn. The resignation was quite unnecessary – he could have had the glass of sherry without it.

I recall this incident because I think it illustrates the problem in the best and sharpest way. There was a view among some senior members of the Service, not quite that it should be done as though it were Buggins's turn, but at least that they should sort out the top posts among themselves and more or less decide for themselves at which particular post they would like to finish their service and then retire. But it must be said for the chaps at the *very* top of the Office that, once I'd explained what I wanted done, they didn't try to obstruct me. They just put what they considered to be the facts before me, and left the decision to my own sense of judgement.

They were, indeed, very good about my whole approach to diplomatic appointments, and even when, for a variety of reasons, I wanted to insert a political appointment into the professional service, they were pretty good. The two instances of this in my time at the Foreign Office were the decisions to put Christopher Soames in Paris and to send John Freeman to Washington.

The Freeman appointment, I think, turned out to be a mistaken one, but not for anything to do with John Freeman. We were then banking on Hubert Humphrey's succeeding Lyndon Johnson as President and bringing in the kind of administration that we knew. And the idea of having an Ambassador in Washington who would be *persona grata* with the liberal-minded Americans whom Mr Humphrey would have appointed was obviously attractive.

But the U.S. election brought in Nixon instead of Humphrey, and Freeman in the past had written some pretty waspish things about Nixon. So although Freeman has succeeded in establishing himself in Washington, he has not had the kind of contact with the President, or even with the administration, that somebody else might have had. With hindsight, therefore, one can look on his appointment as a mistake, but there was no reason to consider it a mistake at the time it was made (but see Appendix II).

Even with hindsight, I think one can say that the appointment of Christopher Soames to Paris was absolutely right. We had a lot to overcome in our relations with France. One problem was to remove a kind of arid frigidity which seemed to have settled down over all official relations between Britain and France. The British Embassy in Paris had come to reflect this – when I used to visit there I seemed to arrive just as they were trying to get the dust-sheets off the furniture; sometimes they didn't even bother to do that.

I felt that if we couldn't succeed in appealing to President de Gaulle rationally, at least we could compete with the Élysée and the American Embassy as social centres, and at least have Ministers and other political figures dropping in from time to time. As things were, our Embassy didn't seem to know anybody outside the normal

channels of the Quai d'Orsay. Yet this obviously is absolutely
essential if the sources of information are to be complete and able
to be tested against each other. One example of the importance of
this will serve to show what I mean.

I have a wonderful old pal in Paris called Harold King who
used to be Reuter's chief correspondent there. Harold had begun
life as the editor of the *Landworker*, the journal of the National
Union of Agricultural Workers, and all his roots were right. In his
years of working for Reuter's in Paris he got to know everybody,
so much so that I used to tell him that he had gone native and
become more Gaullist than de Gaulle.

I remember particularly one occasion when we were still in
Opposition, and Hugh Gaitskell, Aneurin Bevan and I went on a
briefing visit to NATO (the headquarters of which at that time were
in France). We didn't travel in the same plane, or stay in the same
place, and as I was the only one of us who didn't have a bed for the
night, the Ambassador invited me to stay at the Embassy.

About 9 o'clock that evening Harold King called for me. He
wasn't allowed in because he wasn't on those terms, so we went
out together. Harold knew every café where the closest associates
of de Gaulle gathered, and we went from one to the other, seeing
just about everybody who was to be seen, Gaullist and otherwise.
I was convinced at the end of the session that de Gaulle would very
soon become President of France. I also had a pretty clear idea of
the circumstances which would bring it about.

Next morning at the Embassy, while waiting for Gaitskell and
Bevan to arrive so that we could go off together to NATO at Fontaine-
bleau, I discovered that this was not the preferred view in the
Embassy. They were of the opinion that the 'old boy' was on the
decline and that there wasn't the slightest chance of de Gaulle
ever coming to power.

I tried to say, 'Well, I was out last night, and it didn't sound like
that to me.' To which the reply came, 'Ah, you were out with that fellow Harold King. Well, if you will keep that sort of company, so be it.'

A few weeks later de Gaulle was in fact President of France,
having achieved it in the very way I had been told, and retained
his grip for quite a number of years after that.

That sort of incident stuck in my memory when I became Foreign
Secretary – it seemed to me that the Embassy was in all kinds of
ways totally out of touch with what was really going on. When
the time came to fill the Paris post, therefore, I looked with special

care at all the career members of the Diplomatic Service who were held to be available, but none of them seemed quite the right man to change the whole image of the British Embassy in Paris in the way that I felt it ought to be changed.

It needed a man with imagination, a knowledge of and a feel for France and with a particular social flair, and, I am afraid, a man with some money, for Paris is an expensive post – and, alas, we do not sufficiently provide for this in the allowances we afford the Ambassador. Bit by bit I came to the conclusion that this particular job called for an outsider, and I went over in my mind all the outsiders I could think of – industrialists, trade unionists, Socialists, academics – to try to find a man with just the right combination of qualities. In the end I decided that I had found him in Soames.

I knew that people in the Labour Party would complain about such an important diplomatic job being given to a Conservative politician, especially after the Aubrey Jones episode, and I knew that the Foreign Service would not really like to see the plum Paris post going to an outsider. But Soames's qualities in this particular context were quite exceptional.

In addition to his past associations with France during and after the war, he had the inestimable advantage of having Mary Churchill as his wife, plus a young family, so that the Embassy would be peopled and the dust-sheets would have to come off.

So I persuaded him to take the job, and I think that everyone would say now that his appointment has turned out to be a tremendous success.

In addition to changing the system so that I could, as it were, look into the whites of the eyes of the fellows in the Office who were advising me, and try to arrange that the people from thereon appointed abroad would be the ones I knew and was willing to take personal responsibility for, I also embarked upon a system of talking as much as I could on the telephone to the fellows who were in our Missions abroad. I used this system of direct conversation very much more I think than my predecessors had. I felt this had the effect of bringing them much more closely into the making of policy at home, and of course one could pretty easily identify those countries where this was a reasonable thing to do. One of the people I found myself talking to most frequently was Lord Caradon, our representative at the United Nations and also a Minister of State. What I didn't realize at that time was that the telephone line we used was an open one. After a while the Permanent Under-Secretary said to me, 'This open-line telephoning to Hugh Caradon must be giving the Russians and Lord knows who else a tremendous bonus.' So he dragged out of the Treasury some ridiculously small sum of money to put in a direct secure line to our Man in New York. I am still staggered that this thought had never occurred to anybody at all before.

Although not directly concerned with this, I faced another problem at this time. There is an arrangement, which at first sight looks very sensible, whereby one of the Private Secretaries to the Prime Minister is an official of the Foreign Office. I can well understand what was in mind when this practice first began, but certainly in my experience it could be troublesome. It raised considerable conflict on occasions, for we would decide in the Foreign Office on a course of policy on which, if I considered it of sufficient importance, I would in any case have consulted the Prime Minister. But we could quite easily find that the seconded Foreign Office official at No. 10 was simultaneously advising the Prime Minister on the same subject and on a quite separate network. I remember saying on one occasion that it was like someone who had been appointed to be chaplain to the Pope suddenly acting as though he were the Cardinal Secretary of State. This system still applies, and while I would not end it, I hope that by now someone has found the means by which each knows his proper role.

One of the perennial problems of any Foreign Secretary (as I know from talks with my Conservative predecessors), but most especially for a Labour Foreign Secretary in view of the tremendous interest in international affairs that tends to exist in any left-wing party, is that every other member of the Cabinet is a potential alternative. Each knows somebody of importance in a given area or has visited it at some time or other. All are convinced that the Foreign Office is stuffy and prejudiced. The prejudices they accuse it of differ, of course, and are really the subjects on which they are themselves most prejudiced. And so all the views of the Foreign Secretary, however carefully considered, tend to be contested by colleagues who cannot have the same access to all the balancing arguments and may themselves have been exposed to highly sophisticated pressures from the quite powerful lobbies which exist in London as in every other capital in the world.

But what is true in the Cabinet is multiplied four-fold or more in the Parliamentary Party. I found myself very much the target for pressure, attacks, even abuse, on the floor of the House and in the committees, both official and unofficial, which abound in the Commons and are assiduously 'looked after' by outside lobbyists. Very soon it became clear to me that I would have to pick my own priorities, try to make the right decisions, and stick to them. This may seem a somewhat arbitrary way of doing it although the speed of events tends to help. But since it is going to be arbitrary anyway, better it should be done by the man in the chair than by everybody else.

When I came to the Office, one of the issues I felt certain was important, urgent and would steadily become more so, was the Middle East. This was made all too evident by the course events in that area then took. The whole chain of things which led up to the June 1967 war commanded the utmost attention. I could see all too clearly the likely pattern of things to come, and I did everything I could to try to prevent conflict. I could see the build-up on the Israeli side, and I knew at first hand, because I knew the men personally, the kind of doctrine that some of the younger Israeli generals were preaching about a 'pre-emptive strike' as being Israel's best chance of success. I could see also the Russian build-up on the other side. I discussed the situation many times with Russian diplomatists, and I felt then – and think still – that the Russians did not want a military clash. I was less sure of Russian power to control events, to prevent a clash from taking place.

I could see – what some of my colleagues then were reluctant to see – the tremendous price that we in Britain would have to pay if there were another military conflict in the Middle East, and a closure of the Suez Canal. I sent many papers to my colleagues about the effect on us if the canal were to be closed, and I urged the need to reduce the rate of run-down on the coal industry because I felt that I could not, as Foreign Secretary, guarantee the flow of oil from the Middle East. I knew from my experience at the D.E.A. what would be the effect on the British economy of having to find vast sums in dollars to pay for oil from other sources than the Middle East, and to pay the increased freights and charter prices for the emergency rerouting of oil round the Cape. It is interesting to reflect here that the improvement in the British economy that came about too late to save the Labour Government in the election of 1970 could have been brought about at least a year earlier not only if we had changed our economic policy in 1966 instead of at the end of 1967, but had also been able to head off the Israeli-Arab war in June 1967.

This really is the background to the distorted stories which appeared a little while ago about the tremendous efforts which I, with the approval of the Prime Minister, at that stage made to organize some effective outside force to hold events after U Thant's extraordinary decision to accede to Nasser's request that he should remove the United Nations Emergency Force (UNEF). This military force had been stationed on the Gulf of Aqaba and at other vital places to keep the peace between the two sides. To everybody's surprise, and, as I now know, certainly to President Nasser's, the Secretary-General promptly declared the force non-operational preparatory to its removal. I shall never understand how he was advised to come so quickly to this very ill-considered and, I feel absolutely sure, totally unnecessary and unexpected decision. Certainly at that moment, if at no other, the need for a very different character at the head of this vital organization, already so weakened by big power conflicts and the growth of the so-called Afro-Asian group, became very apparent. He did not wait for a meeting of the Security Council, he did not give any of us a chance to discuss the matter, he just said that the rules of the game were that the force could stay there only by permission of the host country (in this case Egypt), and that if the host country withdrew permission he was bound, under the terms of the General Assembly resolution of 1956 which set up the peace-keeping force, to recall it. All of this was legalistically true, but wise men, faced with big events whose possible consequences are immeasurable, shouldn't in my view act as though they were working in a solicitor's office conveyancing property.

The withdrawal of the U.N. force at once increased tension, and prompted the Egyptian closure, to Israeli ships, of the Strait of Tiran, leading to the Israeli port of Eilat on the Gulf of Aqaba. That put us firmly under notice that either we, in the United Nations, carried out what we said we would do after the previous war and let Israel see that she could put her trust in the United Nations, or that the Israelis would act for themselves with their pre-emptive strike.

I didn't give up, but tried all sorts of dodges at least to postpone if not to prevent a military clash. It soon became obvious that the Russians were not going to play in the United Nations team, and if the Russians wouldn't play there was not much that the U.N. could do, because the Russians could veto U.N. action any time they wanted to. The French, alas, also seemed highly unreliable in their approach to the Israeli issue. So I turned to the idea of inter-national action through a body of Maritime Powers. This was an attempt to initiate international peace-keeping outside the United Nations in a form which the Russians couldn't veto. I hoped that a body of Maritime Powers might make a simple declaration that they could not tolerate the closure of the Strait of Tiran because it was an international waterway, like the Dardanelles, and that if necessary an international naval force would be assembled to escort convoys through the Strait.

We never quite settled whether such convoys would include Israeli ships or only ships carrying supplies to Israel. I was clear in my own mind that the Israelis would have to accept that they couldn't expect to have the Israeli flag flying in the very first convoy that went through. The important thing was to try to get some sort of international action under way; details could be dealt with as they cropped up. But this operation never did get under way, partly because of the reluctance of the Americans to support it, and partly because we got overtaken by events. Whether, given more time, we could have assembled an international peace-keeping naval force I do not know. After the sudden Israeli attack annihilating the Arab air force on the ground it became pointless to go on with the idea.

This reinforced in my mind the urgency of something I was already conscious of, namely the need to resume direct relations with Egypt and such other Arab states, who had broken off relations, as we could.

So far as Egypt was concerned, diplomatic relations between us had been broken off over Suez, resumed in 1961, only to be broken off again over Rhodesia in 1965. I felt strongly that we should not tamely allow our influence to be undermined in this way and, on the contrary, should set out to rebuild it. All our interests – commercial, strategic and geographic – seemed to me to require this.

In the case of Egypt this was assisted by the fact that I had known President Nasser since 1952, the year of the *coup d'état* when, although not the titular head, he became to all intents and purposes the effective power. We had kept in close touch and I had met him many times subsequently. It also happened that I knew those around him. And so I turned my mind and that of the Office towards ways in which we might properly bring about the resumption of relations. Although this aroused some horror on the part of those who saw Nasser in quite a different light from that in which I saw him, I persevered. I think their problem really was one which troubled so many in this country after Suez: partly a reluctance to admit that that episode was the disaster which in fact it was, both in terms of policy and practice, but also because they, like so many others, still thought of Nasser as at heart anti-British and opposed to all our traditional friends in the area.

At one point, events – as so often happens – seemed to take over. In November 1966 I was on my way for an official visit to the Russian leaders in Moscow which had nothing specific to do with the Middle East situation. Just before we were due to land (indeed, Gromyko told me later that he was already in his car on the way to the airport) we heard that Moscow was enshrouded in fog and my aircraft had to be diverted to Leningrad. At the airport there, I saw a United Arab Republic plane. I asked who had come in it, and I was told 'Field-Marshal Hakim Amer', then Nasser's No. 2.

I then made inquiries to see where Hakim Amer was staying in Leningrad, and despite the difficulties raised by everybody because of the absence of diplomatic relations between our two countries, I in fact got him myself on the telephone. We arranged to meet the next day in Moscow, to which we were both bound – he to a dacha in the Lenin hills, I to the Embassy. Despite the horrified looks on the faces of some of my party, we spoke again to the Egyptians, and I then went to meet him at his dacha. It was of course a Russian villa, and we both knew what that meant, but we decided not to worry. I explained to him briefly my thinking about Britain and the Middle East and our need of each other, and said how much I would like to resume relations. It was a very friendly meeting, and Amer promised to pass on what I had said to Nasser.

This he did, and it greatly helped the atmosphere in which President Nasser and I then conducted our personal exchange of letters which ended a year later in an agreement to restore diplomatic relations.

One of the problems was to ensure that each country sent to the other as its Ambassador a man of rather specially high standing, known to be close to his home Government, and well disposed to and knowledgeable about the other. I well remember a phrase in one of Nasser's letters saying, 'I don't want any striped-pants faceless diplomat transferred from some South American banana republic.'

The question was, Who? My old wanderings had given me a trump card here, and I was able to write to Nasser, 'What would you say if I sent you Harold Beeley?' He replied at once that he would regard it as a very great honour.

After taking a First in Modern History at Oxford, Sir Harold Beeley (as he now was) had held various academic posts and had worked for the Research Department of the Foreign Office. He had been a member of the secretariat of the San Francisco Conference and of the Preparatory Commission of the United Nations, and he had been secretary to the Anglo-American Committee of Inquiry on Palestine in 1946. In that same year he joined the Foreign Service, and in 1949, when he was serving as Counsellor at the British Embassy in Copenhagen, he and his then wife (their marriage was later dissolved) did me a very considerable service.

I was then Parliamentary Secretary to the Ministry of Agriculture in Mr Attlee's Government, and I made an official visit to Copen-hagen to discuss various agricultural matters with the Danes. The Ambassador was away at the time, and I was, I thought, grossly badly treated by a good many of the British staff, particularly by their ladies, who made it very plain that a Labour Minister was not a welcome sight in the homes of the British community in Copenhagen. (This, it must be remembered, was the period of rigid food controls in Britain, of snoeck, etc.) This hostility was carried to an extraordinary length. During my visit a British frigate put into Copenhagen and a party was thrown on board. As far as I could see every British subject in Copenhagen was invited to the party except the one British Minister who was there at the time. I was regarded as just a visiting seed-grower or swede-basher, and it was made plain to me that I could scarcely expect to have anything to do with the British Embassy or the Royal Navy.

Well, Harold Beeley and his wife gave a luncheon for me, and a fair gathering of British residents in Copenhagen came along. The conversation took the form of diatribes against the wretched Labour Government, and I must have shown that I can get irritated by this kind of talk. I was getting near danger point, when Mrs Beeley called across to her husband, 'We don't really like having *our* Government talked about like this, do we, Harold?' She looked round the room and went on to explain, 'You see, my father was one of the founders of the Labour Party, and when I'm in England I work for it.' I've never seen a hostile gathering so crushed, and naturally I was very grateful to Harold Beeley and his wife.

He had been Private Secretary to Ernest Bevin at the Foreign Office, and I used to meet him when I called to see Bevin. In those days we'd both been much abused for supporting Bevin in his anti-Zionist views, so we had a common link. Beeley had gone on to become a real expert on the Middle East and had served in Baghdad and Saudi Arabia before being appointed Ambassador to the United Arab Republic in 1961. In our younger days he and I

had shared Bevin's anti-Zionism, but, like me, he was in no sense
anti-Jewish, and he understood the real problems of the Middle
East better than almost anybody else. So when, years later, I was
Foreign Secretary and had to find a man for the difficult and
delicate task of restoring diplomatic relations with Egypt, I turned
naturally to Harold Beeley. He was delighted at the opportunity
of going back to Egypt and he did a splendid job there. It was
largely due to him that we were able to open a whole new chapter
in British relations with Nasser.

Recalling those days one is not only impressed, but almost
oppressed, with the sense of how many issues we were faced with and
had to handle at the same time. The question, for example, of the
integration and unification of Europe was currently a very pressing
problem and for me an equally urgent priority.

This was not only a question of Europe's own requirements. It
also involved what was fast becoming a very pressing issue: the
decline, certainly the deterioration, in the provisions made within
the North Atlantic alliance for the defence of the NATO area. To put
it mildly, it was – and I think still is – falling apart. Not only were
the force provisions being made by European countries well below
Treaty obligations, but even then the pressures were building up in
America for a reduction of their European force commitment, and
the whole host of strategic, as well as tactical, decisions were being
taken with Europe in no real position to play a proper role. And
so, although we in Europe were part of the NATO alliance, it wasn't
really an alliance of fourteen powers – it was thirteen little chaps
who couldn't say 'Boo' to a goose, the goose being, of course, America.

As a result of all this, plus the need for Western Europe to be much
more closely organized economically to provide us with the kind
of domestic market which America and Russia have, I have always
seen the question of European integration as not primarily a question
of extending the Common Market. Of course that particular act
is essential in itself and will be the opening symbol of what I wanted
and want to do. This way we begin to unify this continent, getting
common policies – financial, commercial, external and defence – so
that we can stop the polarization of the world around the two
Super-Powers. I shall discuss this whole question in some detail
in my chapter on Europe.

Among other questions which occupied a lot of time was the
question of what role we thought we should play East of Suez and
whether a continued physical presence there was desirable, especially

in view of the feelings of many of those countries who were only too conscious of the old imperialist association.

I came to the view, with my colleagues, that a withdrawal from East of Suez and the dropping of a physical land presence in the Middle East was not only inevitable but essential. However, it must be said in all truth that I did not agree with my colleagues on the speed and the timetable to which we subsequently decided to adhere. And most emphatically I did not agree with those who were really thinking of this, as I suspect some of them undoubtedly were, as a retreat into 'Fortress Europe' or a re-creation of the 'little Englander' concept.

All this in its turn raised the question of our relations with the Americans, who wanted us to play a continuing physical role in that part of the area and at the same time were asking us to help them disentangle themselves from their physical role in South-East Asia. This really meant of course the question of Vietnam. We made tremendous attempts – as the then American administration would be the first to acknowledge – to help them in their search for an acceptable basis on which they could honourably withdraw and at the same time leave behind a reasonably viable situation which could genuinely lead to a non-Communist dictated future for the peoples there. I made numerous visits to America for one purpose or the other, had many conversations with President Johnson and Secretary of State Dean Rusk and others, and both the Prime Minister and I were involved separately and together in talks with the Russians on the subject. The most notable of these efforts, of course, which was abortive in the end, although it seemed at one stage to be tantalizingly hopeful, was made during the visit to London of Mr Kosygin and Mr Gromyko early in 1967.

During and subsequently to all this, I took the view, which brought tremendous fire on my head politically speaking, that we should not join the clamour, which had many dubious origins, for the Americans to withdraw from Vietnam without having achieved at least this result. I had in mind that if we, as a Government, did so, we would put not only ourselves out of court as a possible 'honest broker', but also breach our responsibilities as a co-chairman with the Russians of the Geneva Conference. We would also be creating a rod for our own back so far as Europe was concerned. Far too many of those in America who wanted to disengage from Vietnam had been brought to the view – or maybe had even started with the view – that what had happened showed the folly, as they would put it, of America getting physically involved overseas at all. And I foresaw what is in fact now tending to happen; a demand that, having got out of Vietnam, they should wind up their other overseas commitments, and I could see them putting up a strong case for reducing their commitment on the European Continent. Once these things start one never knows how far they are going to go. I could not get out of my mind the price that Britain had had to pay in the First and Second World Wars in order to try to hold the position until the Americans joined in. This meant that I simply could not face with any degree of equanimity the departure of the Americans from the mainland of Europe again.

The story of those abortive negotiations with Mr Kosygin and Mr Gromyko in 1967 ought, perhaps, to be told more fully, for I think it holds many lessons for us. The hope of embarking on those negotiations began in November 1966 when I went to Moscow. This was not by any means my first meeting with Mr Gromyko, but it was my first official meeting with him in Russia. We had all sorts of things to discuss, but I wanted particularly to talk about Vietnam. My own view was that the right way out of the impasse was to beg, bully or persuade the Russians into allowing Mr Gromyko and myself to reconvene the Geneva Conference with or without the Chinese.

But I took in my bag to Moscow a very different proposition as well, and one on which the Prime Minister was very keen, and which we were supposed to be authorized by the Americans to discuss. The trouble about this was that the Americans had not told us what they were doing with anybody else, so that our attempt to act as mediators ultimately put us in a ridiculous position. But that came later. The secret proposal that I took to Moscow was something that we called 'The Phase A/Phase B Formula'. Under this, we were to make clear to the Russians that while the Americans, for public reasons, kept saying that they could stop their bombing of North Vietnam only after Hanoi stopped sending troops through the demilitarized zone to the south, they were ready to stop the bombing provided that they had a secret undertaking that, as soon as the bombing did stop, Hanoi would keep its part of the bargain. This would appear to meet the North Vietnamese demand for an unconditional cessation of bombing. But that would be only a beginning. When, after the cessation of bombing, Hanoi was seen to stop infiltration through the demilitarized zone, the Americans would respond by halting the build-up of U.S. forces in Vietnam.

Thus Hanoi would appear to win two moves out of three, for the price of a secret agreement to act when the American bombing stopped. What I didn't know when I took this plan to Moscow was that the Americans had already tried it out through various other channels, the latest being the Poles, without getting very far.

Anyway, I duly put it to Mr Kosygin and Mr Gromyko as strongly as I could. Nothing much happened until these two Russian statesmen came on their visit to England in February 1967. By that time our own Government was under tremendous pressure, particularly from members of the Labour Party in Parliament, to reverse our policy of not condemning the Americans and calling on them to withdraw from Vietnam. The Prime Minister was finding it pretty rough going to stand up not merely to the left wing of the Labour Party, but to many other people in the Party as well. We had been defeated at the Party Conference on Vietnam, and he wanted desperately to find a new initiative to take. I, on the other hand, was still concerned to prevent the growth of iso-lationism in America. This led to tensions in the Cabinet, and tensions between the Cabinet and the Parliamentary Party. So it was decided that when the Russians came to England we would make a tremendous effort to mediate on the lines of the plan that I had taken to Moscow three months before. The Prime Minister and I made arrangements to line up our own policy, and we set out to do our damnedest to persuade the Russians to use their influence with Hanoi to bring about a settlement.

The Prime Minister and I met the Russians at Gatwick on the morning of Monday, 6 February 1967, and we had our first session of talks that same afternoon. The next thing that happened was that I learned that the Americans had been putting out precisely the same feelers through Mr Janusz Lewandowski, the Polish representative on the International Control Commission, and that Italian diplomatists in Warsaw had also been involved. I was furious, and so was the Prime Minister, to discover that instead of bringing a bright new plan to the Russians we were being used to peddle ideas that had been put to them already. However, we agreed that the issue was far too important for any sort of pettiness and we went on with the job.

Mr C. L. Cooper has written about our efforts in his *Lost Crusade: America in Vietnam*. He describes the Prime Minister as having been what he calls 'overly optimistic', and adds that I was markedly less so, and that the Americans were even less optimistic than I was.

I think that probably sums up things pretty well. The Prime Minister was optimistic because he wanted so badly some sort of political triumph over Vietnam; moreover, he felt that he had a special ability to negotiate with the Russians that nobody else had, because he had negotiated trade treaties with Mr Kosygin and Mr Gromyko many years before, when neither was so prominent as they became later.

We tried again and again to get the Russians to persuade Hanoi to accept the package deal that was being offered. We got assurances, or thought we had them, from the U.S. State Department and from the President himself. Never before or since has the 'hot line' from No. 10 to the White House been so hot as it was over that period. There was a great argument over the extension or the non-extension of the Tet Truce in Vietnam, which was the cover for stopping the bombing without the Americans actually having to announce that they had stopped it.

The President had appalling political problems. He used to say, 'How can I defend stopping the bombing when my boys are being killed?' What he meant was: How could he explain to American mothers and American wives that he was withdrawing air cover from their men while the Viet Cong were still coming through, still shooting and still mining? I tried to explain to him that air cover in the Vietnam situation was not really very useful, that jungle warfare was utterly different from other kinds of warfare, that you have to fight it on the ground, as we did in Malaya, and that heavy high-altitude bombing, or even low-altitude bombing, may not help much. I had intense difficulty in getting any of these ideas through. Many Americans, regrettably, think that the only thing that matters is the weight of power – they honestly believe that if you flood the world with enough Coca-Cola you are bound to win in the end.

So the Americans had their political problems of how to announce the stopping of the bombing, and we had ours, which was how to go on supporting the Americans when most of the rest of the world thought that they were being extraordinarily ham-handed, inconsiderate, difficult and cruel.

When the Americans heard how angry I was over the Lewandowski affair, they sent an official to London to calm us down. At the request of the Prime Minister, he stayed on over the whole period of the Russian visit, and we were in daily, sometimes hourly, contact. He breakfasted with me several times. He knew of the

Cartoon
by Vicky

Showing Statement of Intent on Productivity,
Prices and Incomes, 16th December 1964

With his National Plan, 16 September 1965

With George Woodcock at the T.U.C. Conference,
Brighton, September 1965

differences of nuance, of sentiment, between the Prime Minister and me, and he understood the similarity of view on many matters between Dean Rusk and me. We were both of us trying to make foreign policy and we were both of us being 'assisted' – in the American case by the White House and in my case by No. 10. All kinds of unofficial advisers were flocking round the White House, and all kinds of chaps flocked around No. 10.

We shared, therefore, a good deal of fellow-sympathy, but this could not prevent a woeful series of misunderstandings. The Americans repeatedly got themselves into a terrible jam, and we all fell foul of the conflict between the White House, with its special foreign affairs department, and the State Department, which is genuinely the American Foreign Office. So far as I could see, never the twain did meet. Every time we were getting something squared with somebody, some sinister figure would emerge from the basement and get the ear of the President, or just say that he had the ear of the President, and everything would get changed.

How serious the Russians were during this period I have no way of knowing. The Americans said that they had an indirect line to Hanoi, but I doubt it. The Russians said that they were in close touch with Hanoi, but I doubt that, too. We were dealing with two groups, each of whom reckoned that it had its own hot line to Ho Chi Minh, but neither of whom in my view really did. So we were bandying about ideas for a settlement without knowing whether they were getting through or not. The Americans were using every channel they could, and using some channels against others. The Russians, I suspect, were trying to prove that they could do better than the Chinese. They wanted the world to believe, especially the Communist world, that they were in the saddle and they were the fellows Hanoi would listen to. Frankly, I think that Hanoi listened chiefly to China, and for one simple reason – the only people who could really do down North Vietnam were the Chinese. Russia was supplying arms, of course, but it was China which could cut off the supply. I think that the Russians were leading everybody up the garden, including us.

However, there came a moment when we seemed on the very brink of achieving something. Through the American official already mentioned whom we called 'The Man in the Tower' because he was incarcerated in the room at Chequers where Lady Jane Grey had been kept, we finally cleared with Washington precisely what we were to say to the Russians. We delivered our

K

message to Mr Kosygin and Mr Gromyko, and both of them looked
interested – but, of course, you never know how much real interest
there may be behind the looks. Anyway, we were full of hope. And
then, at the very last minute, a correction came from Washington.
The Russians had the document which we had so painfully worked
out for them, and I have no doubt that it was in the cypher machine
on the way from London to Moscow. Mr Kosygin and Mr Gromyko
had left for King's Cross to get a train to Edinburgh when the
correction came. The Prime Minister decided to send his Private
Secretary with the message to the Russians, and he managed,
alas, to get it to them on the train with a few seconds to spare
before the train left. Had I been consulted, I'd have said no, let
them get it at Edinburgh in the morning. They don't have a cypher
machine on the night sleeper to Edinburgh and the Russians can't
do anything with the message on the train. If we had waited until
morning we should have had several hours to try to get hold of
Washington, to urge them not to be so bloody silly. But I wasn't
consulted, the American message was rushed off to the Russians,
and you can imagine what they felt. That message changed everything. It convinced the Russians that we were not really in the
confidence of the Americans, and since the French were at it as well
as the Poles, Marshal Tito and lots of others, I suspect that we
looked about as foolish as intermediaries as anyone could look.

So the whole thing petered out. It petered out partly, perhaps,
because we were too anxious to be intermediaries and didn't check
enough with the Americans beforehand. But it petered out mainly
because the American system is what it is, and the White House
and the State Department often seem not to know what the other
is doing. There were doveish officials in Washington who were
trying to help, and hawkish officials, mostly nearer to the scene of
events, who were trying to prevent the doves from helping. The
Prime Minister's hot line to President Johnson was not as reliable
as it ought to have been. I think that the fact of the matter was that
Mr Johnson didn't really like the Prime Minister much, and the
hot line from No. 10 that went allegedly directly to the President
was inclined to go instead to Mr Rostow. Then I'm pretty sure that
the Russians led us up the garden, and that Mr Kosygin never had
any real authority to do what he claimed to be doing.

I don't know whether our attempt to mediate ever had any
chance of success, or whether it was doomed from the start. I'm
fairly sure that even if it had started with some hope of success,

it would have collapsed because of the absurdities of the American political machine and the opportunities it gives for one set of guys in the administration to cut off another set of guys, thereby producing no policy at all. And at that time we had No. 10 Downing Street trying to maintain a private Foreign Office in exactly the same way. We were all stultifying one another.

Our Foreign Office officials worked magnificently over that whole period. Some of them knew far more about things than any of the politicians involved would ever begin to learn. It was they, I think, who reinforced my own natural scepticism, and yet we all put everything we could into the attempt. At the end we were left wondering whether we might, perhaps, have succeeded if everybody on both sides of the Atlantic had been a bit more sensible. I don't think that any individual can really be said to have bitched up that particular episode. I do think that a lot of people in Washington and in London showed up the weaknesses of our particular forms of government machine.

A completely different sort of problem that I had to deal with at the Foreign Office was the Sachsenhausen affair. Sachsenhausen was a notorious concentration camp in Nazi Germany, and a number of British subjects were incarcerated there during the war. They were mostly civilians who, for one reason or another, had been caught in Germany by the war, but a few British servicemen who were prisoners of war and who were recaptured after efforts to escape were also sent to Sachsenhausen.

Long before my time Mr R. A. Butler (now Lord Butler), who was then at the Foreign Office, had negotiated an agreement under which the Germans made available a million pounds for compensation to British subjects for their sufferings under Nazi persecution. Formal rules for the disbursement of this money were drawn up, and it was duly paid out. A million pounds was not really a great deal for all who had to share in it. The understanding was that this money was to compensate people who had suffered the full rigours of a German concentration camp. This might seem to have been a fairly straightforward matter, but so far as Sachsenhausen was concerned there was a small group of people – two civilians and ten servicemen – who had been imprisoned there outside the perimeter. Mr Airey Neave, the Member of Parliament for Abingdon, who had himself been cruelly treated by the Germans in concentration camps during the war, took up the question of this handful of people who had been imprisoned at Sachsenhausen.

They had been detained in a special camp (Sonderlager A) and cell-block (Zellenbau) which had been outside the main Sachsenhausen camp and, in the words of an official report, had 'never been subjected to the well-known inhuman and degrading treatment of the concentration camp proper'. Their position had been considered by every Foreign Secretary before me, and all had come to the conclusion that they could not be regarded as eligible for the particular form of compensation available from the German payment. These men had undoubtedly suffered at Sachsenhausen, and everybody respected their courage, but to include them in the compensation agreement would have created a host of new anomalies. They had not been treated in quite the same way as the civilians who suffered in the camp proper. One or two of them had written accounts of their experiences which showed that, while they had had anything but a joyride, they had occasionally received Red Cross parcels as prisoners of war and had been treated differently from the poor wretches who were incarcerated in the main camp.

I was sympathetic to these Sachsenhausen claims when the matter was first raised with me, and in the minute I wrote then I asked, 'Aren't we being sticky here? Can't we do something for these chaps?' But when I had gone into the whole story I was persuaded that I ought not to go back on what had been the decision of all my predecessors: that, while one naturally wanted to help people who had suffered in the war, to admit this particular group to the compensation scheme would be unfair to a lot of others who had been excluded from compensation.

By the time I had become Foreign Secretary, however, we had got an Ombudsman (the Parliamentary Commissioner, Sir Edmund Compton), and Mr Airey Neave appealed to him. Now, although in law the Ombudsman is not supposed to be concerned with policy decisions but solely with matters of administration, Sir Edmund Compton took the case and found against the Foreign Office in a highly critical report. In my view he proved no real maladministration at all, but simply expressed the opinion that the policy decision was wrong.

I defended the Foreign Office throughout the case, but in view of the Ombudsman's finding I agreed that the department would find the money to pay the compensation to the people concerned in the Sachsenhausen affair. I explained this to the House of Commons on 5 February 1968 by saying that I felt that public opinion would be outraged if I rejected the views of the Ombudsman on an issue which affected personally a few very gallant men. I added, however, 'I want the House to understand that in doing so I am probably being unfair to quite a number of gallant men who have suffered very badly, but who are outside the compensation scheme. It is precisely this difficulty which contributed to my original decision.' I went on to say this, which I regard as extremely important:

'Newspapers talk about bungling and blundering. It is imperative for me to say that no one has blundered or bungled. This was an issue of judgement. The Parliamentary Commissioner's view is that our judgement was wrong. I am willing to accept that. I have therefore reviewed and revised my decision, but this remains a matter of judgement and on a matter of judgement on an issue as narrow as this anyone can be wrong. I would have wished, since it has come out this way, that I had taken this decision earlier. I did not, but there it is. I have taken the decision now, and I hope on this basis we can end what for me is a very unhappy story.'

This ended the particular issue of the Sachsenhausen case, but I would not allow any official of the Foreign Office to be blamed for the earlier decisions. The withholding of compensation from the particular group championed by Mr Airey Neave had been a policy decision; it had been taken originally by Lord Butler when he was at the Foreign Office, and it had been supported by every succeeding Foreign Secretary, including myself. So if anyone was to be blamed it had to be me as the incumbent Foreign Secretary, and not any official in the department.

This led to a peculiarly bitter debate in the House of Commons, in which, for the first time in my experience, the doctrine was seriously advanced that the public should know which Civil Servants had given advice to Ministers, and that such Civil Servants should be named and attacked personally. I resisted this to the end. If it can be shown that a Minister was wrong in taking some decision, then you go for the Minister. If the Minister feels that he has been badly advised, then it's up to him to deal with his advisers; but that's a matter for him. As far as Parliament and the public are concerned, the Minister is the man responsible, and it is the Minister who should be criticized and attacked. This principle is vitally important. No doubt personal attacks on Civil Servants would provide rather juicy meat for newspapers, but if Civil Servants were ever to be subject to such personal attacks it would have calamitous effects on the Civil Service. Officials would be either too frightened to express an opinion at all, or they would themselves turn to the attack and become more public figures than they ought to be. We have seen this happen to some extent in the United States, and the effects on the U.S. Civil Service have been appalling. There you have a Civil Service that is for the most part timid, with officials frightened to death of having to appear before Congress. But you also get top Civil Servants of stronger personality or more intense personal ambition whom you can't tell apart from Ministers. And there's a still more unhealthy development in which you get a President (or, in Britain, a Prime Minister acting like a President) who will play off Ministers against Civil Servants, and vice versa. If this were to come about in Britain the whole virtue of the British Constitution would go by the board.

Some people thought that I was obstinate, silly and unnecessarily provocative in the handling of the Sachsenhausen case. I wasn't really any of these things: I was simply determined to defend a principle that I regarded then and regard still as all-important in our system of government – if something goes wrong, you shoot the Minister.

I had been personally concerned on another occasion when this principle arose – the Crichel Down case in 1954. That was a complicated case concerning land at Crichel Down in Dorset, compulsorily purchased by the Air Ministry in 1940 for use as a bombing range and handed over to the Ministry of Agriculture after the war. Before its war-time purchase, this land had formed part of three separate farms, but after the war the Ministry, with the approval of the Commissioner for Crown Lands, decided to equip it for farming as a single unit, and to lease it to a single tenant.

Other farmers, however, had submitted applications to be allowed to buy back various areas of the land. Among them was Lieutenant-Commander Marten, whose wife, a daughter of Lord Alington, had succeeded to certain rights in the land previously owned by her father. Commander Marten and these other applicants felt that they had not been able to get satisfactory replies to their requests, and in September 1953 they sent a petition to the Minister of Agriculture, Sir Thomas Dugdale, asking for a public inquiry. The petition was at first rejected, but after further consideration and a personal interview with Commander Marten, the Minister agreed to the inquiry.

This inquiry was conducted by Sir Andrew Clark. His report, published in July of the following year, found no trace of bribery or personal dishonesty, but criticized the handling of the matter by various government departments. In particular, an under-secretary at the Ministry of Agriculture was criticized for what was described as 'a grave error of judgement' and of 'a regrettable lapse from the standard of conduct the public is entitled to expect from responsible Civil Servants'. The then Permanent Commissioner of Crown Lands was also criticized personally, as were some junior officials.

Having been Parliamentary Secretary to the Ministry of Agriculture from 1947–51, I was chosen to speak in the debate on the Crichel Down case and I had planned a terrifying speech, which I hoped would rock the Government benches, demanding the resignation of the Minister of Agriculture. Just before the debate was due to start, Sir Thomas Dugdale called me behind the Speaker's Chair and said, 'George, don't be too rough, because when I come to speak I'm going to tell you that I've resigned.'

I had about thirty seconds to throw away the speech I'd planned and start again. I described the Crichel Down case as 'a very sad and very sorry story', but I emphasized that it reflected 'the failure of government at every level' and that responsibility could not be 'shuffled off' on to Civil Servants. I also criticized the form of Sir Andrew Clark's report, particularly for the way in which it denied the Civil Servants the protection which they ought to have. I felt then precisely as I felt about the Sachsenhausen case when I was the Minister involved fifteen years later – if there is to be blame for a decision on policy, the Minister must take it.

Sir Thomas Dugdale took it, and he took it very well indeed. He knew perfectly well – everybody in the House knew – that he was in no way personally responsible for the decisions over Crichel Down, but he took the traditional, old-fashioned view, 'You don't go for my officials, you go for me.' Rather than see his officials – who couldn't answer back – accused in public he took the whole blame on himself and resigned. Whether the incident really demanded the resignation of a senior Minister is another matter, but Tommy Dugdale's self-sacrificing defence of the doctrine of ministerial responsibility was a noble one. I am sure that it is the right doctrine, and that we ought all to defend it. Ideally, a Minister ought to be so good that he can't be misled by his officials. If he is misled, well, it may not be personally his fault, but he's got to carry the can. That is why I was obstinate and stuck to my guns in the Sachsenhausen case – I was not going to have Civil Servants pilloried for what was a ministerial decision.

8

Government:
Diplomatic Reflections

A CONSIDERABLE PART of a Foreign Secretary's time is taken up by problems of security. I'd had brushes with the security services before I went to the Foreign Office, and my work as Shadow Minister of Defence brought me in touch with various members of the C.I.A. in the United States and with some of their opposite numbers in Europe. So before I went to the Foreign Office I was fairly attuned to the various threats of espionage that we face, and the methods used to counter them. But it was not until I got to the Foreign Office that I became at all deeply involved. Almost as soon as I got there people from the various security departments came to talk to me about their problems, within the Service, within politics, and in the country at large. This is a tremendous burden for a Foreign Secretary to carry. The Home Secretary is also concerned, and there are occasions when the Home Office and the Foreign Office clash to some extent. Oddly enough the Ministry of Defence comes into it very little, except on questions of strictly military intelligence.

I came to the conclusion that although the theory which links security with the Foreign Secretary because he has to deal with foreign states is logical enough in a way, it isn't really a sensible approach. I wouldn't like to see an independent agency, like the C.I.A., set up in Britain because I think it imperative that there should be political responsibility at every stage, but I do think that security should be the particular job of a specific Minister, on good terms with his colleagues, and himself reporting directly to the Prime Minister.

For obvious reasons I can't say much about the various agencies we have and the things that are done, but I can say that I don't think we manage the security side of affairs very well. This is partly, or even largely, because of our national scrupulousness. It is hard to come down on a member of the Diplomatic Service about whom there may be doubts or suspicions without violating his rights as an individual. Inevitably, much of the evidence in such cases is hearsay or almost unprovable deduction, and one must reckon with the natural wish of colleagues to protect, as it were, a fellow-member of the club, especially when they don't know, and can't really be told, the full extent of the matter. This clearly happened in the case of Burgess and Maclean.

Where I think we really could do something to improve matters is in recognizing the extent of deliberately hostile propaganda against us. This goes on all the time, in industry, in the universities, in all kinds of institutions whose legitimate aims are perfectly good. We are so reluctant to be accused of seeing Communists under every bed, or of being unfair to anybody, that we give people who really are hostile to Britain and our way of life almost a clear run. Mixed up in a number of recent events in universities, for instance, appears to be deliberately fomented hostility to Britain. We do next to nothing to identify it, and we are frightened to death of using public money to conduct our own propaganda against this really dangerous subversion.

We are in a particular difficulty with the BBC. Every Foreign Secretary comes up against the BBC's refusal even to listen to, let alone take, guidance on some matter that is causing concern. This is because of the BBC's insistence that it must be free from any suggestion of the taint of government control. That is a fine. conception, but there are occasions when the Foreign Office, or some other Ministry, may in fact know more about a subject than the BBC's own reporters or commentators. If what the BBC broadcasts is known to be wrong, or is known to be doing actual harm to British interests in some other country, should there not be some method of inducing the BBC to accept guidance? I make no allegations against anyone in the BBC, but this is a twilight world, and when X says 'I won't have this because it will be a breach of *our* independence', he may well, without even realizing it, be threatening our national independence.

This not only affects our ability to counter the enormous amount of propaganda that goes on against us, but it also affects our relations with close allies on whose co-operation we depend. I'm sure that people just don't realize the extent of the subversive effort against us. This is not merely directed to what is generally understood as espionage, the collecting of information about our affairs; it includes an immense operation for getting hold of people in what are thought to be useful or influential positions. If we could ever dare to publish a total of the members of various embassy staffs whom we suspect to be here for subversive purposes, simply because there just can't be enough work for all that number of cultural or trade attachés, it would be terrifying. Perhaps we should publish such a list.

I don't for a moment suggest that we should try to mount the same kind of subversive operation in other countries. It involves doing things that we in Britain simply do not do. But we could and should keep our eyes open. When I first went to the Foreign Office I was given a briefing on the various devices that are known to exist for 'bugging' conversations. I don't suppose that in any Ministry dealing with a really sensitive subject there are many rooms which can be reckoned absolutely secure. As I dictate this, I have no means of being *absolutely sure* that somebody hasn't arranged for everything I say to be listened to some distance away. I think it improbable, but I can't be *sure*.

We do not permit our own M.P.s' telephones to be tapped. If we were to start opening M.P.s' letters, following M.P.s about, checking and reporting on all their contacts, it would debase our whole conception of democracy. I have no great solution to propose, except that the appointment of a Minister of Security might enable the actions of those who behave unwisely to be spotted before great harm is done. That, to my mind, is the chief lesson to be drawn from such unhappy affairs as the cases of Burgess and Maclean. It ought not to have been possible for Burgess and Maclean to have gone as far as they did before *somebody's* suspicions were aroused, and action could be taken. What a Minister does with his own time is, I suppose, his own business, but before a Minister's indiscretions become of any embarrassment to security the Prime Minister ought to know enough at least to be able to warn him. On the whole we are a nice people, and I should not like to see our general decency in not suspecting one another changed. But this is not a particularly nice world, and national decency can be abused and betrayed. I do advocate, therefore, a little more realism in our approach to these matters.

I now turn to one of those 'happenings' which I don't suppose occured only during my tenure of office, which, while very serious and important, nevertheless provided the light relief without which life in such an office would be totally insupportable.

The United Nations, through one of its Special Committees, had established a mission of three, not so much to help Britain end our rule in Aden as to do the job for us. The mission consisted of Dr Mañuel Pérez-Guerrero (Venezuela) as chairman, Mr Abdul Satar Shalizi (Afghanistan) and Mr Moussa Leo Keita (Mali) – all very distinguished in their way, but I cannot honestly say that they struck me as being either high-powered enough or well-assorted enough to be of much effective use. However, we did our best to work with them and to get their assistance. One Sunday I had them all to the country house, Dorneywood, which is made available to Foreign Secretaries. It was an absolutely fascinating day. There were arguments with all the Foreign Office officials who had come down. These were broken at intervals while they met my family, who were also there, and played clock-golf on the lawn. The whole account of that tragic/comic day would in itself fill a book. But it was an absolutely essential ingredient in the working out of the whole scene and could not have happened without the use of that house. Let me say something about it.

Dorneywood is by no means a distinguished house – it is mock Tudor, built after the First World War – but is in a beautiful setting on the edge of Burnham Beeches in Buckinghamshire. It was given to the nation by the late Lord Courtauld-Thompson to be used in much the same way as Chequers – which provides a country house for the Prime Minister – and by custom is allocated to the Foreign Secretary.

In 1951, when I was Minister of Works, I met Lord Courtauld-Thompson during discussions on the conveyance of Dorneywood to the nation and, indeed, signed the trust deed as Minister. I had lunch with him there, taking my family – the girls were then very young. Lord Courtauld-Thompson played with the children, and I recall his saying to me, 'One day, my boy, you will live here, and all the things you want, your papers, your cigars, everything, will all be provided for.'

That had certainly been his intention – he gave an endowment for all the personal needs of the Minister in residence. It was a generous thought, recognizing that not all Ministers are rich men. But by the time I became the incumbent the lawyers had somehow got around this generous intention. It was ruled that the endowment was not valid as a charitable bequest, and so a Minister who lives there has to pay for whatever he has.

When we went there for week-ends it used to cost the earth –

I don't think I've ever seen such enormous bills. This was mainly because of the way in which the place was run. In my time – there have been changes since – it was looked after by an elderly couple who had been family retainers to Lord Courtauld-Thompson. They were nice people, but they lived in an age that is simply gone. If my wife and I had gone down for a week-end by ourselves, they still wanted to wait on us at every meal, he in black coat and striped trousers, she in a beautiful little old-fashioned pinny with blue and white spots on it. It took a long time to persuade them that we really could serve our own meals when we were alone.

I once asked this major-domo to get in some beer for Christmas. In fact he couldn't think of anything less than four dozen and, of course, I had to pay for – though happily not drink – the lot. If I had official guests I could get the Government Hospitality Fund to take over. Then everything would be brought down from London, with every bottle carefully labelled so that anything left over could go back. If I had only one or two guests it wasn't worth going through all this rigmarole, so I would pay for things myself. It was expensive, but it was a wonderful place to retreat to.

Looking back on my period in the Office certain impressions prevail. One is the fantastic tempo at which one lives; the crashing weight of problems which in the end, no matter how much you ask somebody else to take responsibility, are going to end up on your own desk again. I suppose to a large extent one's ability to withstand this depends on one's temperament and degree of involvement. Others I know have lasted much longer and apparently weathered the storm much better. Without passing any unhappy reflections, I can only wonder to myself how much of the tide they have allowed just to flow by. Certainly in my case it was the toughest, yet the most exciting, period of my political career.

I have already discussed how we reorganized the approach to diplomatic appointments. More fundamental is the structure of the Foreign Service itself. Nowadays the Civil Service Commission recruits for both the Home and Foreign Services, but only a very foolish man would allege that its writ runs as strongly in the Foreign Service as it does at home. By a system which was invented (or so, at least, some people would assure me) by God, it so happens that most of the recruits to the Foreign Office come via Oxford or Cambridge. Now I'm not in any way anti-Oxford or Cambridge, but it does seem to me that at a time when traditional political

work abroad is giving way to much more sharp-ended work the
Foreign Service is losing a lot of chaps from redbrick universities
who might have a good deal to contribute. I was told that this
problem arose solely because the principals of redbrick universities
just didn't advise their chaps to apply for the Foreign Service: what
the people at the F.O. wouldn't admit was that the *reason* they didn't
advise their chaps to apply was that their chances of getting in were
a bit thin. I can't say that I myself achieved much in the way of
widening the range of intake for the Foreign Service because I
didn't have time, but I think I did help to promote a climate of
thought in which such a broadening will come about. It is much
needed.

Another problem is that too much of the Foreign Office's work
in London is done by 'birds of passage' – by this I mean ambassadors,
Ministers, counsellors, First Secretaries and so on who are doing
a home term of duty before going on to their next foreign posting.
There are departments of the Foreign Office which are essentially
specialized, and which need long-term specialists to staff them.
The economic departments, for instance, really ought not to depend
largely on birds of passage who may or may not have any real
understanding of economics. The F.O. needs an Economic Department of the topmost quality, which can stand up to and argue with
the other economic departments of the Government on equal terms.
I was particularly conscious of this when trying to deal with oil
policy. I knew that there was a powerful oil lobby in London and
that much of the information coming through the Board of Trade
or the Ministry of Fuel and Power was really what the oil lobby
was telling them. Now it may have been good information, but at
the Foreign Office I had no means of evaluating it and I had to
take on trust views which I sometimes felt were not necessarily
correct. The same applied to the cost-effectiveness of defence policy.
The Ministry of Defence would put up arguments about the cost-
effectiveness of some particular line of policy, and we at the F.O.
had nobody who could really pull the arguments to pieces if they
needed to be pulled to pieces, as I felt sometimes that they did.
If I'd had more time at the Foreign Office, and more freedom from
other problems, I'd have done my best to reform the whole system,
to establish departments which would be known as specialized
departments and which would be staffed by people who would
make a career in them instead of appearing at intervals between
tours abroad. Of course such specialists might go abroad from time

Sophie, April 1966

With Sophie and grandchildren
in Derby, 1970

Surveying the world
on becoming
Foreign Secretary,
1966

to time, but their jobs would be essentially in London, and would
be seen to be in London. The Foreign Office may tell you that this
breaks all their traditions and challenges their dearest thinking,
but I'm quite sure that it needs to be done if the place is to become
relevant to its modern problems in modern terms.

There is a kind of class distinction between the Foreign Service
and the rest of the Civil Service which makes cross-fertilization and
transfers between the Foreign Office and other Ministries exceptionally difficult. Recruits to the administrative grades of the Foreign
Service are given what they call the Queen's Commission, which
is a piece of paper appointing them to Her Majesty's service in a
rather special way. No other Civil Servant has this 'commission',
and the Foreign Service officers are very proud of it. To my mind
it is a considerable barrier to the effective deployment of the Foreign
Service, for it inhibits bringing in experts from other Ministries,
and the temporary employment of people with particular qualities
who happen to be outside government service altogether. Of course
this is done from time to time in special cases, but it is always much
more difficult in the Foreign Office than in any other government
department. It ought not to be; the whole system should be much
more flexible.

Then there is tremendous room for improvement in the Foreign
Office's sources of information. Whole volumes of paper pour in
telling you what some embassy has gathered from the Third Secretary of the Ruritanian Legation, but what is picked up in this way
may often be a good deal less than reliable. I tried to set up a special
relationship with the T.U.C., because the T.U.C. is in touch with
Labour movements all over the world, with men who are either
in their own Governments or who are actively organizing to become
the Government. These people really do know what is going on,
but the F.O.'s links with Labour movements overseas seem to me
to be ludicrously inadequate. My personal efforts to improve things
here did achieve something, for there is now an Overseas Labour
Consultative Committee which is chaired by a Foreign Office
Minister. It is also usually attended by the Parliamentary Under-
Secretaries from the D.E.P. and O.D.M. and also has official
representation from these Ministries. It has a Foreign Office Secretariat. This committee was set up after I left the Foreign Office,
so my thinking on the subject can be said to have been followed up,
although the committee itself is not the instrument I should have
chosen for the job. I had in mind consultations at once more

L

continuous and much less formal. However, George Woodcock, the General Secretary of the T.U.C., insisted on having things on a formal basis, hence the committee.

Another area where it seemed to me the Office could be improved is in the use it makes of political Ministers. If Ministers serving there were chosen not merely because they were important members of their Party and of ministerial calibre, but much more with a regard for the job they would be asked to do in the Office, I think that the whole system would be much more effective. I tried to organize the work of the Ministers who were working with me in such a way that each one took responsibility for some part of the Office functionally and some part of the world geographically. This, I am sure, is essential if the Foreign Secretary's task is to be eased, and it should mean that these Ministers are chosen for the particular work they are going to be asked to do.

Next, there is the question of trying to reduce the vast load of paperwork. In my time at the Office I did try to tackle the problem of people writing millions of words to each other, which would eventually land on my desk. Instead I invited all those concerned to meet in my room and thrash out particular issues. Each could put forward his own view in front of the other, and each view could be argued and discussed. For example, if the subject were the Middle East, then we would have whoever was looking after the Israel end, whoever was looking after the Egyptian end, whoever was looking after the French end, and so on.

It took a bit of time to get this system working, but I think that people grew to like it. It didn't reduce the written work all that much, but it did mean that when the files came to me, with long telegrams from all over the world, I had enough knowledge from our discussions to be able to assess the personal opinions offered. It also meant that I developed a scheme of management in which people were always having to come up, always having to defend, and decisions could be given – and were.

There was another advantage in this system. As anyone will realize, a Foreign Secretary's day is incredibly full. Virtually no half-hour is unfilled. I was seeing people in the Department, receiving visiting statesmen and other groups who thought they ought to see me, attending Cabinet Committees, and so on. As Deputy Leader of the Party I was of course also very involved with Party work both in Parliament and outside it. And quite often I would have to be at the House of Commons, either for Questions or to speak in a debate not only on our own but often on other business. And so by the evening I had already worked a very full day.

But round about 6 p.m. the bowler-hatted chaps would start wending their way home or to their clubs, depositing as they went the papers, the minutes, the telegrams which they thought I should deal with that night. The people in my own office, who of course themselves had already worked a full day, had now to start hours of hectic work quite unknown in outside industry in order to 'process' these papers so that I could receive them in relays from then on. Again and again it seemed that the first red box I got wherever I was – at home or in the House – did not turn up until about 8 p.m. Then there would be a succession of further red boxes crammed full of telegrams, files and minutes. I could be pretty sure of enough work to keep me at it until 2 a.m. at least. The system of briefing I had instituted therefore gave me the background I needed to understand the problems and get through the mountain of paper-work.

I instituted much the same system for my speeches. I was often delivering several a week and therefore had a speech-writer in the excellent person of John Margetson. For this we had similar meetings, the only difference being that the whole discussion was recorded on tape. In this way John Margetson was able to draft a speech for me, using my own words during the discussion on it beforehand. This resulted in a more personal speech.

Many organizational changes in the Office still need to be done. Bevin wanted to do some of them all those years ago, got too immersed in the immediate problems and finally left too soon to carry out many of them, although he originated big changes. I tried to do my share of carrying that on, but for much the same reasons did far less than I should have liked.

I had high hopes of the Duncan Commission in this respect. Sir Val Duncan (chairman, Rio Tinto-Zinc Corporation), Andrew Shonfield (the eminent economist and journalist) and Sir Frank Roberts (former H.M. Ambassador in Bonn) made a most impressive team. Yet I must record my sad feeling that when I read their report I felt this was possibly the most missed opportunity of quite several decades to bring about a genuine reform of the Foreign Service. It is a job somebody still has to carry out.

The third, and in its way the most important, reflection is that it is only when one goes there and has responsibility for the job that one realizes just how much all the critical international issues interact on each other. However much one has privately studied; taken part in debates and discussions; gone on missions and visits abroad; in this context, one tends to see the issue of the moment, the place one is visiting at the moment, the delegation one is talking to at the moment, as the big event. And part of the conflict between what the Foreign Office is doing about this or that issue, and what other people in Parliament or out of it think it should be doing, arises from this quite natural misunderstanding of the degree to which one issue conditions the responses to be made on others. Each problem has its own inherent merits, virtues and difficulties. But Europe relates to the Middle East, the Middle East relates to the Far East, the Far East relates to relations with America, as does Europe, as does the Middle East. They all relate to relations with Russia, and relations with either Russia or America not only relate to each other but obviously ultimately involve relations with China. Wherever one turns, the issue of one's attitude and ambitions for the future of the United Nations arises. Unless a British Foreign Secretary ever emerges, which the Lord forbid, who really thinks we can return to the days of gunboat diplomacy, then the creation of a world authority, effectively able not only to decide but to enforce its decisions, must be the aim of any occupant of that post. Therefore, how we maintain the present United Nations, keep it operating and seek to build up its authority must be present in one's mind at every point and in every issue which arises.

The fact of the matter is that foreign affairs, whether for Britain or any other nation, are not just a catalogue of unconnected events. They most certainly aren't just a question of relations with this or that foreign power. They are a kaleidoscope of inter-related pieces, all of which must somehow be juggled with, virtually at the same time and certainly in relation to each other. It is a fascinating study and a great corrective to ending up with a series of independent passions and prejudices.

The manner of my leaving the Foreign Office I discuss in the next chapter. Before doing so, however, I should like to return briefly to the domestic side of being a Minister of the Crown. I have described what Dorneywood meant to us when I was Foreign Secretary – it was a place of respite for us, but, of course, it was not our home. When people read of Cabinet reshuffles and of the comings and going of Ministers, they seldom think of the personal domestic upheavals that these involve. I was continuously in office for three and a half years, two years at the D.E.A. and eighteen months at the Foreign Office. During all this time we lived in the flat at Carlton Gardens. It was comfortable and rather splendid, but that, too, was like a tied cottage – we had no security of tenure. I'd always had a feeling that one day we might suddenly find ourselves on our own again, so all through the years of office I kept on our little flat at Marble Arch. This was quite a problem, for under the terms of my lease I wasn't allowed to sub-let, and I couldn't afford to go on indefinitely paying for a flat that we might or might not want to use. A whole series of friendly devices helped me to work out things. First, my daughter and some friends lived in the flat. Then they went off for various reasons, and I found a friend in business outside London who wanted a place to come to instead of always going to hotels. So I gave him the use of the flat while we didn't need it. This was a very casual arrangement, and it was understood that the flat remained ours to go back to whenever we wanted to. So it was always there, with all our own furniture and belongings, and this was a comforting feeling. On the night of my resignation from the Foreign Office we slept at Carlton Gardens, but I said to my wife that we'd better get out on the very next day. And we did: we simply got into a car with our suitcases and drove back to the flat in Marble Arch.

But Dorneywood had given us a taste for week-ends in the country, and Sophie and I had long discussions about what to do. Our flat at Marble Arch is comfortable enough, but it's pretty small and gives no sense of being in a house or a home of your own. We discussed whether to try to get a bigger flat, or whether to go back to living just outside London as we used to do at Dulwich or Potters Bar. Finally we decided to get our little flat done up, to acquire some new furniture and change its character a bit, and to look for a cottage in the country which we could have as well. We thought that we should probably have to buy a cottage, but we met a friend who was doing up some old farmworkers' cottages in Sussex which he no longer required for this purpose, and he was willing to let one of them to us. So we got our cottage, and it has proved a godsend. It provides just the same respite that Dorneywood did, except that it's on a tiny scale – and a very great deal cheaper.

There's another aspect of life as a Minister that people seldom think about, and that's the question of getting secretarial work done. When I went to the D.E.A. I was Deputy-Leader of the Labour Party, which involved a lot of political work, and I had all my constituency work as well. None of this stopped when I became a

Minister, but it became vastly more complicated. As Deputy-Leader of the Labour Party I had a secretary provided by Transport House, and when I went to the D.E.A. I took her with me and she became a fourth secretary in my Private Office – that is, the Minister's Private Office, which houses the personal staff to assist him in his duties as a Minister. She was allowed to help in my parliamentary work, but the Accounting Officer at the Ministry fixed a sum of money which I had to pay to the Government personally for that proportion of her time which was spent on party-political or personal work for me. After a time she became an established Civil Servant, and the Establishment Officer then said that the system of paying separately for personal work would be frowned upon, and that I ought to get a separate secretary to do such work outside my office in the Ministry. So I did, and my new secretary was equipped with a desk and a typewriter in the House of Commons.

Now I don't think that the public gets any bargain by making it so difficult and expensive for a Minister to deal with the political side of his work. The idea that in some way you are a 'purer' Minister if you walk over to the House of Commons to deal with your parliamentary work and then walk back to the Foreign Office to deal with your work as Foreign Secretary is just nonsense: you are in no sense 'purer' as a Minister, and you certainly are much more tired as a man. If a Minister is to be trusted with all the responsibilities of a great department of State, then I think that the nation should not grudge him secretarial help to enable him to deal with political correspondence from his desk in the Ministry. If this could be put to the nation, I don't for a moment suppose that anybody would grudge it. The present system is one that has come down from days when Ministers and M.P.s had far less work to do; it is quite unfitted for the very different needs of today, and adds unnecessary extra business to the inevitable strain of serving the community as a Minister of the Crown.

The whole question would of course be solved if we could make up our minds that M.P.s need to be serviced. One of the services they need in our present day is efficient secretarial provision. Offices and secretaries I would place highest on the list of provisions which should be made for all M.P.s.

9

Resignation

THE NIGHT OF 14/15 March 1968, during which I resigned from the Foreign Secretaryship, was certainly a watershed in my own life and, I think, in our recent political history. The reasons for my going have become clouded in the dramatic stories which newspapers and television nowadays weave around news, but they were in fact simple and straightforward. I resigned on a matter of fundamental principle, because it seemed to me that the Prime Minister was not only introducing a 'presidential' system into the running of the Government that is wholly alien to the British constitutional system – others have been tempted to do it that way too – but was so operating it that decisions were being taken over the heads and without the knowledge of Ministers, and far too often outsiders in his entourage seemed to be almost the only effective 'Cabinet'. I put this plainly in my letter of resignation, written to Mr Wilson on 15 March:

> The events of last night and the long hours of this morning have brought to a head a really serious issue which has, as you know, been troubling me for some time.
> It is, in short, the way this Government is run, and the manner in which we reach our decisions. You and I have discussed this more than once.
> I regard this general issue as much more fundamental than any particular item of policy.

The particular incident which brought things to a head was the Prime Minister's decision to ask the Queen, at a hurriedly called meeting of the Privy Council late at night, to proclaim a Bank Holiday in order to meet a request from America which had to do with arrangements being made internationally to steady the chaotic gold situation which then existed. No announcement of this had

been discussed among Ministers and no statement had been made
to the House of Commons. The statement that was subsequently
made at 3.20 a.m. on the following morning was only made because
of the events of that night leading to my declared intention to resign.
Whatever may be said as after-thought, there had been no intention
to make a statement and there would not have been any announcement that night to the House of Commons. There have of course
been attempts since by quite sincere people to say that this really
was a very technical matter – simply a question of whether you
have a Bank Holiday on a particular day in order to be able to
shut the banks and stop financial manœuvring. But the 'techni-
cality', if that's what it was, cloaked two very serious issues: the
first one was what it was all about, who asked for it or authorized
it, and were we in fact doing something which the Americans
wanted which nobody else over here in authority knew very much
about; and the second was this grave, as I saw it, departure from
constitutional practice which allowed the Prime Minister and two
other Ministers to act as though a decision which should have been
that of the Cabinet as a whole had in fact been taken. The proclamation was reasonable enough – had the Cabinet been consulted in the
ordinary way it may well be that we would have supported it. The
point was that the Cabinet was not consulted. Although I was
Deputy Prime Minister, Foreign Secretary and a member of the
Economic Committee of the Cabinet, I for one knew nothing about
it. Other Cabinet Ministers learned by chance that Mr Wilson, Mr
Jenkins and Mr Peter Shore had gone to the Palace to attend a
Privy Council to have the holiday proclaimed. We had no idea
what was happening, whether another devaluation was imminent,
what on earth was afoot. It was a decision taken by Mr Wilson in the
'presidential' manner, without consulting us, without even informing
us. That was what made it so important. It was the *way* in which the
decision was taken, not the decision itself, which seemed to me then –
and seems now – to mark a clear breach in constitutional practice.

But the events of the night of 14/15 March cannot be considered
in isolation. In order really to understand the impact this particular
issue had on me it is necessary to look back a little in time to other
occasions when I had found myself in difficulties which seemed to
me seriously disquieting as a result of the Prime Minister's method
of running the Government. One of the more serious of these – but
I must emphasize there were a number – was the way in which the
ultimate decision was reached not to accede to the South African

Government's request for further deliveries of certain categories of arms which we had previously been supplying.

This question, which I had been discussing on behalf of the Government with the South Africans over a period of a year or so, became very urgent, partly because the South Africans began to put pressure on us and set a deadline for a decision, and partly because Ministers were once again very busy putting together a 'package' of deflationary measures involving cuts in expenditure and of course increases where we could get them in exports. This exercise too was subject to a very short time-scale. The supply of arms to South Africa was obviously very relevant to this, both because of the amount of money involved in the order and because of the uncertainty of the effect a refusal would have on our large and growing commercial trade with that country.

The arms in question included Buccaneer aircraft and other items of mainly naval equipment such as frigates, for South African defence and the implementation of the Simonstown Agreement between us and the South Africans. This was of course a much wider issue than just the defence of South Africa since she had taken over a large part of the responsibility for the defence of those seas which we ourselves used to provide.

To my mind the issue was clear. We detested apartheid in South Africa, and it would have been unthinkable for a British Government to supply a South African Government, operating the internal policies which the current South African Government was, with the kind of weapons which could be used for internal repression. But the question of the external defence of South Africa and the protection of those waters, so essential for ourselves in view of the closing of the Suez Canal and the consequent dependence by us commercially upon that route, especially in face of the growing Russian advance in the Indian Ocean, was another matter.

I did not see how the argument could be sustained that the sort of arms and equipment which the South African Government was anxious to obtain from Britain could really be said so to jeopardize the position of black South Africans as to make it wrong for us to be willing to supply. There was also of course the little point that, if we didn't supply, France or someone else was waiting on the doorstep pressing the South Africans to let them do it at our expense. However, this is a matter on which people hold – and hold sincerely – opposing views, and within the Labour Party all questions of trade with South Africa have long been somewhat explosive.

I had throughout this time various meetings with the South Africans on the whole subject, including of course the question of their influence in Rhodesia and over Mozambique. These meetings took place both in New York and in London, and there was certainly one at No. 10 at which the Prime Minister was in the chair. It was subsequent to all this that I sent a telegram, dealt with between the Foreign Office and No. 10 in the normal manner, to our Ambassador in Pretoria saying that I was sending to him a letter for Dr Muller, the Foreign Minister, which I would be obliged if he would hand personally to him. In that letter, again after a brief reference to Rhodesia, I explained the complications politically for us and suggested that, if they would understand all this and not press us too much on timing, while I could not give a commitment they might find it worth their while to await the outcome. This was what came to be known in various leaks which have occurred since as the 'nod and wink' letter, meaning that it was accepted that I should tip the wink to Dr Muller. I repeat that this was done wholly with the knowledge of the Prime Minister, and I therefore felt entitled to regard it as a policy that was both authentic and proper, and of course the whole subject had been discussed again and again and again at meetings of the appropriate Cabinet Committee, and indeed of the Cabinet itself.

On 11 December 1967, I had to go to Brussels to attend a NATO meeting. Throughout this meeting I was of course in close touch with the Foreign Office and those of my colleagues most closely involved. In particular Mr Healey, the Minister of Defence, kept me in touch by telephone and letter on what was happening in London. I thus learned that the whole issue had suddenly become 'live' again, that there had been a great row about it in the Parliamentary Labour Party, that the Prime Minister was now taking a different view, and that there was to be a meeting of the Cabinet at which a decision was likely to be taken against supplying the arms. On December 13 I telephoned to the Prime Minister from our Embassy in Brussels asking that the Cabinet should not meet until I got back, and saying that I would get back next day – 14 December. I arranged for a government aeroplane to fly me back from Brussels.

When the plane came, however, Brussels was shrouded in dense fog. While I was sitting in the NATO building having coffee we heard an aeroplane, and I said, 'Well, that is my plane coming in.' We heard it, but in the fog we never saw it. We sat there listening to it going round and round, round and round, and finally the captain of the aircraft spoke by radio telephone to the control tower and said that he had come to the point of no return – unless he set off immediately for England he would not have enough fuel to get back. He made one more circle of the airport to see if he could get down, but he couldn't so he had to go off home. And I was still stuck in Brussels.

As it turned out, the only way I could get back to England was on the night boat-train from Belgium. It was fearfully cold, and as all arrangements for the party had to be made at very short notice we had to travel in whatever accommodation we could get. My wife and I were given berths in a first-class compartment, but the rest of the party had to cram in as best they could.

In England, the train stopped at some station on the way to Victoria, and Donald Maitland, then my Principal Private Secretary and now in charge of public relations at No. 10, got out and brought back the early-morning editions of the newspapers. This was probably a mistake, in a way, for the papers were full of such headlines as 'Wilson puts Brown on the spot', 'Wilson isolates Brown', 'Brown out on his own'. And so, by the time I got off the train at Victoria, I was already feeling pretty sore, and I was met by an enormous crowd of reporters who wanted to know what I felt! I said that it all seemed to be in the papers, but what I really felt was that there was something wrong – that it wasn't like this at all, that it was all bloody silly.

After a short call at home I went straight to the Cabinet meeting, and the atmosphere at the meeting was, to say the least, pretty tense and hardly conducive to a reasonable re-examination of the whole issue. However, the final decision was not taken then. During the week-end, however, the press publicity, the leaking and the briefing continued and by Monday morning it was pretty evident that it was no longer possible for a balanced argument to take place, or for there being any chance of a decision on merit being taken.

And so there it was. Mr Healey and myself, who had jointly submitted the original memorandum and recommendation and those others who were originally in favour of supplying these limited arms, had become a pretty small minority, and we were no longer able to carry our colleagues with us.

There is one other thing that I remember very clearly about this period, and that is that all attempts, by those in favour of supplying, to take it to the Parliamentary Labour Party were resisted and refused. After hearing about the emotion which was said to have arisen at a previous meeting which none of us had attended, I volunteered to put the case to the Parliamentary Party to test whether the feeling in the Party was as strong as we were being told, and I had colleagues who were willing to support me in order that the issue could be tested. This was never done and we had no more to go on so far as the Party was concerned than the stories of the atmosphere and the emotion about an issue on which they were never genuinely consulted and never properly informed.

I now learned in much more detail from colleagues in the Government and members of the Parliamentary Party of the extraordinary lengths to which they said the Prime Minister had gone in the House of Commons, not merely to *bow* to the feeling of the Party on the arms issue but, as they saw it, to *organize* the feeling of the Party. It was very firmly alleged, and most certainly widely believed (although denials were made later and have been recently renewed) that the Whips went into action and encouraged the drafting and signing of a motion against the supply of arms. Whatever the truth of these allegations, and I find it hard to discount them in view of the weight of evidence then given to me, and since put into writing by one of those concerned, an atmosphere was provided in which the Prime Minister and others could put before the Cabinet what appeared to be a plausible reason for turning down what up until then had been gone along with. Among the particular events I was told of at that time was a visit by the Prime Minister to the Northern Group of M.P.s, where he was said to have given the assurance that there would be no provision of arms to South Africa, thus pre-empting any decision in that way by the Cabinet meeting for which I was especially returning and to which the decision had been deferred in order that I should be back.

That, I think, was when I came to the conclusion that the Prime Minister was capable of working in a way that made effective co-operation almost impossible. It looked as though, no matter what one did, one could never be sure that if events seemed to him to make it appropriate the whole thing wouldn't be changed.

From then on, a whole series of issues arose on which I found myself increasingly unhappy about the decisions which were taken and again, almost without exception, at the manner of their taking. One of these came, for example, in the next phase of the financial squeeze, when the question of going back on our decision to raise the school-leaving age from fifteen to sixteen came up. The decision

to do so for a ludicrously small and highly dubious saving of money
made me exceedingly angry – I thought it was one of the greatest
betrayals a Labour Government, so overwhelmingly composed of
University graduates, could make of the less privileged people who,
after all, had elected it. At the same time there was the question of
the reintroduction of the Health Service Charges which we had
abolished in 1965, and with one thing and another I found myself
more and more in a minority in the Cabinet.

So we come back to the events of that night, 14/15 March 1968,
to which I referred earlier. In his letter accepting my resignation
Mr Wilson wrote:

> You refer to the events of last night. As you know, unsuccessful
> efforts were made to get in touch with you at a critical phase, so that
> you could be brought into the immediate decision, which had to be
> taken with great urgency if most serious consequences for the nation
> and for the international community were to be averted.

That letter was written for publication, and it not merely implied
but said categorically that I could not be consulted on the decision
to proclaim a Bank Holiday because I could not be found – that
'efforts were made to get in touch with me', but that these were
'unsuccessful'. I feel I must set this justification by the Prime
Minister of why he acted as he did against the actual recording of
events that night.

The House was debating the Transport Bill. In the early part of
the evening I was in the House and, so far as I knew, nothing special
was happening. I was in my room at the back of the Speaker's
Chair, saw my secretaries and dealt with ordinary business. At
about 8 o'clock I decided to go home for supper in my official flat
at Carlton Gardens.

Now a very relevant part of this story is that the telephone at
Carlton Gardens was an extension of the Foreign Office switchboard
– it was not an outside line. If you rang the Foreign Office and
asked for me, you could get the extension in my room in the House,
the extension in my flat and the extension in my office. All the time
I was having supper in my flat the telephone never rang. I therefore
had no reason to suspect that anything was happening at all.

There was a three-line Whip on at 10 p.m., so after supper I went
back to the House – if it hadn't been for the Whip I wouldn't have
gone back and would presumably still have known nothing of the
events that were taking place. Because of the Whip I did go back,

went into the Chamber and sat on the bench. I voted in the division, and having voted returned to my room. Later I went back to the Chamber and again sat on the bench. Around 11 o'clock or so I got a note from one of the Prime Minister's secretaries saying, 'My Master has asked me to give you a message. Can I see you?' So I left the bench, went outside, accompanied him to my room and said, 'Now what is it?' He then told me that the Prime Minister wished me to know that he was on his way to the Palace to arrange for a Privy Council meeting to declare tomorrow as a Bank Holiday, so that the banks would be closed. I said, 'What's it all about?' He said, 'Well, I don't know any more than that; that is what I have been asked to tell you.'

I telephoned No. 10 and asked to speak to the Prime Minister, and there was one of those long lulls which led me to believe, rightly or wrongly, that the Prime Minister was, in fact, still at No. 10. After this long pause I was finally told that he had left for the Palace or was in his car on the way there.

About this time my brother Ronald (the Member for Finsbury and Shoreditch) came to tell me that he had heard rumours that something was going on. Another division was called while I was talking with him, and I went again to vote. As I went into the division lobby I met some members of the Cabinet and said, 'By the way, do you know that there is a Privy Council going on at this minute? Do you know that there is going to be a proclamation issued? Do you know that tomorrow is going to be a Bank Holiday? Have *you* heard anything about it?' One was Tony Crosland, then President of the Board of Trade, and he said, 'No, certainly not.' Another was Michael Stewart, the Secretary of State for Economic Affairs. He said, 'Of course not, I would know about it.' I said, 'Well, my dear friend, I'm awfully sorry, but I've just been told.'

We walked down the Lobby, each of us talking, and I said, 'Look, come back to my room and we'll have a chat about this. And if you see any other members of the Cabinet, ask them to come back as well.' So we went back to my room, and it is interesting that Willie Ross, the Secretary of State for Scotland, told us when he arrived that he had just heard of it from a couple of Scottish Members who had approached him and told him that they had seen it on the tape. As it happened, most of the members of the Cabinet came along – but not on any formal summons. This is important – they just came along informally. Indeed, so informal was it that if my life depended on it I couldn't now say which members of the

With Willy Brandt, Mayor of West Berlin, 1966

With the Prime Minister, Harold Wilson,
and President de Gaulle, 1967

With Emile Bustani in the Middle East

With the Soviet Foreign Minister,
Mr Gromyko, at Moscow Airport

Cabinet weren't there. All I can remember is that there was a large number of us, just as I can remember some of those who took a personal part in some of the arguments.

We gathered in my room and discussed among ourselves what had happened – not one of us knew *what* was supposed to be happening, nor *why* anything was happening at all. We thought of the most dreadful things, like a sudden new devaluation.

It was then about 1 o'clock in the morning. I decided to telephone No. 10 again to try to find out what was happening. I got hold of the Prime Minister and asked, 'What the hell is going on?' A somewhat angry exchange took place, and finally I said, 'I've got a number of our colleagues here, who are interested to know.' At this point Mr Wilson started to accuse me of trying to engineer a palace revolution behind his back. I said, 'Well, why don't you talk to Michael Stewart?' having it in mind that he would be hardly likely to harbour such a suspicion of him. Stewart took the telephone from me, and said in his precise and very careful way, 'But Prime Minister, you can't do it like this. I wouldn't have known anything about it if George hadn't seen me. Other colleagues wouldn't have known anything if they hadn't met Members in the House who had got it from the tape. Really, we can't do it like this.'

Subsequently I spoke again to the Prime Minister and said 'Look, I think it would be better if we had a proper meeting. Shall we come to your room here?' After all, we did quite commonly hold meetings in that room when parliamentary affairs made it more appropriate than No. 10. His response was, 'Well, you know, it would be better if you all came over to No. 10 if you want to see me.'

I pointed out, 'If we all get into our cars and drive to No. 10, it could start the most awful speculation. The easiest thing would be for you to come over here. Nobody's going to think that odd, because the House is still sitting.'

At this he agreed to come across, and said that if we just waited a few moments in the House he would be in his room there. But a few minutes later – presumably having discussed things with other advisers – he rang back and returned to the accusation of being summoned by an irregularly called Cabinet meeting, called by me. He said that he wasn't going to have it, and that if we wanted a meeting we must all go over to his house.

So over we all went, taking such care as we could to avoid drawing attention to ourselves. I walked and went round the back way,

M

and my recollection is that this was what most other people did. But once there the conversation again went right off-beam. Instead of us dealing with the questions in all our minds, the Prime Minister simply went on and on about my having tried to engineer his dismissal, about my calling an irregular 'Cabinet' meeting, and so on, until I was sick of it. Finally, I said to him, 'Look, it's pretty obvious that you want my resignation, and, brother, if this is the way you are going to run affairs, you can have it.'

At this there was a sort of general hubbub, with other people midst it all urging me to let it go. But the Prime Minister simply went on saying that he was not going to have a pistol held to his head, and so on and so forth, and in the end I said, 'O.K. Well, you've asked for it, you've got it, and I'm going,' and I left.

It was then about 2 o'clock in the morning. I went back to the House, where I saw my brother again and we had some coffee in the tea room. Incidentally, there was subsequently a story that what had happened owed a lot to the fact that I had been drinking heavily. Of course, there is no doubt that there have been occasions on which I have drunk alcohol, and I see no reason to deny that, but on this particular occasion ironically enough it was not so. There had been very little opportunity to do so even if I had wanted to, and in any case, when the issue began to arise I was so clear in my own mind that this was a critical moment that I took great pains throughout the rest of that evening and in the early morning to drink no alcohol, whatever the others were doing.

I then started trying to check up on the alleged efforts that had been made to find me earlier in the evening, for the Prime Minister had said in front of the other Ministers that it was only because I was 'otherwise engaged' (and he managed to make *that* sound sinister!) that he had been unable to get in touch with me. I learned that there had indeed been a call for me a little before 9 p.m., but that about ten minutes afterwards – whilst a search was being made for me in the House and before it was discovered that I had left to go home for supper – there had been another message from the Prime Minister's office telling them not to bother, that the Prime Minister didn't particularly want me after all so there was no need to go on looking for me. Because of that second message, I wasn't even told at the time that anybody had been looking for me.

The final outcome of the evening's events was that the Chancellor of the Exchequer at 3.20 a.m. made his statement to the House about the gold situation and the decision to proclaim a Bank Holiday.

What we were not told, and have not been told to this day, is who took the decision. The Cabinet didn't, and wasn't told. The Economic Committee of the Cabinet didn't take it, because I was a member of that Committee and would have known. A number of us suspected that the decision had simply been dictated to the Prime Minister from across the Atlantic. And this is in part why I felt so strongly about the way in which a British Government had apparently been committed to a major decision affecting Britain without the British Cabinet's being given any inkling of what was happening.

I felt – and feel still – that this was a major constitutional issue. Government simply mustn't be conducted in this way if the British democratic system is to be maintained. I had already that evening drawn a parallel between Wilson's going to the Palace with Roy Jenkins and Peter Shore, and Ramsay MacDonald's conduct of affairs almost alone with Snowden and Thomas in 1931. I said, 'You know, we've all read this history, and we've repeatedly said that if only the Party or the Government had stopped Ramsay, Snowden and Thomas from behaving on their own, the events of 1931 and the subsequent Labour disaster need never have happened.' The particular issue in 1968 may not have been of critical importance, but that did not matter. What *was* of critical importance was that decisions – which might have been decisions of appalling gravity – had been taken without the knowledge of the Cabinet. What had happened once in breach of constitutional practice might happen again.

These reflections were in my mind as I went back into the Chamber on that early morning of 15 March. I did not sit on the Front Bench, but went to the third bench back. That, of course, made it obvious that I had resigned. People came up and asked me about it, and I said, 'This is the end. The Prime Minister wants me to go – he has made that crystal-clear. And I'm damned well not going back on that. And in any case, there is no *point* in sitting in a Cabinet where things can be done in this kind of a way.' Later, many of my colleagues came to talk to me in my room, but I felt that the decision had been made, the die cast, and that I was right to take the view that I couldn't work with a Prime Minister who would conduct things in this way, that indeed it was not in the interests of the nation to allow things to be conducted in this way without protest.

About half past five in the morning I went home, and spent the rest of the day at home, discussing things with my family. I didn't want to give any impression of acting hastily, or in a fit of pique, so I didn't send my letter of resignation until 5 o'clock in the afternoon. That meant that I gave myself ample time to think it over, and I gave the Prime Minister ample time to see me and to talk to me if he had had any second thoughts. By 5 o'clock nothing had happened to change the situation in any way, so I sent my letter. At 8.30 p.m. in the evening I got the Prime Minister's reply. So that was that.

The week-end intervened, and on Monday, 18 March, I made the customary personal statement on my resignation to the House despite much interesting effort to discourage me from acting in accordance with normal precedent. The statement was not a long one and, as it is important in this record, I give it here in full. I said:

> I do not propose today to go into the history of my various disagreements with Government decisions, and, even more, with the way in which they have been increasingly made and the considerations on which they were so often based. There will be time enough for all that. But in view of some of the wilder speculations and exaggerations over the week-end, I feel I owe it to the House and to my right hon. Friends on this side of the House, in particular, and, if I may say so, to myself, to say why I decided to resign at this time.
>
> It was not despite the gravity of the situation; it was, in a sense, because of it. It is in just such a situation that it is essential for Cabinet Government to be maintained if democracy is to be assured, and equally it is in just such a situation that temptation to depart from it is at its greatest. Power can very easily pass not merely from Cabinet to one or two Ministers, but effectively to sources quite outside the political control altogether.
>
> It is open to anyone to challenge my judgement of the situation on Thursday night, when it was learned that the Prime Minister and two other Ministers were already at the Palace, or to feel that I exaggerated the dangers in it. But I am very conscious of past parallels in my own political lifetime, and felt strongly enough on the issue to gather some of my colleagues together and to protest then. When that protest was virtually brushed aside on the basis that what I had done was in itself irregular, I felt that the time had come to leave the Government.
>
> But for what I have read over the week-end, I would feel it quite unnecessary to say that, of course, my purpose in the action I have taken is not to challenge the Prime Minister or to set out to lead a left-wing revolt against the Cabinet.
>
> I had a feeling that that suggestion might have amused and surprised some of my hon. Friends, as it did me.
>
> I do, however, feel most strongly that if the authority and success of this Government is to be re-established, as, indeed, it must be, then

the basis on which they take their decisions must be changed and their communications within the Government and with those outside must be greatly improved. Just making what are called touch decisions on occasions, valid as they may be, is not enough. There must be a thread of continuity evident in all that is done.

Whether I can help to bring about the necessary change by my resignation and by acting outside of the Government only time and experience can tell; but I shall loyally try. I believe that restoring the morale and the enthusiasm of those who elected this Government with such high hopes in 1966 is a most vital and urgent task facing us. It has seemed increasingly to me over a period that we were ignoring the basic reasons for the decline, that we were misreading all the political signs and refusing to recognize that we ourselves were at least partly responsible for the mood of cynicism in the nation which, whatever our future policy decisions may be, is Britain's greatest threat.

I completely accept that so long as I remained in the Government I fully shared the responsibility for all this, whatever my private or semi-private reservations. I have decided by this action to end that responsibility.

To those who say I did it on the wrong issue and at the wrong time and in the wrong temper, let me just say this. There never could be a wholly right issue or a wholly right time, as those who before me have walked this unhappy road and made statements from this seat can no doubt testify, and if one waited for the cold, calculating considerations of all personal and other consequences one would probably never move at all.

In my view, there is no practicable alternative to this Government which would not be infinitely worse for the nation, to put it mildly. Our business is to try to make this Government very much stronger and more effective and, meanwhile, to campaign as powerfully as we can in the country to restore confidence in and support for this Government. I propose to do all that I can to those ends.

Some people felt at the time – perhaps still think – that I was too gentle in my resignation statement, that, feeling as I did, I should have been much more specific and firm. My statement did, I think, make things as easy as possible for the Prime Minister. This was not because I wanted to be particularly nice to him, but because I wanted to minimize so far as I could the effect of my resignation on the Party. I could have fought that night for some other resignations – quite a number of my colleagues in the Government also felt very affronted by the affair. But I didn't want to provoke other people into leaving the Government – that might have broken the Government completely. I didn't want that. I felt that loyalty to the Party must come first. I was making a personal demonstration, because I genuinely felt that Prime Ministers must not be allowed to act in that way, and partly because my personal relations with Harold Wilson had deteriorated to a point where neither of us was really trusting the other. When other colleagues, some of them younger colleagues, talked of joining me in a general resignation, I discouraged them all and said, 'No. I'll make the stand, *you* see to it that it doesn't happen again.' That was why, in my personal statement to the House, I did not blow things up into a major confrontation between me and the Government.

That has worked to my disadvantage since, because it led some people to think and others to imply, that I had resigned on some rather minor issue. I have even read in articles that it was simply because Peter Shore was asked to go to the Palace and not me. I have never felt it necessary to answer such rubbish, and I hope I have been able to explain here that, far from being a minor matter, it was quite simply the overriding principle of collective Cabinet responsibility. The essence of Cabinet government must be its collective responsibility. That is not a matter of the exercise of personal power or working through small groups currently in favour – it means running the Government on lines that the Cabinet is prepared to go along with. As it became steadily more evident that this was less and less the case, and that I had no way of stopping or preventing it, it seemed better to take myself off. I saw my resignation not so much as giving up something for myself, as leaving a Government that wasn't being run in the way I thought it should be run. That is why I stressed in my statement to the House that I was leaving the Government not so much because of the decisions that had been taken, but because of the *way* in which decisions were taken.

You must have effective Cabinet Government if democracy is to survive. If you don't have it, and you have instead all the powers of patronage, of 'leaking', of manipulating the Parliamentary Party against whichever of your colleagues is for the moment out of favour, it doesn't seem to me that you can have effective democracy.

I came to feel that Mr Wilson preferred something akin to the presidential system, that he really did prefer to have his own outfit at No. 10, rather like the way in which the President of the United States has his own outfit in the White House. In my view, one of the arguments against the White House system, and I speak as one who has been allowed to see it operate under more than one President and who has many friends who have served in it and

suffered from it, is that it places too much power in the hands of
one man. It also places power where it shouldn't be, in the hands
of friends or unofficial advisers to the President or Prime Minister,
who are not accountable to Congress or Parliament while reducing
the real Cabinet to the level the others should occupy. And indeed,
the greater the pressures – quite apart from the temperament of
the man – the greater the chances are that the effective decisions
will be taken by these friends or unofficial advisers.

I suppose it could be argued – and no doubt some people would
argue – that concentrating things in this way at No. 10, in these
modern rather hectic times when events move so fast, may well be
better than our traditional system, just so long as the man at No. 10
runs things well. And it may be said that, whatever the constitutional niceties, no great damage has been done. But what if he
doesn't run things well? – after all, the more hectic the pace the
greater the chance that one man, with a handful of irresponsible
advisers around him (using the word 'irresponsible' in its proper
meaning) will go wrong. Look at what we have been allowed to
know of Mr Eden's actions and relations with his then Ministers
and, in consequence, the way Britain got into the Suez disaster.
If you look into this, even with our limited information, it seems
uncannily reminiscent of the events that culminated in my resignation. How many members of the Cabinet at the time of Suez knew
that Mr Selwyn Lloyd was outside Paris with the Israeli Foreign
Minister of the day and Monsieur Mollet, the French Prime Minister,
presumably arranging the implementation of the ultimatum given
to Israel and Egypt? The relevant document, which was effectively
a declaration of war against Egypt, wasn't even signed by Selwyn
Lloyd as Foreign Minister – a Civil Servant was left behind to sign
it. I am not even now at all clear on whose say-so he did sign it,
apart from the Prime Minister and Selwyn Lloyd. This seems pretty
analogous with the events of 1931 and 1968. For it isn't the merit of
the particular decision that matters. What matters is the way in
which you do things. You can do enormous damage or you can do
little damage, but once allow the British constitutional system to
be flouted in this way, and we may end by finding that system
has been irrevocably breached.

That some people, at any rate, understood the point I was trying
to make by my resignation was shown by the number of letters
I had after my statement in the House. I had between 800 and 1,000
letters, wholly supporting my point of view.

Looking back, I am sure that it would have been better for me politically to have resigned before I did, on some issue that could have been grasped more readily. There was the occasion that I have written about in an earlier chapter, when the Prime Minister decided, against the strongest advice, not to devalue the pound in 1966. Perhaps I really ought to have gone then. Or on South Africa; or on health charges; or on education when Frank Longford did go. My own explanation is that I wasn't on any of these things thinking of my own political future. There were obvious dangers of desperately splitting the Party on any of the others. On the issue I finally chose I knew that by going I would create a situation where my colleagues in the Cabinet would see to it that such a position would not occur again. And I also knew that, even though I would keep quiet at the time, there would come a day, as I said in my statement, when I could properly and validly bring into the open the whole situation as I saw it.

10

Picking up
the Threads

Now THERE AROSE for me the agonizing position that everybody has to face at some stage in life – from being a man who, over many years, had worked from 6 in the morning until 2 or 3 o'clock in the following morning, with never enough time to get through all the various jobs that needed doing, I suddenly found myself at the age of fifty-four a retired gentleman of leisure. I was still, of course, a Member of Parliament, and being an M.P. is regarded by many people as a pretty full-time job. But I have never seen it like that. I have always worked hard in the House, and done everything I could for my constituency, but it has also seemed to me that one is a better M.P. for having an active life in the world outside the House as well as in it. The sudden transition from holding one of the great offices of State to becoming simply a private member was a difficult one for me. You never, I think, realize quite what a change of this sort means until you find yourself getting up in the morning, shaving, putting on your coat to leave the house, and your wife says, 'Where are you going today?' And suddenly you say to yourself, 'Well, where the hell am I going?' I had an absolute horror of this going on for a long period.

I need not have worried. From the moment of my resignation I was in the thick of things again. The first thing that had to be decided was whether I should make a statement in the House, and there was a good deal of pressure on me from various sources not to do so. But I took the view myself that I could hardly just leave the Government (after all, I was the Deputy Prime Minister) and treat it as a minor occurrence. I took the view all the more strongly because of a story that was being put around at the time that I had left in a fit of pique over the question of whether Mr Peter Shore or I should have gone to the Palace with the Prime Minister. So

I decided that I would make a short statement, but I promised
everybody in the Party who was talking to me that, to avoid doing
harm, I would make it as colourless as I could. This I did in the
statement I have quoted in the previous chapter.

The next question was what I should do about being Deputy
Leader of the Labour Party. In my statement to the House, and
in my letter to the Prime Minister, I had said that I wanted to do
everything I could to continue to serve the Labour movement and
to support the Labour Government, and I meant this. If I gave up
the Deputy Leadership I should be off the National Executive of the
Party, and out of all the channels of influence, authority or responsibility. If I stayed on as Deputy Leader, it was bound to seem
anomalous – it would scarcely seem logical to have a Deputy
Leader not in the Government when the Party itself was in Government. Somebody else would in fact be acting as Deputy to the
Prime Minister, whatever we said about the Deputy Leadership
of the Party. Arguments about this, both in my own mind and with
other people in the House, went on for some time. I tried to consult
the Prime Minister, but elicited only a somewhat frigid response
indicating that he didn't care one way or the other. Finally I came
round to the view that, however illogical it might seem, there was
more to be said for my staying in the job than for not staying. The
House of Commons in any case is a Palace of Illogicalities and
I didn't think that one more or less could matter much.

There were solid reasons for this decision. One was that, if I went,
there would have to be another election for a Deputy Leader, with
the possibility of all kinds of warfare breaking out in the Party
and between leading members of the Cabinet over who should
have the job. There wasn't any one natural successor then obvious,
and if I stayed it would keep things quiet until a more convenient
moment came for the election of my successor.

Another important reason was that if I went, and there had to
be an election for my successor, the Prime Minister would have
had to stand for re-election as well. This came about through a
change in the procedure for Parliamentary Party elections which
the Prime Minister had himself instigated when we took office in
1964, though it was not much noticed at the time. Previously the
Leader and Deputy Leader were elected separately by the Parliamentary Party at the beginning of each session, but in 1964 Mr
Wilson proposed that the Leader and Deputy Leader should be
elected together in one resolution for the lifetime of a Parliament.

So the odd situation arose that the band of brothers who wanted to put down a motion forcing me to resign from the Deputy Leadership could only succeed by forcing the Prime Minister to resign from the leadership as well.

I put my views in a letter to Mr Douglas Houghton, the chairman of the Parliamentary Labour Party, on 26 March 1968. I wrote:

> I recognize that continuing as Deputy Leader, will be, in House of Commons terms, anomalous. Nevertheless, it seems to me that it would be, as you put it, the least troublesome way out for the Party.
>
> But there are more positive reasons than this, for me just carrying on.
>
> As I said in my Statement in the House, I want now to do all I possibly can to help the Party in the country, and to contribute to the development of a statement of policy which will help us to win the next election.
>
> To do the latter, I really need to stay on the National Executive, and to continue the work which I have already begun, as Chairman of the Home Policy Committee. I would, of course, be very much helped in doing the former, if I held a position in the Party.
>
> Therefore, despite the anomalous situation which will arise, in purely House of Commons terms, I have come to the conclusion that I should in fact just carry on.
>
> It is, of course, open to the Parliamentary Party to reject this, and no doubt, if they wish, they will.
>
> I do not propose to issue any statement, but it will no doubt become known that I am doing this. Therefore, I think it would be better for you to have a formal letter from me to this effect.
>
> I have been encouraged to take this view from consultations I have had within the Parliamentary Party, and even more, from the letters, many hundreds of them, which I have received from Party supporters in the country.
>
> The Prime Minister knew, a few days ago, that this thought was in my mind, and I have no reason to think that it is inconvenient to him. But I am sending him a copy of this letter.

I haven't regretted this decision, and I think that, on the whole, it worked out remarkably well. There have obviously been times when it was rather embarrassing. At meetings of the P.L.P., for instance, I couldn't sit, as it were, in the body of the kirk, yet it seemed to me ridiculous to sit as Deputy Leader among Ministers when I was not myself a Minister. So I usually made what Mr George Woodcock has described as a 'shoddy shabby compromise' by sitting on the platform, but in the second row instead of at the front. In the House, I chose to speak from the front bench below the gangway, and that came to be accepted. On occasions I criticized the Government, but that came to be accepted too, because in the Labour Party there are always groups who want to criticize the Government on some particular issue. It is no bad thing to have a Deputy Leader of the Party free to criticize the Government, and in a way I think people came to like it. In the country I was completely accepted as Deputy Leader – outside the House few people saw anything anomalous in it. And my not being in the Government had one directly good effect in that I could say things at meetings, and get other people to talk, with a freedom that would not have been possible had I remained a member of the Cabinet.

Soon after the question of the Deputy Leadership was settled, the General Secretary of the Labour Party, to my absolute astonishment, and, I suspect, that of many other people, was suddenly chosen to be the Governor-General of Mauritius. Nobody, in his wildest moments, had ever thought of Len Williams, whom we all admired, as the Governor-General of one of our outposts of empire, but such he was to become, and so we had to replace him as General Secretary. The constitutional position here is interesting. The General Secretary of the Labour Party is, in the first instance, appointed by the National Executive, voting in secret at a closed meeting. His appointment is subject to confirmation by the next annual Party conference. If he didn't get a majority of votes there he would, of course, drop out again, but confirmation of the appointment in the past has always been a formality, so that to all practical purposes the General Secretary is elected in secret by the National Executive.

As we were required to do by rule, we advertised the post, and appointed a sub-committee, of which the Prime Minister as Leader of the Party and I as Deputy Leader were both members, to consider the various applicants and to make a recommendation to the full Executive. We had various meetings, but nobody of really the right stature emerged, and gradually it began to appear that the favoured candidate of the Prime Minister himself was Anthony Greenwood, then in the Government as Minister of Housing. A good deal of canvassing went on to get the post for him, but setting aside all personal feelings, some of us took the view that we didn't think him quite the man for the job. There was no animosity about this: the General Secretaryship of the Party is an immensely important post, and we were concerned solely to find the candidate whom we felt to be best suited to it. So we began looking around for other possibilities.

At this stage we learned that Harry Nicholas, who had been acting General Secretary of the Transport and General Workers Union while Mr Cousins was in the Government, but who had had to step back to being Assistant General Secretary when Mr Cousins left the Government, would be willing to be considered for the Party Secretaryship. The difficulty about Harry Nicholas was that he was sixty-two – wasn't that a bit old for the appointment? I had in fact had an earlier conversation about him with the Prime Minister, saying what a jolly good General Secretary Harry would make, and what a pity it was that the job hadn't come up when he was a bit younger. Because of his age, we rather dropped him out of our considerations.

Now when the canvassing and the pushing and shoving went on for Anthony Greenwood, I and one or two others discussed all this, and we came to the conclusion that if Harry Nicholas would stand he would be a man worth having in spite of his age – he was an able administrator, a very active man and exceedingly well-liked in the trade unions; we felt that at least he could hold the post until after the General Election, by which time one of the younger men might have emerged as the natural successor to the secretary-ship.

Then came a meeting of the sub-committee at which I wasn't present, because I had to go out of London for a Party engagement. At that meeting it was decided unanimously to send an emissary to Anthony Greenwood to find out for certain whether he would accept the post if it were offered to him. Jennie Lee was the chosen emissary, and the understanding was that if Anthony Greenwood said 'Yes', then the Committee would recommend him unanimously to the Executive.

I was told about this as soon as I got back to London by members of the sub-committee, who obviously regretted that they had voted with the majority to make the decision unanimous, and who now had all sorts of explanations about why they had not stood up to oppose it.

Well, I wasn't committed to it. I was the only person not committed, and therefore I was the only person who could re-raise the matter at the next meeting without being accused of a breach of faith.

The meeting duly came. Miss Lee reported that Mr Greenwood had said Yes, and she therefore proposed that the recommendation as agreed upon by the sub-committee should be made. To which I said, 'I'm awfully sorry and I don't want to be a nuisance, but

I am not committed to any recommendation you may have decided to make. And quite frankly, I think that this is the wrong one.' I gave my reasons for thinking that Mr Greenwood would not be suitable, and said that I should like to suggest that Mr Nicholas be asked whether he would accept the post. I added that if Mr Nicholas was willing, I myself would like to propose him.

Mr Greenwood and Mr Nicholas were both members of the sub-committee. At this point Mr Greenwood got up in a dignified way and left the room so that we could discuss things in his absence, and when I began to talk about Mr Nicholas, he, too, got up and left the room. I think that was the first time that the Prime Minister realized that there was any other candidate involved, and I remember feeling that the way things were happening was a tragedy, for it now seemed certain that he would gather his forces to make sure that the Nicholas proposal was defeated at the full Executive.

But for some reason that I shall never understand, this was the one occasion when the Prime Minister didn't take a challenge seriously, presumably thinking that it was a purely private enterprise by me. Anyway, the outcome of that meeting was that we decided that we couldn't make a unanimous recommendation and that Miss Lee, who was then chairman, would have to report to the full Executive that we had two candidates who were both excellent and that the Executive would have to choose between them.

So we went to the National Executive. I took no further part in trying to organize support for Mr Nicholas, but I did discuss how we should handle things at the meeting of the full Executive and it was evident that because of the previous unanimity on the sub-committee I was the only one who was still free to nominate Mr Nicholas.

Miss Lee reported the whole situation faithfully and fairly. She did not name me as the dissentient, but she did say that but for a member who had not been at one meeting of the sub-committee there would have been a unanimous recommendation to appoint Mr Greenwood. She went on to say that she would like to move from the chair, and did move, that Mr Greenwood be appointed. Mr Greenwood, according to custom, then left the room.

There was a long pause. I wasn't particularly anxious to step in, and hoped that some member of the full Executive who had not been on the sub-committee might say something, but nobody did. Miss Lee had just got to the point of saying 'And now, if there is no other nomination . . .' when I said that I did want to make

With
President
Kennedy,
1963

With
President
Johnson
1967

With Sophie, his daughter Pat, and her fiancé (now her husband),
Derek Knowles, at Dorneywood, August 1967

With Sophie,
relaxing by their cottage
at Jevington, Sussex

another nomination. I explained that I was the member who had dissented from the unanimous recommendation, that I was sorry to intervene again but that I wished to propose Mr Nicholas for the General Secretaryship and that I asked leave to test my colleagues' opinions on the matter. At this Mr Nicholas in his turn got up and left the room.

The Prime Minister then said that he, too, did not want to intervene, but that he felt it necessary to explain the reasons that led him to the view that it should be Mr Greenwood and not Mr Nicholas. He put a lot of emphasis on the need for a young man in the job, and he made Mr Nicholas look so old and Mr Greenwood look so young that my impish sense of humour got the better of me and I asked, 'Would you regard me as a young man in this context? And if you wouldn't, would you like to say how much older than I am Mr Greenwood is?'

Well, he didn't know precisely how old Mr Greenwood was, so I said, 'Mr Greenwood is at least two years older than I am, which means that he is approaching fifty-seven against Mr Nicholas's sixty-two. There doesn't seem to be such an awful lot of difference between one old man and the other, except that in my view one old man is better for this job than the other.'

We sent for reference books and discovered that Mr Greenwood is in fact three years older than I am. So we got rid of the young man argument against Mr Nicholas, but another impediment was raised – the question of his retirement. The Prime Minister agreed that perhaps there wasn't all that difference in age between the two of them, but Mr Nicholas would have to retire at sixty-five, which meant that he might even have to go before the next election.

At this I asked, 'Why should he have to retire at sixty-five?' I was told that that is the retiring age in the Labour Party. However, one or two of us who had taken the trouble to look up the rule-book pointed out that there was no retiring age in the Party. There was an age at which you took your pension, but that would not apply to Mr Nicholas because he would have a pension from his union and so would not need to join the Labour Party's pension fund.

The rule-book was very busily turned up, and it proved that our argument was right – as far as the rules were concerned, a General Secretary could carry on until he was ninety or 190 if he could stand the pace. So that obstacle fell, and one by one all the other impediments dropped. Finally, after long and tedious argument, it was time to vote.

N

Then an attempt was made to abandon secrecy and have the vote on a show of hands. But secrecy was essential if we were to have a fair chance of getting our candidate adopted, for a show of hands would have been embarrassing for everybody, particularly the junior Ministers present. Again we had to go back to the rule-book, only to find that the point about the precise method of voting did not seem to be covered. So we turned up the minutes of past meetings of the National Executive concerned with the appointment of General Secretaries, and these established that it had been the practice of the Executive to make the appointment by secret ballot.

At last the scraps of paper were handed round, the vote was taken and Mr Nicholas won by two votes over Mr Greenwood. Then the two candidates came back into the room, and Mr Greenwood made a very graceful speech withdrawing his candidature so that we could then have a unanimous decision in favour of Mr Nicholas.

That should have been the end of the matter, but we all had to go on to a send-off luncheon which we were giving to Mr Williams on his becoming Sir Leonard and leaving our service to go to Mauritius. At this luncheon the Prime Minister made a speech congratulating Len Williams on his becoming a Knight Grand Cross of the Order of St Michael and St George. Without thinking of the events of the morning, I called out – as I hoped humorously – 'Don't let's have too much of the St Michael. Can't we concentrate on the St George?' At this the Prime Minister said immediately and very loudly, 'Those of you who know your Gibbon will know that Michael was an angel and George a crook.'

This would hardly have mattered had the Executive been alone, but in fact the Press had been invited in to hear Mr Wilson's speech and therefore heard these exchanges. Although considerable pressure was subsequently exerted to damp down any references to them, this was only partially successful.

This whole business had its ludicrous side, but there was also a serious point at issue. I took the view that it was bad constitutionally, and would be bad in practice, for the Secretary to the Labour Party to be regarded in any way as the Prime Minister's nominee. I had already resigned from the Cabinet on the ground that the Prime Minister was exercising too much individual power: if he could put his own nominee into the Party Secretaryship, he would in fact be controlling, in one person, in one pair of hands, every piece of apparatus in the Party as well as in the Government. I had made the comparison with Ramsay MacDonald in 1931 over the incident which had led to my resignation from the Cabinet, and I felt that it could fairly be made again: it was imperative that the National Executive of the Party should not only be, but should be seen to be, independent of the Prime Minister, whoever he might be. There was no question of personalities here – my feeling was simply that it was wrong for one man to have all that patronage within the Party as well as in the Cabinet and Government. It was not a matter of personality; it was a matter of constitutional belief.

The major business of the Labour *movement* in the end must always be that it shall survive. One would like to think that a Labour *Government* will survive, but democracy being what democracy is, you can't always be sure of that, for a Government may get dismissed. At that stage, unless the Party is independent and can act in its own way, the Party may go down with the Government. In 1931 the Prime Minister and two or three of his colleagues were able very effectively to bring down a Labour Government and to reduce the Parliamentary Labour Party to a mere handful in the House. What they were not able to do was to destroy the Labour movement outside Parliament, and after 1931 the Labour movement was restored not immediately in the Government, not immediately in the House of Commons, but in the country. It took us a long while to come back, but we did come back, and we had another Labour Government in 1945, just because there was this difference between the Labour movement and the Labour Government in 1931. If the Prime Minister in 1931 had been able to force the Executive of the Party, and the staff of Transport House to follow the line that he took in Parliament, he would have destroyed the Party in the country as effectively as he destroyed it in Parliament. That is a situation we have always to guard against.

If the Labour movement had not been independent of the Government in 1931, there would not have been a Labour Government in 1945. We should never have got back. The Party in the country would have split like the Party in the House, there would have been more than one Labour Party. We should have gone the way of the Liberals – it would have been the Asquith–Lloyd George split all over again. I suppose it is because I began active Party work in 1931 that the events of that period made such an impact on me that they have coloured so much of my thinking since. Inside and outside the Government, constantly and without any variation, I have taken the view that the National Executive of the Party must be free to disagree with whatever the Government is doing. Even though it made things much more difficult for me on occasions, I stuck to this view all the time I was doing the most unpopular job of, for example, dealing with prices and incomes policy at the D.E.A.

The election of a new Party Secretary in July 1968 turned on this question of principle. I felt that the Executive *must* be free to select among those available the candidate whom a majority considered to be best fitted for the job. To this end a secret ballot, ignoring if necessary what were assumed to be the Prime Minister's wishes, was imperative. As things have happened since, I imagine that the Prime Minister himself would now agree that on sheer merits we were righter than we knew at the time. Harry Nicholas has turned out to be probably the most effective and efficient General Secretary we have had since Arthur Henderson.

My decision to carry on as Deputy Leader of the Party after my resignation from the Cabinet had one effect which I did not foresee when I made it, and which became a continual embarrassment: it kept alive in people's minds the idea that I should be going back to the Government. This may be a convenient place to record the facts about the various rumours and Press stories suggesting my return to the Government.

Relations between myself and the Prime Minister since my resignation, while never barbarous or really impossible, never rose much beyond what might be called a civilized level. At some times we were friendlier than at others, but, broadly, our relations remained those of two civilized chaps who feel happier when the other is not too obviously present. Rumours that I might rejoin Mr Wilson's Government often embarrassed me, and I think also embarrassed him, because every time he contemplated reshuffling the Government the prospect of my return was always canvassed, and when it didn't happen it assumed an even greater significance.

The events surrounding the election for the Party Secretaryship in July 1968 did not exactly endear me to the Prime Minister, and in fact the possibility of my return to the Government was not discussed between us until I came out of hospital after an operation for hernia in July 1969. The Prime Minister then came to see me at home, told me that he was thinking of making substantial changes in the Government, and sounded me about the possibility of my coming back. But we discussed it without ever coming to the point of his saying, 'Well, here you are, that's what you can do, would

you like to do it?' or of my saying, 'I'm ready to come.' We just
discussed it in vague and general ways, on the lines of, 'If it were to
happen, would you want to come back as a Secretary of State with
a department, or would you want to come as a non-departmental
Cabinet Minister?' This led to a discussion about what my role
was to be in the next General Election, and I think we both felt
that if I were to do all the work I wanted to do in the country there
was a lot to be said for my not having a department in the Government.

Then these discussions rather faded out, and we didn't do anything
about them. We had three talks in all, and at the third he raised
the issue of what he called 'the pecking order' in the Cabinet,
remarking that he couldn't do anything about it. Until then I
hadn't even considered this particular complication, but at this
point it became clear how additionally embarrassing the whole
thing could be. I was still the Labour Party's Deputy Leader –
I could hardly resign as Deputy Leader in order to go back into
the Cabinet when I hadn't resigned as Deputy Leader in order to
leave it! Yet if I went back to the Government as Deputy Leader,
I should not, in the Prime Minister's then thinking, be the second
man after the Leader. We clarified the position, and I discovered
that what he really meant was that he did not want to disturb the
then order of seniority, with Michael Stewart as nominally his
deputy and various other people taking precedence over me.
Envisaging myself sitting somewhere down the bottom of the table
I said, 'Well, that would be really rather silly. It would be even
more embarrassing for my colleagues than for me if I were to sit
in the Cabinet like that than to be outside it. Really, you know,
I think that there is not much point in it. We are managing quite
well as we are, and I'm doing just about as much work for the
Party as Deputy Leader outside the Cabinet as I could do inside.'
However, I added, 'I leave it to you. You think about it, and if
you really want to make me a proposition I won't be difficult about
it, provided that you don't make the situation more embarrassing
for everybody than it is now. My position is simple. I'm not particularly anxious to rejoin the Cabinet, but equally, if you think
my coming back would help, I'm ready to come. It's up to you, and
I shan't be a bit upset whichever way your decision goes.' Subsequently I put this in a letter to him, adding that while I didn't
want to try to force his hand, I did find the degree of speculation
then going on in the newspapers very embarrassing indeed. This

was added to by some flattering remarks he made about me on a programme with David Frost. So, I went on, would he make a decision soon? I emphasized that, as far as I was concerned, there would be no ill-feeling whatever he decided – all I wanted was a decision.

Then followed a series of events that still seem to me to be extraordinary. Not for the first time they took place when I was making a short trip abroad. Before leaving I came to the conclusion that there wasn't much immediate likelihood of the Prime Minister's inviting me to come back. My wife wasn't all that keen on my returning to the Government, and before leaving I said to her, 'You needn't worry, because the whole thing seems to have gone off the boil.'

On 9 September 1969, a front-page story appeared in the *Daily Mail*, headlined 'Cabinet Job for Brown'. This stated that my return to the Cabinet was 'the outcome of a slow but steady reconciliation' with my 'old adversary the Prime Minister'. This was attributed to Mr Walter Terry, who was generally thought to be very close to No. 10. On that day there was a meeting of the Campaign Committee of the Labour Party. At this meeting I was warmly praised by the Prime Minister, who suggested that I should undertake the big Party Political Broadcast on television which was then being planned. The Prime Minister did not mention the *Daily Mail* story and I went straight from the meeting to London Airport to start my visit to Yugoslavia.

Next day another story appeared all round the Press saying that I was not going to be recalled and that I was not going to be invited back into the Government.

I got Bill Greig, my public relations adviser, to make inquiries about all this, and it turned out that the second round of stories were the outcome of a full-scale Press conference called by the public relations staff at No. 10 to make the usual off-the-record announcement that can be written about but not attributed to anybody. The announcement on this occasion was that I was not to be asked to rejoin the Government, and it went on virtually to make clear what had been my discussions with Mr Wilson – that I should be having an increasing influence on the Labour Party's affairs during the run-up to polling day, and that I could do this job as effectively outside the Government as within it.

The No. 10 public relations staff could have acted, of course, only on the instructions of the Prime Minister. Why he failed, as a matter of common courtesy, to tell me of his decision, or the fact that such guidance was to be given to the Press, must remain a mystery to me. Our inquiries indicated that the first guidance was given to a London evening newspaper just as my plane was taking off.

I was therefore to learn of the decision that I was not to be invited back in a telephone call that evening from Bill Greig to my hotel in Yugoslavia. A strange way indeed for the Leader of a Party to treat his deputy.

We were getting near the Annual Party Conference, at which the Prime Minister and I as Leader and Deputy Leader had to share some of the major debates and, of course, to do all we could to encourage and inspire other people. I can only suppose that the Prime Minister found it embarrassing to think that he might be asked why his chief lieutenant was still going to be out in the wilderness and wanted to make it clear that it was all my own fault. But I don't know this, and I still don't know why the announcement was made in such a devious way. There was no need to make a public statement at all. It was a queer business.

In our different ways the Prime Minister and I each had a considerable success at the conference, and we came rather closer together than we had been for a long time. Then, out of the blue, he raised again the question of my coming back into the Government. 'This hasn't really been the last reshuffle,' he said. 'I'm not now going to do the very big shuffle that I discussed with you, and I'm not going to move people around in the way I thought I would, but perhaps January [1970] would be a good time for you to come back.'

I said, 'Well, again, it's entirely up to you. But I wouldn't want the thing to be speculated about all over again. I'd rather that we either did it or put it to sleep, so I do trust that you won't indicate to anyone that you have this in mind until you are ready to do it.' I had to make another point, which was that the nearer we got to the election the more difficult it would be for me personally to rejoin the Government: I had undertaken the job of Productivity Counsellor for Courtaulds, and it would not be right to abandon all the work I had started there to return to the Government for perhaps only a few months before an election.

This is another problem that the Minister who resigns from office has to face: you give up not only a job into which you have been putting everything you've got, but also you surrender overnight your official residence, ministerial car and all the other things

that go with the great offices of State. I have already explained
that I'm not sufficiently in love with the House of Commons as
such to want to spend my whole time hanging about the place:
I needed something else to do, to use up, as it were, the energy
left over from the House. I had some remarkable offers from newspapers. One Sunday paper offered me a fantastic sum for ten articles
a year on subjects which, they said, could be of my own choosing:
and I was to be allowed to decide when to write – I could write
four articles in a row and then have a gap of a few months, I could
fit in the writing as I pleased. It seemed an absolutely fabulous
offer. But I didn't want to become a journalist on anybody's pay-
roll. I had watched what happened to other people in politics who
got in that position; no matter what an editor might say in order
to get you to sign a contract, once you have signed up the fact of
the matter is that you have got to write when it's wanted, and on the
subject that's wanted, otherwise the paper just doesn't want your
contribution. I've seen M.P.s on both sides of the House obviously
having to create a sensation on a Thursday in order to have a peg
on which to hang an article for Sunday. I didn't want to drift into
that position.

So I decided that while I would write from time to time, it would
be when I wanted to write, and because there was something that
ought to be written about, and not as a hired journalist tied to
some particular employer. But if I wasn't going to be a regular
journalist, what else was there?

Various concerns offered me directorships, but I felt that becoming
a company director really would be embarrassingly incompatible
with my then position as a trade union official. For at that point
I had not ceased to be an official of the Transport and General
Workers Union on leave for parliamentary duties. I did not con-
sciously rule out the possibility of accepting some directorship,
and I would never say that all directorships would be impossible,
but I preferred at that moment to avoid one if I could. In looking
round, it became evident to me that the thing I could do best
would be to advise some company on industrial matters about which
I really do know something, without having a board-room vote.

While I was thinking in these terms and talking to colleagues
and friends about it, Frank Kearton of Courtaulds quite independently made an approach to me along the same lines. We knew
each other well, we had worked closely together when I was a
Minister at the D.E.A., and he came along with an offer on almost

exactly the lines on which I was myself thinking. He said that if I would like to come to Courtaulds as a consultant, not as an officer of the company, not on the board, not receiving a salary but being paid what he called 'a fee' for the services I could render, they would be happy to have me. Since I liked him, and I liked the company, and it covered so many industries that I knew a good deal about, I thought the idea worth trying. I came originally for a trial period, during which I said that I would take no fee at all and we would see how things worked out, whether there was enough to do, and whether we could all get on with one another.

For the first six months I took no money at all, except for train fares when I travelled about the country visiting factories. We then decided to make a longer-term arrangement, and I accepted the fee that was offered in the position of Productivity Counsellor. I'm not part of the Labour Relations Department at Courtaulds, and they have their own Director of Personnel on the main board of the company. I have no more to do with the Labour Relations Department than I have with any other aspect of the company's work. My job has developed into that of being a kind of roving inspector. I go round and visit factories, talk with their managements, talk with the work-people, look at the practices they are following and see if I can suggest improvements without treading on too many corns. I have no executive responsibility at all, I can't hire, or fire, anyone. All I can do is to wander in and out of other people's offices, saying, 'Why don't you do it this way?' or, 'Why don't you stop doing that and try doing this instead?'

I have been criticized, of course – a politician can expect to be criticized whatever he does. But I have got to meet my own conscience, and it seems to me that my work for Courtaulds is at least as much for the benefit of those I represent in the Labour movement as for anybody else.

So the time since my resignation from the Government has passed quickly. I didn't realize then just how quickly my life would fill up. Instead of beginning what looked like years of emptiness, I found very soon that I was just as hard put to find time to do things as I'd ever been before. The only difference has been, as I've sometimes said jokingly, that whereas once when I pressed a button a cannon fired, now if I press a button I'm liable to find that it's not even connected to a bell – but you take as long over doing it!

II

Reflections
on Europe

HIGH ON THE list of things I wished to press the button on and
hoped the bell would respond comes the integration of Europe.
I have devoted much of my political life to that and had to work
very hard in the Labour Government to persuade the Prime Minister
of the tremendous importance of this for British interests – economic, industrial, strategic and defence. With the help of my
friends I didn't do too badly at this and so when I was Foreign
Secretary the Prime Minister and I made a tour of the six Common
Market capitals, having obtained a mandate from the Cabinet
to do so.

That tour was between January and March 1967. It would have
been logical for such a tour to be made by the Foreign Secretary
alone, who, after all, is the Minister most directly concerned with
Britain's relationships with other countries. In the special circumstances of the time it might have been logical for the Prime Minister
to make a round of visits to the Common Market capitals. For us
both to go introduced that element of tension which so often touched
the relations between the Foreign Office and Downing Street
during Harold Wilson's Government.

The story of Britain's efforts to join the Common Market had
followed a somewhat zigzag path since Wilson had become Prime
Minister after the General Election of 1964. I, as Deputy Prime
Minister, was known to be committed to 'going into Europe', and
I had continued to take a line consistent with this all the time I was
at the D.E.A. In the election campaign of 1964 Mr Wilson had been
a good deal less committed, and many of his friends in the Party
and in the Cabinet were strongly anti-Common Market.

As soon as he took office the Prime Minister began to change –
I think he was genuinely convinced by what he saw in office of the

arguments in favour of joining the Common Market. The tour was his suggestion, to explore, as he put it, the climate of opinion and to find out what the chances were, after we had received the authority of the Cabinet, reinforced by the evident majority view of our colleagues, that unless the demands were clearly impossible we should in fact join. It remained true, however, that the Cabinet was very much divided on this issue, and the Prime Minister could sell the idea of the tour only on the basis that he and I should both go. If I went alone the anti-Marketeers would not believe what I brought back. If he went alone, the pro-Marketeers would be rather suspicious because of his late conversion. So it was agreed that we should go together, but even so, the Prime Minister had to promise the anti-Market members of the Cabinet that full records of all our talks would be taken and circulated so that everyone could see what was happening.

We began with a visit to Rome on 15 January 1967, and made our rounds of Paris (23–25 January), Brussels (31 January–1 February), Bonn (14–16 February), The Hague (26–27 February) and Luxembourg (7–8 March). Gradually our line got firmer and firmer, and by the time we had finished we had virtually decided to make our application. Then came a great battle in the Cabinet which ended with a majority decision in favour of applying to join.

It will be useful, I think, if I now go back a bit in time to describe my own approach to Europe and the Common Market.

Soon after Mr Attlee's Government fell in the election of 1951, I was invited to be a member of the Labour part of the British delegation to the Council of Europe at Strasbourg. This body was the outcome – the somewhat vestigial outcome – of all the ideas for a European Parliament which were canvassed after the Second World War. Sir Winston Churchill had been closely associated with them at the great Hague Congress, but Bevin stoutly opposed the whole thing, and so did Sir Anthony Eden (Lord Avon). The nearest that Bevin, who was then Foreign Secretary, would go to anything approaching a European Parliament was to agree to the setting up of a purely consultative council, without any executive powers. And the only place he would accept for the headquarters of the council was Strasbourg. Strasbourg is not easy to get to, and I sometimes privately suspected that Bevin had felt that if he made the meeting-place as difficult to get to as he could the thing could be relied upon to die.

However, the Council of Europe duly came into being. Paul-Henri

Spaak became its President. He was a great internationalist and became widely known as 'Mr Europe'. The fact that he looked a little like Winston Churchill didn't go unremarked. Patrick Gordon Walker was leader of the Labour delegation, and I became deputy leader. With us we had Alf Robens and Arthur Bottomley. We were quite a strong team in a way, but in those early days we acquired a reputation for being somewhat 'anti' – our line was for practical organization between countries to tackle specific and realistic tasks, and against federal political organization.

I got rather disenchanted with Strasbourg and left the delegation at my own request. But this didn't mean dropping all the associations I'd made at Strasbourg. I'd met a good many European Socialists there, and I went on meeting them. I also visited various international Labour organizations on the Continent. After an interval I was asked to rejoin the British delegation at Strasbourg, and this time I took a much deeper interest in its affairs. I became chairman of the Agricultural Committee of the Council of Europe, and in that capacity had a good deal to do with agricultural developments in various countries and with the resettlement of refugees on agricultural land. I also became interested in the European Steel and Coal Community and in various plans for European economic development.

At this same time I became the Labour Party's spokesman in the House of Commons on defence, and this got me more and more involved with European colleagues, in NATO, in the Western European Union, and in an American–European consultative body called the NATO Parliamentarians. Quite without planning I became a main spokesman for the Labour Party in all these various bodies, and I began thinking of Europe on a much wider basis than at Strasbourg. I began to think deeply about European defence, and about European and American relationships. Gradually my views changed and I became a convinced 'European'. That is something much more than being merely a Common Market man. My belief that Britain should join the Common Market developed out of my thinking on European integration. Important as it is, the Common Market in my view is only part of the wider process of creating a politically integrated Europe, capable of standing up both to the Russians and the Americans.

It seems to me that a politically united Europe is the only bridge over which the problem of a divided Germany can ever be settled. I cannot imagine the Russians ever agreeing to a United Germany

if that Germany is to be free to march off, rearm and do all the
things that a purely nationalistic Germany has done in the past.
That is a view which many people in other lands would share with
the Russians. One of the great arguments for a politically united
Europe is that, in such a Europe, the Germans would act in concert
with the rest of us. Whether Germany should be one unitary state,
a federation or a confederation of two Germanies is an issue to
be discussed, and it is really beside the point. What matters is that
the German people as a whole would be part of a united Europe.
A politically united Europe also seems to me to be the only chance
for the Eastern European countries to free themselves from close
control by Russia.

I get rather irritated sometimes when people talk of Britain's
'joining Europe' and I want to ask, 'In what other Continent has
Britain been over the past few thousand years?' A 'little Englander'
point of view is, perhaps, just tenable, if you are prepared to accept
the consequences. The late Hugh Dalton was a passionate anti-
European. There were one or two peoples in the world whom he
liked – he had a particular love of the Poles – but apart from these
special cases he didn't think much of anybody who lived on the
other side of the Channel. As I have already described, I was
Dalton's Parliamentary Private Secretary for a time, and I remember
his saying to me in private (though considering the voice he was
blessed with, it is hard to think of Dalton's saying anything in
private), 'My boy, the right thing to do is to cut down the population
of Britain to 26 millions by sending all the others away on assisted
emigration, and then we could live happily and not have to get
tangled up with a lot of bloody foreigners.' Well, that's at least a
logical argument, for if we in Britain were ever to try to live on our
own a population of the order of 26 millions is about the most we
could hope to support.

There are present-day politicians of both Parties whose ideas
seem to be in the same mould. Some of them declare it pretty
openly, others try to hide it under a great cloak of humanity. I am
bound to say that I don't think it would be much of a life for the
British people or do much to further the contribution we like to
think that Britain has made to the world.

There's the argument that Britain's role in the world is to be the
leader of the Commonwealth, but that's largely make-believe. Most
of the new Sovereign States that have emerged from the Commonwealth have no tie with Britain except that they were once colonized

With George Thomson, Bill Rodgers and the
U.N. mission on Aden, Dorneywood, April 1967

With
King Hussein
of Jordan,
1967

With Sophie at 2 Carlton Gardens
after resignation as Foreign Secretary,
March 1968

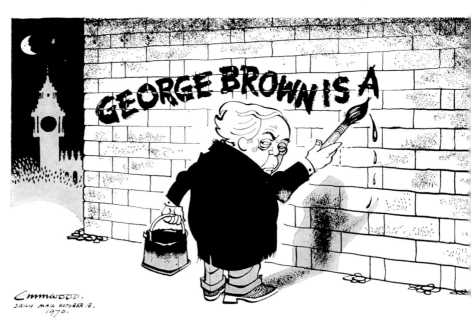

Cartoon by Emmwood

from here. They now, quite properly, do their trade with and obtain their arms from those who are willing to supply them. If we tell the absolute honest truth, there is no such thing as a united British Commonwealth. The old white dominions are looking more and more to the United States both for their defence and their trade, and our traditional ties with them are being weakened. It seems to me that a purely Commonwealth role for Britain is now unthinkable.

A third anti-European role for Britain which is sometimes canvassed is that of forming an Atlantic union or Atlantic trading area with the United States. Even if that were practicable, and I don't think it is, it could not offer a satisfactory role for Britain. The U.S. Congress is never going to allow anybody to export easily and freely into the United States in ways that might put the jobs of a Congress-man's constituents at risk. We've seen this happen over motor-cars, bicycles, aeroplanes, everything that we've ever tried to sell in the United States on any scale. Scotch whisky is, perhaps, an exception – the Americans might permit us a role as whisky suppliers, though even there a strong Bourbon lobby would be hostile. The only possible place for Britain in an Atlantic union would be as a 51st U.S. State. For all purposes, political, economic and cultural, we should become nothing but a vassal of the United States. And perhaps a not very important one at that.

Geographically, historically and in every other way the British are among the leading nations of Western Europe. I have always quarrelled with Dean Acheson's much-repeated remark about Britain's having lost an empire and not found a role. We *have* a role: our role is to lead Europe. We are, and have been for eleven centuries since the reign of King Alfred, one of the leaders of Europe. It may be that Britain is destined to become *the* leader of Europe, of Western Europe in the first place, and of as much of Europe as will come together later on. The little bit of water that comes between us and the mainland is a help in the sense that it provides a point from which you can stand back and observe without getting too involved in the passions of States in the centre of the Continent, but it is no longer a barrier because wars will never again be fought in a way that makes the Channel a barrier.

It is our business to provide political leadership, to provide the stability that for so long has eluded the democracies of the mainland of Europe. I have as much arrogant patriotism in me as anybody else, and I don't want to see Britain's becoming just one of a number of small European States. That is why I feel that we must support

o

the idea of a united Europe, play our full part in bringing it about, and offer leadership wherever we can. I don't see where else leadership can come from other than from this country. For historic and all sorts of other reasons, it is impossible for Germany to be the focal power point of the Continent: that would not be acceptable to her Western neighbours, and it would so consolidate the whole of her Eastern Communist neighbours that it would offer a challenge that the Soviet Union could hardly avoid picking up. That would be the likely road to another war. I don't think ultimate leadership can come from France, again for historic reasons. I think that the only counterbalancing force to all the old tensions of the mainland can come from Britain.

I think that this is Britain's role, but I don't want to argue it from any selfishly nationalistic point of view. With the possible exception of France under de Gaulle – and de Gaulle has now departed from the political scene – all countries in Europe fear for their own survival politically, economically and culturally unless we can build one Europe with leadership and full participation from Britain. And they don't fear only for their individual selves: they recognize that Europe itself, the whole tradition of European culture, will go under unless European peoples can unite. The Communist party is still the largest single party in several European countries and a really concerted effort at a Communist takeover could swamp the democratic heritage of Western Europe without any military adventures at all. I think it was the student power movement in 1968 that really brought home to people on the Continent the narrowness of the margin that exists between maintaining present democratic institutions and losing them, perhaps for ever. France, in particular, realized how near she came to complete disaster. The way in which de Gaulle rescued France from disaster then was one of his greatest triumphs, but there won't always be a de Gaulle around to come to the rescue. The threat to European institutions is very real and very present. There are some Englishmen who look to that little bit of water that separates us from the Continent and see in it an illusion of insularity. They think of our cultural inheritance as being our own, not part of Europe's heritage. This is wholly self-delusion. The British people have done many great things in history, but the moral and cultural inspiration behind our achievements comes from Western Christendom, which belongs to Europe as a whole. The Dutch, the French, the Germans, the Belgians, the Luxemburgers and the Italians see as clearly as we should that we share a common culture and a common heritage, and they see more readily than some of us are willing to see that we face a common danger.

Some people in Britain seem to think that by keeping ourselves to ourselves we can keep out of the way of danger. That is not only an immoral and unattractive argument, but it offers an alternative that in any case is not open to us. We can't keep out of the way of danger. If the cultural front, the democratic front, the humanitarian front, the literary front, any part of our common heritage, gets eroded on the mainland, it will be eroded here. If the rest of Europe falls to modern barbarism, we shall fall to barbarism.

So I am convinced that Britain's role is in Europe, that it is a powerful role, an influential role and one which will pay us great dividends in every way. This is what makes so much of the argument about the Common Market frustrating and irrelevant. It is not the price of butter which in the end really matters – it's the size, stability, strength and political attitude of Europe that matters. We have got to get a new kind of organization in Europe. We *must* succeed in this, and our children's children will wonder what on earth all the argument about the market was even about: to them it will be so natural a part of the scene as not to be visible. If we don't succeed, I doubt if there will be much of a Britain for our children's children at all.

But there are other practical arguments for our joining the Common Market, arguments which appeal to me strongly as a trade unionist and which should appeal to all trade unionists. If we were to try to go it alone, we should be restricted to the investment capacity that we could ourselves generate, and the job potential which our domestic market could support. Our domestic market is, for this purpose, ourselves, and the other countries which make up EFTA, the economic organization established when we failed to join the Common Market at the very beginning. Now it's true that this is quite a sizeable group, comprising a population of about 100 million. What is often forgotten, however, is that we in Britain form more than half of it. We are some 55 million, so that the EFTA extension to our domestic market was only about another 45 million. Moreover, these are people in countries which, on the whole, are not complementary but competitive with one another and with us, all making or growing and trying to sell much the same sort of thing.

By bringing Western Europe together we should provide a domestic market of some 300 million people and be associated with countries whose economies are in many ways complementary to ours. That would give us an economic base big enough to stand up to anything that the Americans or the Russians can do industrially. At present, for instance, when we invent something – let us say the computer or the hovercraft – our own requirements are so few you could almost say we take about half a dozen and that is that, and so the whole cost of research and development has to be borne by that trivial domestic requirement. Then we try to export, but our prices have to meet the enormous capital investment which cannot be recovered from domestic sales. With a domestic market comparable to that available to the Americans we could do as they do – order a sufficiently large number of 'first copies' of anything new to spread research and development costs, and so be able to export very much more cheaply.

That is one powerful argument for going into the Common Market. Another, at least equally powerful, is to question the extent to which we could afford to stay outside it. To sell British goods to the Common Market countries from outside would mean having to jump a tariff fence of 25 per cent. Now it seems to me that businessmen, certainly large international corporations, would plan their investments and provide new jobs inside that tariff fence rather than outside it. This means that all the new job opportunities would be in Rotterdam or the Ruhr or Milan rather than in the North-East or North-West of Britain, or in Scotland or South Wales. That would be a grave risk to our economic future.

So the bread-and-butter arguments as well as the moral and political arguments all add up to the necessity of our being ready to take our place in Europe. There is a more compelling reason still – the provision of a common defence for our survival.

No area of political life has changed so much – not merely for Britain, but perhaps specially for Britain – as the question of how to provide for military defence. In the years immediately after the war it was still practical to think in terms of national provision for military survival, and many people did so think. Around the middle 1950s the picture changed radically, and it became no longer sensible to think in terms of national provision at all. This was not so much because of the development of more sophisticated nuclear weapons as because of the development of delivery systems for such weapons. There can be platforms orbiting the earth from which anything they may be carrying can be brought down to any point on earth at the touch of a button. To maintain such a system of defence is certainly beyond the resources of the small nations of

Europe. This again is a powerful reason why we must make a reality of the alliance. If there are people prepared to blow up the world and to risk blowing up themselves as well, then there is no defence and considerations of defence become simply irrelevant. But so long as one assumes that statesmen are going to act rationally, then this issue remains relevant for Europe.

I doubt, however, if any of the present major countries in the world would really want to risk blowing itself up with the rest of the world. The real danger is of some grotesque accident – of misunderstanding the readiness of an adversary to carry out a threat, of a miscalculation, perhaps, of one's own capacity to wage or to survive a nuclear war. The only real defence left to the world is to prevent such a war from ever being started. This is where conventional forces, foot soldiers, people on the ground, tanks and ordinary aeroplanes are still relevant. If some nation thought that it could get away with a military attack on someone else without turning the adventure into a nuclear war, then it might be prepared to risk it. The problem, therefore, is not to provide conventional forces to fight and win a conventional war, but to provide conventional forces in sufficient strength to contain an attack for long enough to make the attackers pause before invoking nuclear retaliation; in other words, to warn any would-be aggressor that if he persists he will run the risk of tripping over the wire that will trigger off a nuclear response. But how much force is 'sufficient', and how long is 'long enough'? Most of the argument that went on when I was doing defence for the Labour Party, and has since gone on in NATO, was about these questions.

As I went more deeply into these questions I came more and more to the conclusion that democracies like ours, and those on the mainland of Europe, are simply not made to provide enough military forces for really adequate defence. My colleagues in the Labour Party, for instance, even some of the most realistic and distinguished of them, seem to think that it is a good electoral point to stress that we are spending more on education than on defence. It is doubtless a good thing to be spending more on education, but why relate this to the expenditure on defence? The attitude of mind which considers expenditure on defence a bad thing in itself makes it next to impossible to provide a sufficient force to give us even a minimum chance of containing a serious attack. If, therefore, something serious were really to happen we should have no choice but to give in or to threaten nuclear retaliation. But with the delivery systems now in being for nuclear weapons, there isn't one of us in Europe who could really carry out such a threat. If there were to be any chance of doing this, then a united Europe inside NATO provides the only possibility.

So it seems to me that our defence policy must be tied in with the Americans. It is unthinkable that we should ever go to war with America, and the only two peoples in the world we could conceivably go to war with are those of Russia or China. When I was defence spokesman for Labour I received a grant from one of the American Congressional Trusts which enabled me to spend six weeks in the United States doing anything I liked. There were no strings of any sort attached – grants like this are among the most generous and far-sighted benefits that any country could provide. I chose to spend my six weeks visiting American and NATO defence installations. I travelled right across the United States and I was shown a very large amount of what the U.S. Defense Department had at that stage to show. I was also able to begin discussions, which I have kept up ever since, with American military leaders and thinkers. When I got back to Britain I got together a team of people to advise me. They were not all Socialists, indeed, I don't think that many of them were. The late Basil Liddell-Hart played in this exercise the role that many years earlier he had played for Churchill and later for Hore-Belisha. Many top serving officers as well as retired officers also took part. Because I saw the connection between this and the rest of our life I brought into these discussions industrialists and others. I think that all of us came to the conclusion that the requirements of defence are now so changed that it is pointless to consider them in national or small-group terms. We also concluded that any major war in Europe is almost certain to involve a quick recourse to nuclear weapons unless we are to be overrun.

Thus our defence *must* be related to the defence system of the United States. But the Americans will not be willing to keep a large standing Army in Europe indefinitely. One of my worries about Vietnam was always that if the Americans were to be kicked out there, a wave of isolationism would sweep the United States, followed by a quick withdrawal from Europe. But whatever happens in Vietnam, the Americans one day will reduce their standing army in Europe to a small token force. When that happens there will be no force that could withstand an attack coming from the Eastern half of the Continent unless the rest of Europe can unite to provide its own defence. This means that Europe must be a joint partner with the United States in a common defence provision and a common defence attitude.

The idea of a European Defence Minister and a European Defence Force still frightens many people in Britain, and it will be some time before it can come about. But I have no doubt at all that it has to happen and the sooner the better. The real argument here isn't just about Europe. It concerns the provision of an American-cum-European defence provision, defence strategy and defence staff. It would be terrifying to have that if it meant only that the Pentagon did all our thinking for us. And the only way of avoiding that is to have a European equivalent of the Pentagon, not, I hope, in size, but certainly in power and influence. I don't see any possible alternative to this, and the question is simply, how soon can we bring it about?

With Britain leading a defence-organized Western Europe we should be in a position to argue plainly and bluntly with the Americans; indeed, to commit the Americans if it were ever necessary to do so. We should be big enough, and powerful enough, to have a respectable deterrent force of our own. It wouldn't be much use for the Americans to ring up Moscow and say, 'Please do understand that that rocket which has just landed on the Kremlin didn't come from America'. The fact that Europe would be in a position to commit the United States would mean that the U.S. Government would be under great constraint to agree political policies with us, and to take account of our requirements.

All this, I feel absolutely convinced, means that Britain's future rests upon her emergence as the leader of a new bloc in the world: not General de Gaulle's old 'third force'; I'm not suggesting a neutralized Europe, but a new European bloc which would have the same power and influence in the world as the old British Commonwealth had in days gone by. This is the future of our British people – vastly bigger and more important to us, our children and our children's children than petty squabbles about temporary fluctuations in the price of butter.

Until comparatively recently, the Labour Party was pretty well opposed to any involvement in Europe. There are historical reasons for this, and it says a great deal for the loyalty and fundamental common sense of the simple people of Britain that a Labour Government was able to formulate a policy of applying to join the Common Market.

In the years of Opposition up to 1964, when Mr Macmillan was trying to negotiate Britain's entry, Labour feeling, on the whole, was hostile. There were some of us who were consistently pro-European. Sam Watson, the miners' leader on the National Executive of the Labour Party, for example, was always a totally reliable colleague on this issue. But the bulk of the Party was anti-Common Market.

In the early 1960s Gaitskell himself began to waver. As he studied the problems of European defence and became more interested in NATO he couldn't help moving towards acceptance of the need for European unity. I was Deputy Leader to Gaitskell, and we talked a great deal about Europe. I knew that his line would never be as passionately and as full-bloodedly pro-European as my own, but I thought that he would support a cautious but favourable attitude towards opening negotiations for joining.

The Party, at any rate officially, was moving in the same direction. At the Party Conference in 1961 the National Executive took the line of refusing to pass judgement on the abstract question of whether or not Britain should join the Common Market, insisting that the matter could not be judged until the precise terms of entry were known. It accepted a cautious resolution, declaring:

> This Conference does not approve Britain's entry into the Common Market, unless guarantees protecting the position of British agriculture and horticulture, the EFTA countries and the Commonwealth, are obtained, and Britain retains the power of using public ownership and economic planning as measures to ensure social progress within the United Kingdom.

At the same time, however, the National Executive made it clear that Labour would support Britain's entry if those terms were met. In a broadcast in May 1962 Gaitskell elaborated this in terms that were, on the whole, favourable, saying:

> To go in on good terms would, I believe, be the best solution to this difficult problem. . . . Not to go in would be a pity, but it would not be a catastrophe. To go in on bad terms, which really meant the end of the Commonwealth, would be a step which I think we would regret all our lives, and for which history would not forgive us.

For the Party Conference of 1962 the National Executive prepared a long policy statement, setting out broad conditions which, in its view, would 'constitute reasonable terms of entry' to the Common Market. Gaitskell was to introduce this policy statement to the Conference, and I was to wind up.

Shortly before the Conference I went to France on holiday, and I'd arranged to go on to Strasbourg to make a major speech outlining what Labour policy on the Common Market was. While I was on holiday there was a meeting of Commonwealth Labour leaders in London, and when I got to Strasbourg I was met by some of our Party officials, who told me that they were not happy at the way things were going, and that they thought Gaitskell was moving back.

In the light of what they said to me I telephoned Hugh from my hotel in Strasbourg early in the morning on which I was due to make my speech and asked him whether the policy on which I thought we were agreed still held. I talked about my speech, set out the lines that it would cover, and we agreed on the telephone that I should go ahead and make it, which I did. To my considerable embarrassment a communiqué from the Commonwealth Labour leaders was issued soon afterwards, and this, to put it mildly, was hardly in keeping with the line I had taken. This was a little reminiscent of the situation in which poor Maxwell-Fyfe found himself when he had been put up by the Tory Government to make a pro-European speech at Strasbourg almost at the same time as Mr Eden, then Foreign Secretary, spoke in the totally opposite vein in Rome. That had completely flattened poor Maxwell-Fyfe and did a lot of harm to the reputation of the British among all the delegations at Strasbourg.

My situation wasn't quite as bad as that, but it was a little uncomfortable. When I got back to London I found that Mr Nash, who was then Prime Minister of New Zealand, and who was a specially close friend of Hugh's, had done a tremendous job to persuade everybody of the dangers which would come about for New Zealand if Britain joined the Market, and that he had been backed up by the delegate from India, with a passionate plea on behalf of the poor and downtrodden peoples of Asia if they lost their markets in Britain. Gaitskell had an Indian background – his father had served in India – and he was always susceptible to emotional pressure from India. The result was to put a distinctly different interpretation on what I had believed to be the Labour policy.

Nothing much happened, however, because we had to go off to our own Conference in Brighton, where the National Executive's policy statement was to be introduced. Harold Wilson at that time was very active in public in leading the anti-Marketeers in the Party, and we'd had a lot of difficulty in drafting the statement. But we had got it drafted in the end, and although it was too cautious and too hedged around for my liking, it did favour a policy of trying to get in. I went over it all again and again with Hugh, and since I had to wind up the debate I kept asking if I could have a look at the speech with which he was going to open it. Like Wilson, Hugh was given to reading his speeches, so that written texts were always available. He continually said, 'Of course, certainly', but he didn't show me the speech. We were staying at the same hotel for the Conference, and very late on the night before the Common Market debate was due to open I went up to him and said, 'You know, I'm getting a bit suspicious of what you are going to do tomorrow. You obviously aren't going to show me your speech, and I'm asking myself, Why? You are not going to switch the line, are you?'

He put his arm round my shoulder and said, 'You know me better than that. I'd never do a thing like that.' And I have no doubt that is how he thought of it at that moment. Anyway, we all went to bed.

Next morning, he made an hour-long speech of tremendous force and power, which, while it did not formally close the door on the possibility of negotiations with the Common Market, was emotionally totally opposed to Britain's having any involvement with the Continent of Europe. This was the speech containing the famous phrase that for Britain to join any form of European federation 'means the end of a thousand years of history'.

Emotionally, intellectually, and in the manner of its delivery this speech was most compelling. It was followed by a standing ovation, led to my horror by Wilson and all the anti-Gaitskellites. Frank Cousins, of the Transport Workers, who had been bitterly anti-Gaitskell, was one of the leaders of the demonstration, and he announced that his union would pay for a million copies of 'this great speech' to be printed and circulated throughout the country. Sam Watson and I, who had led the fight in the National Executive to get the policy document, unsatisfactory as it was, into some sort of European context, looked at each other, wondering what on earth we did next. We did, as a matter of historical fact, drag ourselves to our feet, but without any obvious enthusiasm, as the photographs of the occasion show. Then we adjourned for lunch.

I went back to the hotel in an absolutely raging temper. Sam Watson, Gerry Reynolds and Sidney Jacobson, who was then political editor of the *Daily Mirror*, joined me in my room. I remember flinging my glasses across the room and breaking them, so that I was in the position of having to make a new winding-up speech from notes that I couldn't even read. My wife was so scared of all the noise that was going on in our room that she decided to go down to lunch, and promptly fell down the staircase. We laugh at it now, but it wasn't so funny then.

The rest of us sent for some sandwiches, and decided that however silly it might look we should just have to continue to fight for the policy set out in the policy document. Somehow we concocted a new winding-up speech, and I made it during the afternoon.

Reading it now, I think it must be one of the worst speeches I have ever made. But, somehow, without getting howled down by anybody, I succeeded in stating the case for going into Europe, and somehow persuaded the Conference that that was what Gaitskell had really been intending to say all the way through. The anti-Europeans looked bloody thunder, but the pro-Europeans were delighted, and my speech got quite a reasonable reception from the audience. At the Executive meeting which followed that day, Peggy Herbison moved that the Party should accept Mr Cousins's kind offer to reprint and circulate the Gaitskell speech, provided that my speech, and the policy statement, were printed with it. Nobody could see any way of stopping this, so this wonderful pamphlet went out, containing Gaitskell's speech, my speech, and the policy we were supposed to be supporting.

This may seem ludicrous now, and in a way it was ludicrous then, but the outcome of that conference was really exceedingly important. If it had gone the other way, the Labour Party would have been tied to an anti-European position, and not even Harold Wilson could have embarked upon the policy which he subsequently did. In the early months of 1967 Harold Wilson, now converted, and I were enabled to make our trip round the capitals of Europe as a direct result of that debate.

In our talks with Common Market statesmen the Prime Minister took a surprisingly firm line in favour of Britain's applying to join the Market. Voluminous records of all our talks had to be taken to satisfy suspicious colleagues in the Cabinet.

In Europe the main opposition to the idea of Britain's joining the Common Market came from France under de Gaulle. A month or so before the Prime Minister and I called on General de Gaulle in January 1967, I had made an official visit to Paris as Foreign Secretary to attend a NATO ministerial meeting. At a dinner given by the French Foreign Secretary, M. Couve de Murville, I naturally discussed the Common Market, and, rather pulling Couve de Murville's leg, I remarked to him, 'Of course there's not much point in my putting all these questions to you, because you're not the chap who can give the answers.' To my surprise, he said, 'Would you like to see the chap who can give the answers?' I said, 'Yes, rather,' though I still thought that he was joking.

But next morning I was invited to the Élysée Palace and there received by de Gaulle himself. De Gaulle was alone except for his interpreter, and we had an hour-long talk about the whole question of Britain and the Common Market. I argued as strongly as I could about all that Britain meant to Europe and the great part that she could play in Europe, but it was very clear that de Gaulle was adamantly against us. He regarded the Continent as France's place and the Atlantic Ocean and the United States as Britain's place. It was at this meeting that de Gaulle made his famous remark about the impossibility of two cocks living in one farmyard with ten hens. He said that he had had a lot of trouble getting the five hens to do what France wanted, and he wasn't going to have Britain's coming in and creating trouble all over again, this time with ten.

All this, however, was exceedingly friendly. De Gaulle made himself most agreeable to me; indeed, when I went he made quite a fuss of me, and insisted on coming out to see me off.

There were no observers present at that meeting, and no minutes kept, which brought a fairly cool breeze around me from anti-Market members of the Cabinet when I got back. When the Prime Minister and I made our official visit to de Gaulle on 24 January 1967, we had a retinue of advisers and observers with us. Everything was exceedingly formal. De Gaulle had his Ministers ranged alongside him and we sat opposite, ranged alongside of the Prime Minister. There was no conversation, there were no discussions in the ordinary sense. We said our bit and we listened to what de Gaulle had to say, and that was that. After this de Gaulle and the Prime Minister had a short private chat, and the visit closed with a sort of foursome between de Gaulle and Couve de Murville and Harold Wilson and me. There were no officials present at this final meeting, and it went on for some time. There was no shaking de Gaulle's opposition to having Britain in the Common Market, but again he was friendly and he went out of his way to say how impressed (as he put it) he had been by his meeting with me in the previous month.

The outcome of our tour round Europe was that we persuaded the Cabinet to recommend to Parliament that Britain should make a formal application to join the Common Market. This was tabled as a resolution and it received an overwhelming vote in the House.

This time our application was hedged around with practically no conditions at all. One of the things that had always worried people was what Britain might commit herself to by adhering to the Treaty of Rome, but I'd long ago discovered that the Treaty of Rome, like the Bible, takes account of any possible sin, provides the antidote and thereby offers ways and means of obtaining sanctity afterwards. On our tour of Europe the Prime Minister also learned this. We found that other people bound by the Treaty of Rome had managed to provide for all their private troubles, and it was pretty obvious that we could provide for ours, even within the terms of the treaty.

But now we met a really absurd difficulty. We in Britain had agreed to make an application to join the Common Market, but France refused to have our application tabled before the Commission which is the controlling authority for membership. How, then, was our application to be brought officially to the attention of the Commission? It couldn't discuss an application that it was not allowed to see. How were we to overcome French opposition and make sure that the Commission did see it?

An opportunity arose in July. It would require, perhaps, a little diplomatic sleight of hand, but I thought it could be done. This is how it came about.

On 4 July 1967 there was a meeting of the Council of Ministers of the Western European Union at The Hague. By tradition, one session of these W.E.U. meetings is always devoted to a debate on the European economy, and this is attended by members of the Economic Commission for Europe, the Common Market Commission. I had been invited to open this debate and I decided to use the occasion to put forward our application in such a way that official notice would have to be taken of it. It was a tricky business. First, I had to get my speech approved by the Cabinet, and this was not easy. It was the only speech I ever made as a Minister where every single word was vetted by the full Cabinet beforehand. It was an absolute work of art to get the speech into a form which was sufficiently enthusiastic to please the Commission and the other countries in Europe, and could yet carry my more doubtful colleagues in the Cabinet with me.

However, this was done. Then the speech had to be made, and I had to use a good deal of subtlety here. If I tried to hand in our formal application during the debate, the French representatives would have objected that this was not the right occasion for making it. So I made my speech in two parts. The speech contained fifty paragraphs, and the first forty-nine were all about our reasons for wanting to join Europe. The fiftieth paragraph said,

> I hope that the statement which I have made to you this afternoon will help the Community in its consideration of our application and enable negotiations to open as soon as the opinion of the Commission has been given. . . . I am, therefore, formally conveying the text of my statement to you, Herr Brandt, as Chairman of the single Council of Ministers of the European Communities. I shall also convey copies to the President of the Commission. I am also arranging for the text to be made public in the United Kingdom.

When I opened the debate I delivered the first forty-nine paragraphs of my speech. I knew that by custom at these W.E.U. meetings the opener of a debate is always invited to have the last word, so when I was called upon to wind up I delivered the fiftieth paragraph containing the formal conveyance of our application, and I duly handed the full text of all fifty paragraphs – printed as a whole, with no asterisks or anything to separate the last paragraph from the rest – to the Chairman and the President, Jean Louis Rey. Herr Brandt, the Chairman, was, of course, well-disposed to us, so our formal application was put in before the French realized what was happening.

I cannot conclude this chapter without saying a little more about Sam Watson, who was my staunchest ally in the early years of persuading the Labour Party to support a pro-European policy. Once Bevin and Arthur Deakin had gone, Sam Watson was the outstanding intellect among trade unionists. He was the Durham miners' leader, and I always felt it a great pity that his love of Durham prevented his coming to London as a national officer of the Mineworkers Union. He was a member of the National Executive of the Labour Party and of many national bodies, but Durham was his home and where he had his heart. If he had ever cared to seek national office many things, I think, might have turned out differently. As it was, his national influence was considerable. He was a great thinker and must have been one of the most widely read men in the whole Labour movement.

His formal schooling ended when he left an elementary school at Bolton to work underground in the pits, but he made himself highly educated in every sense. This was recognized by the University of Durham when it conferred an honorary doctorate upon him in 1955. Sam had his emotional prejudices, no doubt, and sometimes he was too uncritically pro-American. But such prejudices as he had were open, and could be discounted. He brought his great intellect to bear on every issue that cropped up, and he was a wonderful counsellor and friend. He never raged and tore around like Bevin and some of the other great trade union leaders; indeed, he hardly ever raised his voice. But once he had given his loyalty to a cause or course of action that he was intellectually convinced was right, he had a rock-like stability that nothing on earth could shake. It didn't matter what anybody tried, cajoled or bullied, Sam would stand firm. He had a rare integrity, and our Labour movement owes much to him.

12

Reflections
on the Middle East

WHAT FIRST PROMPTED me to become deeply interested in the problems of the Middle East I do not know. It is a question I have often asked myself, and for all my probing I cannot wholly answer it. Some part, unquestionably, is due to my feeling for British interests in the area and the impact on those interests of events in the Arab world. Some part is certainly due to my oddly inherited Irish background, which made me an anti-imperialist and gave me sympathy for other people who were trying to throw off the yoke of imperialism – sympathy and, I hope, understanding of the dangers of throwing out the ox with the yoke. As my life developed it is good, I think, that I had these sensitivities – good, I mean, not just for me but for the work I was trying to do. Whether all these interests would have 'jelled', as they say, without one of those odd coincidental happenings that have marked my life I don't know.

When the Labour Government fell in 1951, I found myself somewhat at a loose end. I was still young, but I had been a full Minister in the Government and the sudden return to an almost completely private life left me restless. This is where the coincidence comes in. I have written earlier of my friend Mont Follick, a rich, eccentric and remarkable man who was a Labour M.P. It would be hard to think of anything that could link me with Mont Follick had it not been for the fact that in the early 1930s I had spoken for him on a famous 'spouter's corner' known as Effie Road when he had stood for West Fulham.

Not long after I found myself in the wilderness in 1951 I was telephoned one day by a man, now dead, called George Newport. I didn't know him, but he explained that he was the agent in Britain for a big contracting firm in the Middle East known as C.A.T. (the Contracting and Trading Company), one of whose main

owners was an Arab called Emile Bustani. George Newport explained that he had been given my name by Mont Follick. Bustani,
for whom Newport was acting, wanted to invite some British
Members of Parliament to visit the Middle East as his guests.
Bustani was Lebanese, but he had come originally from Palestine. He
was a man of great idealism, and one of his chief purposes in life was
to try to get people to understand the realities of the situation in
the Middle East. It was for this reason that he was trying to arrange
for British M.P.s to visit the area.

Much as I respected Mont Follick, I saw no particular reason
why I should go to the Middle East, so I turned down the invitation.
But it was repeated, Mont Follick thought that I ought to go, and
finally I agreed to join him and Dr Reginald Bennett, then Tory
M.P. for Gosport, in visiting the Middle East as guests of Emile
Bustani.

Emile Bustani, now alas buried under the waters that lap the
beaches of Beirut after an air accident in March 1963, was one of
the most fascinating characters I have ever met. In these days the
word 'millionaire' is tossed about rather easily, but Bustani really
was a millionaire, and many times over. He was a fierce businessman,
and from contracting originally for the British Army he had built
up an enormous trading empire, owning hotels and goodness
knows what – there seemed to be hardly anything he wasn't involved in. As well as all this he was pretty well a full-time politician.
He was a member of the Lebanese Parliament and organized all
sorts of political events. He was also a genuine idealist with vivid
ideas on how the Middle East could be made peaceful. Although
he was a patriotic Arab, he was no anti-Jew. His concern when I
first met him was that people in the West should have some real
understanding of the fact that there *was* an Arab case in the Middle
East. He felt that there was general Western knowledge of Israel's
case and of Israeli sufferings, but little conception of the Arab case
and of Arab sufferings. It was this that had prompted him to invite
us as British M.P.s to visit the area.

It was through Emile Bustani that I first met King Hussein of
Jordan; through Bustani that I met Nasser in the year he came to
power; it was through Bustani that I met Nuri Pasha of Iraq,
later to be ignominiously hanged in the costume of a woman because
we in Britain made the mistakes that Bustani feared we would make.
It was through Bustani that I came to know all the characters, the
revolutionaries as well as the members of the establishment, who

With Mrs Golda Meir,
Prime Minister of Israel, 1970

With President Nasser
of the U.A.R., 1970

With constituents,
Swadlincote, May 1970

made history in the Middle East over the next ten years. I used to go out every winter and spend weeks talking to them all, getting to know them so well that when they came to Europe they would talk to me, helping me to understand what they wanted and try to reconcile this with what our interests really required. Although married into a Jewish family, and on terms of intimate friendship with many Arabs, I never took on either a Zionist or an Arab colouring. I had in fact opposed the establishment of a Zionist state in Israel in the early days because I was then close to Bevin and saw things through his eyes. But that didn't make me anti-Israeli. The state of Israel having been established, it seemed to me crystal-clear that the state would have to live.

My Arab friends never expected me to take a different position, and were always willing not only to have me as a visitor, but to receive my wife too. The idea that Nasser, or, indeed, any of the leading Arab statesmen are anti-Israeli is, in my view, wrong. They were – and are – fighting for an arrangement in their homeland which would give them all the kind of rights that any people would ask for themselves. And they were all conscious, as Bustani used to explain to me, that if too much time went by without a settlement in the Middle East, they would lose control of the situation and extremists would arise who would not be willing to make statesman-like arrangements.

My first visit to the Middle East stays vividly in my mind. It came just after Christmas in 1951 – I arrived in Beirut for the first time on New Year's Day, 1952. On the eve of the Eastern Orthodox Christmas, which is celebrated on 6 January, I was in Amman and feeling excruciatingly ill. This had nothing to do with Arab feasting, but was because I had been vaccinated for the first time just before leaving England and in Amman the vaccination 'took'. For some reason that I have never understood, my parents were against vaccination on some mysterious ideological grounds. So I had never been vaccinated before. The effects were horrible. I felt fearfully ill, and had we not had Dr Bennett with us, I don't know what might have happened.

But the chance of visiting Bethlehem on Christmas Eve was too great an opportunity to be missed, so although I felt more dead than alive, I got in a car with Bustani and set off on the drive from Amman to Bethlehem. I slept for a time in the car and suddenly woke up to one of the most wonderful sights I've ever seen. It was a frosty, bright moonlit night, and the fearsome road was tooled on the edge of the mountainside. In the light of an enormous moon we passed a string of donkeys and camels, and suddenly, right ahead in the cold, clear night I saw a huge star blazing in the sky. 'There,' said Bustani, 'is Bethlehem' – and there was the star. In my half-awake, half-drugged state it was hard not to think that some time-machine had taken me back to the very first Christmas Eve. All my knowledge of Bible scenes then came from picture books, and this was a picture-book scene. The donkeys, the shadowy people march-ing along leading them, and that wonderful, shining star . . . surely it *was* the first Christmas Eve.

The star, in fact, was a plastic one, placed over the church in Bethlehem, but we couldn't see the church when we first saw the star from the winding road in the hills and it gave an extraordinary impression that we really were following it, like the shepherds of old.

We came to Bethlehem to find the place packed with visitors and pilgrims, assembled to attend the midnight Mass in the Church of the Nativity, which is said to be built right over the Manger. I remember being received by a tall Arab, who was then, I think, the Military Governor of the province – years later, I am sad to say, he was rather badly wounded in the Six-Day War. He greeted us with the little cups of coffee that I came to know so well, and then we proceeded to the church. The service was a strange experience, for not only the Eastern Orthodox Christians, but every other sect that regards that day as Christmas Eve seemed to be holding services simultaneously. All had microphones and loudspeakers, and in the babble that went on, it was hard to keep one's mind on the service. Because there were so many competing Christian sects, the church then was administered and looked after by Moslems – perhaps no one else could keep the peace! That is how it came about that an Arab leader took me in. Of course, not all Arabs are Moslems, Bustani, for example, was a Christian, and his family are still Christians.

After the service we went down to the Manger. It is said to be on the site of the original Manger – at any rate, there is still a Manger there. A little service took place beside it, and then everybody lined up to kiss the relic. This was an intensely moving experience, far more moving than I can hope to convey in words.

On that and on succeeding annual visits I met most of the people who mattered in the Middle East. I found Nasser a most attractive personality, and I liked his lack of ostentation and modest way of living. In those days his family were young and we sat and talked round his lunch-table, with babies crawling in and out under the table, exactly as one might sit in anybody's home. Nasser was very proud then to look like a British Army officer, and he certainly had no hostility to the British as such. One of my great reasons for admiring him is that he went with the tide as much as any politician needs to, and yet never lost sight of the dangers he was running. When I first spoke to him about his involvement with Russia he was sharply clear about it. We were talking about arms and he said to me, 'I am going to get what I have to get as an Arab leader from wherever I can get it. I shall always ask the West first' – at that stage Nasser thought of himself more as a British officer than anything else – 'but if the West refuses me, well, I shall still get it. You must understand, Mr Brown, that we are no longer a colonial people.' In the end he did what I had warned him that he would do, and he became over-involved with the Russians. I recall sadly what turned out to be my last meeting with him in January 1970 when I asked him what he felt about that conversation we had had almost twenty years before. He smiled wryly and said: 'I will tell you a little story, Mr Brown. Some time ago now Mr Khrushchev attacked me in public, and I answered him back in public. He repeated the attack – I answered him back again. If Mr Kosygin were to attack me now, I would not say a word.'

After a number of my visits to the Middle East some people in the Labour Party began to feel that I was in danger of becoming too involved with the Arab case. Hugh Gaitskell was among them. He never tried to discourage me from visiting Arab countries, but he was passionately pro-Zionist, having married into a prominent Zionist family. No pressure was ever put on me to desert my Arab friends, but efforts were made to enable me to meet Israeli leaders. I welcomed these meetings and got to know men like General Yigal Allon, who became Deputy Prime Minister of Israel, and General Moshe Dayan, later to be famous as the Israeli hero of the Six-Day War.

In 1955 I was invited to visit Israel, and accepted the invitation gladly. I was warned by everybody, because I was still a relatively new hand, that I must have two passports, one to show to the Israelis, the other for the Arabs, the argument being that no Arab State would ever admit you on a passport with an Israeli stamp on it. This made me feel intensely pro-British, and I remember hitting the table hard and saying that I proposed to travel on one British passport and that if anybody wouldn't let me in on my British passport then they could damned well shut me out.

Against everyone's advice I took one passport with Arab and Israeli visas in the same book, and I have shown this passport all the way round the Middle East without meeting any trouble. On that particular trip I'd arranged to go on from Israel to Jordan. I entered Jordan by the Mandelbaum Gate in Jerusalem, which was then one of the exits from Israel into Jordan, though it is now incorporated in Israel. My wife and I went to the Gate in a British car, and I had one foot in Israel, saying good-bye, kissing, and being kissed by, all the Israeli officials, and the other foot in Jordan, where a group of Jordanian dignitaries were holding out their hands to me. My farewell to the Israelis and my welcome by the Jordanians were carried out in full view of each side, and as far as I could see everybody was entirely happy about it.

This passport business is symptomatic of the things that people invent or exaggerate out of all proportion to exacerbate the bitterness that is said to exist between Arab and Jew. Of course there is bitterness and bad feeling, but talk about the impossibility of getting Jew and Arab to live together is simply not true. It may be harder now after the Six-Day War than it was then, but there is still no fundamental reason why Arabs and Jews should not be able to live side by side.

On that trip I made an extensive tour of Israel and saw the wonderful things that the Israelis were doing then, and are doing still, to reclaim the desert and to increase the fertility of the country. I saw the towns of Beersheba and Curiagat and went to a place that until then I had never heard of but which was to become very familiar in my subsequent career – the Gulf of Aqaba with its port of Eilat. I had talks with most of the leading politicians in Israel except Ben-Gurion. He was one of the few political leaders in the whole world who have declined to meet me. He had been briefed, I suppose, about my activities and had misunderstood them, and perhaps he had been reminded of my admiration for Bevin. Anyway, whenever I was in Jerusalem or Tel Aviv and tried to see him, I was told that he had just gone to his *kibbutz*, and when I was on my way down south and suggested that we should make a slight detour and call on his *kibbutz*, I was informed that unexpectedly he had just gone back to Tel Aviv. So I never met Ben-Gurion.

I was Foreign Secretary during the Six-Day War between Israel and the Arab world. I did everything I could, first to try to prevent the war from breaking out, and afterwards to devise some basis for a peaceful settlement.

The Israelis had by now annexed *de facto* if not formally, large new areas of Arab land, and there were now very many more refugees. It was clear that what Israel, or at least many of her leaders, really wanted was permanently to colonize much of this newly annexed Arab territory, particularly the Jordan valley, Jerusalem and other sensitive areas. This led me into a flurry of activity at the United Nations, which resulted in the near miracle of getting the famous resolution – Resolution No. 242 – unanimously adopted by the Security Council. We took over the drafting of this resolution when pretty well everybody else had failed. Lord Caradon (Hugh Foot), who was then British Minister at the United Nations, and his deputy, that indefatigable man Leslie Glass, did an absolutely monumental job of sounding out all the other delegations to give us an idea of what we might be able to get in the way of agreement on our resolution. There were some who didn't want us to table a resolution at all for fear that we might go down, but we persevered, and when the time came for us to table our resolution we felt that we had a chance of getting it through. Much to everybody's surprise, on 22 November 1967 we did.

This resolution set out in a most carefully balanced way what the Israelis and the Arabs would have to do to secure both peace in the Middle East and recognition of the State of Israel. I have been pressed many times to spell out exactly what the resolution meant, but I've always refused to go farther than what it says. It declares 'the inadmissibility of the acquisition of territory by war' and it also affirms the necessity 'for guaranteeing the territorial inviolability and political independence of every State in the area'. It calls for 'withdrawal of Israeli armed forces from territories occupied in the recent conflict' and also for 'termination of all claims or states of belligerency'.

It does *not* call for Israeli withdrawal from 'the' territories recently occupied, nor does it use the word 'all'. It would have been impossible to get the resolution through if either of these words had been included, but it does set out the lines on which negotiations for a settlement must take place. Each side must be prepared to give up something: the resolution doesn't attempt to say *precisely* what, because that is what negotiations for a peace-treaty must be about. However unpromising it may look, the fact of the matter is that Resolution 242 is the *only* basis on which negotiations for a peace-treaty can ever be started. It is both interesting and important that, whatever is said by anybody, the one thing on which all parties are agreed is that they still claim to accept Resolution 242. (I give the text in full as an appendix.)

But perhaps my greatest effort to bring about a settlement in the Middle East came after I had left office, when I made my Middle Eastern journey in the three weeks from 28 December 1969 to 19 January 1970. That was not exactly an attempt at personal diplomacy, but it was a personal diplomatic effort that was made possible only by my friendships in the Middle East. I went as a private citizen, although I was, of course, a Member of Parliament and Deputy Leader of the Labour Party. The official purpose of the trip was a fact-finding mission for the Labour Party, and it was made possible by a generous grant from the Ariel Foundation, established in 1960 'to encourage by practical means understanding between countries'. This splendid grant, with no strings of any sort attached, not only enabled me to go, but also allowed me to be accompanied by Mr Gwyn Morgan, assistant general secretary of the Labour Party, and by Miss Jean Elliott, my secretary. I could not commit the British Government in any way and I was not a spokesman for the Government – in that, it may be, lay the value of the tour. Although I had no official position, I was received everywhere like a visiting statesman; Heads of State and leading Ministers made time to see me, and talked frankly of their problems. The Foreign Office, while not in any way responsible for me, courteously extended to me the facilities of our embassies and missions in the countries I visited.

As I went from capital to capital on this tour I realized just how much we had missed our opportunities over the past decade. The Russians had built up a powerful position. The sheikhly families, although still strong in some places, were mostly on the defensive. The idea of a British physical presence was anathema to everybody, and although we had rebuilt some part of our original goodwill as a result of reopening relations with Nasser, we were not really in the picture. For some odd reason that I cannot explain, the French were. My visit came shortly after the famous 'escape' of the frigates from Cherbourg. My Arab friends seemed able to accept this without much anxiety, and I asked what they would have said if the same ships had 'escaped' from Devonport and proceeded to Israel. It seemed a reasonable question, but there were no clear answers.

Why the Arab world seems able to adopt a double standard so far as the French are concerned I do not know: it is a severe criticism of the way we have conducted our political affairs in the Middle East.

One of the greatest stupidities of British foreign policy has been to underrate Nasser. I think back to my last conversation with him a few months before his death and I remember him as a sophisticated, careful, Western-orientated man. As I recall my travels from country to country, and think of all the people I met in different places, I feel more than ever strongly how vital it is that there should be a settlement which will establish Israel's rights and yet deal with the undoubted grievances of the Arab peoples. How will the Gulf be organized after Britain's departure? People in Britain are inclined to half-laugh at Arab sheikhs in their robes and wonderful head-dresses, but these leaders are wise and worried men. They are trying to work out arrangements for mutual survival against much traditional hostility and dislike. This brings me to one of the world's greatest men – Mohamed Reza, Shah of Iran.

I had met the Shah once or twice in England, but had never spent any real time with him. In January 1970 I was able to talk to him at length, at first with officials present and then for a considerable time alone. The Shah carries on his shoulders an enormous responsibility. He has to face internal problems and the presence of the Russians on his border: he has to try to secure peace in the Gulf without invoking any of the old hostilities between Iran and the Arab world. He has built up an arrangement with Israel and contrived to avoid unpopularity as a result. I think of him as one of the wisest and most courageous men I have known, and I treasure the remark he made to me when I left. He said: 'Mr Brown, I am so glad we have had this talk. I wish I had known you better earlier.' I can but echo his sentiment.

Many other people come to mind. In a unique position is King Hussein of Jordan. It is natural for people to say now that he has shown unbelievable courage. But if you say this sort of thing often enough it ceases to sound valid – yet it is true. From the day when his grandfather King Abdullah was shot at his side because some people thought that Abdullah was willing to make an arrangement with the Israelis, King Hussein has remained loyal to Abdullah's vision and loyal to his Western (dare I say British?) connections. By sheer personal physical courage, King Hussein has quelled every revolt in his country. Nasser needed Hussein greatly, and Hussein

needed Nasser. Both wanted a settlement in the Middle East. Now
Hussein has to go it alone until time shows what leadership the
U.A.R. can produce to succeed Nasser. The Western world must
recognize the weight on King Hussein. A new dimension has arisen
– an Arab state that knows no physical borders. We know it as the
Palestine Liberation Organization. It includes many faces, many
forces, many ideologies. From it comes a threat with which not only
King Hussein has to contend, but the precariously balanced Leban-
non as well. The Palestine Liberation Organization has been moder-
ately led – people laugh at me when I talk about moderate leaders
in the Arab world, but I use the word with care and meaning.
I would place Arafat in that category. If the West does not understand the situation and enable moderate leaders to establish their
position, their principles and their rights, if Israel does not grasp
the opportunity, we may find all the moderates swept away. I am
sure that the Russians do not want a bloody conflict to start in the
Middle East, but they are quite happy with the situation in which
they seem to be the only people capable of making any real headway.

I think back particularly to my visit to Baghdad. Since my visit
to Poland referred to in an earlier chapter, I have never seen a more
obviously Soviet-controlled armed camp. The tanks at street corners,
the long barrels of the guns, haunt me still. And yet in Baghdad
I met and talked to men who really understand the nature of the
threat facing them, and the nature of the whole Middle Eastern
problem. I imagine I would do nobody any good if I were to
identify people by name. But one important Minister stands out.
If he reads this book he will know who he is. I can say only that
I wish him all the luck in the world in trying to bring Iraq, so vital
to the West as well as to the Middle East, through its present unhappy
involvement with the Soviets.

We wound up our tour in Israel, spending five very crowded
days there. I had two meetings with the Prime Minister, Mrs Golda
Meir, and at one of them we had a rather passionate clash because
I thought that she was being unrealistically determined to have a
military victory. I told her plainly how disappointed I was to meet
this attitude. Two days later I got a message from the Deputy
Prime Minister, General Yigal Allon, inviting my wife and me to
dine with him alone at his *kibbutz*. He wanted to talk to me without
others to hear everything that was said. What I didn't realize at
once was that it wasn't any of our people whom he wanted to shut

Talking with constituents, Swadlincote, May 1970

Electioneering, Stevenage, June 1970

Setting off on his election campaign
tour, 1 June 1970

out: he wanted to get me away from some of the people who had been accompanying me around on behalf of the Israeli Government, and whom I had naturally treated as being fair-thinking because they had been selected to talk to me. What I had not realized was the extent of the division between the hawks and doves and the suspicion that each side had of the other. General Allon was the leader of the moderates, and Mrs Meir had specially asked him to see me, to explain exactly what the situation was and, as she put it, 'to disabuse my mind of any idea that she herself did not desperately want a peaceful settlement'. A similar message was later conveyed to me by Mr Reuven Barkatt, the Speaker of the Knesset (the Israeli Parliament).

General Allon discussed with me at great length, just as President Nasser had done, the kind of timetable for a peace settlement that might be possible, the things that were negotiable and the things that it would be very difficult indeed to regard as negotiable. It became clear to me that there was in fact little that the more moderate Israelis wanted which would seriously disturb Nasser if he were free enough to make an agreement which could not give all *his* colleagues everything they wanted. I was told that Mrs Meir was satisfied that she could carry the country overwhelmingly in support of a peace-treaty, and that she could carry her Party in Parliament by a large majority, though not quite such an overwhelming one. I was also authorized, if I could find some way of getting negotiations started through my personal associations with President Nasser and King Hussein, to go ahead and do so. Later, after I had got back to England, General Allon came to London on a much-publicized visit to see the Prime Minister and Foreign Secretary. He also made a completely unpublicized visit late at night to my flat, to repeat and to confirm the proposition he had made to me at his *kibbutz*.

It was the divisions between the Israeli hawks and doves that led to the widely reported row at a dinner given to me by the Foreign Minister, Mr Abba Eban, on my last night in Israel. Eban is known to be a moderate, and earlier in the evening of his dinner-party I had had a long private talk with him. He knew all about General Allon's discussions with me, and he wanted to reinforce what I had been told about Mrs Meir's real attitude, to make sure that I had not misunderstood the messages that had been sent to me. So we went to dinner, to what I imagined to be a sort of family party. It still hadn't struck me that there would be representatives of the other

side, as it were. I had a fairly relaxed evening, and when conversation round the dinner table got under way I tried to get some further
views on the sort of timetable for peace that the people there would
accept. But among the guests was General Chaim Hertzog, whose
wife is a sister of Abba Eban's wife. The more I tried to get a general
discussion on a timetable for peace, the more he and some who
apparently thought with him refused to accept any kind of timetable at all. I felt that they were trying to tell me that Eban, who,
after all, was Foreign Minister, did not really have the influence that
I was led to believe he had. I got rather fractious and rubbed up by
all this, and particularly irritated by the thought that all my private
talks with the moderates had apparently been monitored by the
hawks. I thought back to a talk I'd had a bit earlier with General
Ezer Weizman, who had recently become Minister of Transport,
and who had formerly commanded the Israeli Air Force. He had
said, 'It's nice to see you here, it's nice of you to take the trouble to
come, it's nice of you to be interested in our problems, but I wish
to God you'd go away, George.'

I had said, 'How charming. Why?'

To this he replied, 'Well, you see, these silly so-and-so's' – that
was the language he used meaning the politicians – 'can be talked
into thinking that we should pay some price for peace. I don't want
to pay any price for peace. We've won the war already.'

I felt that the hawks were trying to make sure that I went away
from Israel with the hawkish tale ringing in my ears, and I was
hurt and angry that these views should be put to me at what I had
supposed was a private dinner party given by my friends. The only
thing to do was to go away. So I pleaded that I was tired, my wife
reinforced the plea, and I went.

Back in London I thought deeply over what to do. General
Allon had left me, saying, 'If you get in touch with your friend, I'll
go anywhere to meet anybody, so long as it is somebody of similar
authority and standing.' He named a person in Egypt who would
be acceptable to him on the assumption that President Nasser
wasn't ready to make a start. General Allon's assumption was that
I would go to see him myself, but this I ruled out on two grounds:
firstly, it would have been too dramatic, and secondly, it would
have set every trail alight.

I thought of approaching Nasser through the Foreign Office, but
then I thought that the more the Foreign Office was kept out of
things officially at that stage, the better. If things went wrong, it

would be preferable to be able to disown my efforts as a private episode.

Then I thought again of Humphrey Trevelyan, who had come so nobly to the rescue in Aden. Lord Trevelyan was back at work in the City, but he knew Nasser, who had a great respect for him. I asked Trevelyan whether he would go to Cairo, ostensibly on business, and deliver a letter for me. After a little hesitation he said, 'Yes'.

Somehow the mechanics of the journey were arranged and shortly afterwards Lord Trevelyan took a plane to Cairo carrying my notes with him. They were headed 'Speaker's Notes', and he had complete authority to speak from them, keep them to himself, or hand them to Nasser as a memorandum.

Now comes an apt illustration of the difference in attitudes of people in our Foreign Service. I wanted to warn Nasser that a message was on its way to him, and I also wanted to explain to King Hussein what I was doing, so that he would learn about the message to Nasser directly from me and not hear about it first from other sources. So I wrote letters both to Nasser and King Hussein, and sent them via the Foreign Office in the official bag to our respective ambassadors in Cairo and Amman, asking that they should be delivered as soon as possible. The ambassador in Amman, then Sir Philip Adams, was an exceptionally bright, sympathetic and energetic person. He took my message seriously, and he delivered my letter to King Hussein at once: I had a reply from King Hussein before Sir Philip's colleague in Cairo had even got around to delivering my letter to Nasser. I'd guarded against Hussein's being upset by hearing about things first from Cairo: what happened now was that Cairo heard from Amman. Lord Trevelyan arrived in Cairo on a Saturday, and my letter to Nasser warning him of his visit was not delivered until the Monday after he got there. Nasser agreed to see him at once, and an interview was arranged for the following day, but what should have been a very full week-end turned out to be one interview at the very end of his visit.

Alas, the message that Lord Trevelyan brought back was a disappointing one. Nasser had been ill since I had seen him in January, and he seemed physically changed, with much of his enthusiasm gone. And then, of course, the situation had changed, with a great increase in the activities of the Palestine Liberation Organization, and an apparently narrow escape by King Hussein from being ousted. The upshot of all this was that Nasser was not at all

forthcoming about the idea of anybody's attending a meeting with
the Israelis, but he didn't tell me, like General Weizman, 'Thank you
for coming, I wish to God you'd go.' He sent me a message telling
me who was in his confidence if I wanted to get in touch with him
again, and I felt that, in an ambiguous way, he was trying to tell
me, 'Don't take this too seriously, don't chuck it all up.'

But that wasn't wholly the end of this attempt at peace-making.
A little later I had, I suspect, a more than normally significant lunch
with the American Ambassador in London and his advisers, and
soon after this came the cease-fire which implemented the proposals – the Rogers proposals – which had been put forward by the
American Secretary of State.

As I write the outcome is still in doubt. As I close these reflections
the thought uppermost in my mind is that both the Israelis (the
young hawks apart) and the Arab statesmen (the extremists apart)
want desperately to make progress towards an agreed settlement.
In the last months of his life Nasser said to me, and I try to quote his
words exactly, 'I would have no problem sitting down with the
Israelis and signing a treaty. What I cannot do, Mr Brown, is to sit
down in the room with them and negotiate it. That must be done
some other way.' As long as the four Powers pursue – to put it
mildly – different policies in the Middle East, I do not see how any
initiative which depends for its authority upon the four Powers can
possibly work. The initiative will have to be separate from them. I
recall very clearly what Golda Meir said to me: 'We need an inter-
mediary. It can be anybody. It could be you. But we are not going
to have the four great Powers, or any one of the four great Powers...'
and I saw what she meant.

13

Personalities
Recalled

ᛩ

ONE OF THE joys of having lived a life as full as mine so far is that I have been privileged to meet so many people – some loved, some disliked, but most with qualities that commanded respect and inevitably had their effect on my own developing views, attitudes and philosophy. I have written elsewhere about many of the men with whom I have rubbed shoulders on my political journey. Some obviously stand out more than others in my memory and justify, I think, an attempt to make a special assessment of them.

There can be no doubt that Ernest Bevin stands out among all the people I have met. He is in a place by himself. He was a man with little or no taught advantages, who relied wholly upon his own brain, his imagination and his capacity for envisaging things and people. In this capacity he was not surpassed and I think not even matched by anyone else I have ever met. The Churchills, the Attlees, and most other leaders, political or industrial, had all the advantages which their social position and long formal education can bestow. Bevin had none of these advantages, but I have seen him in every kind of situation – trade union negotiations round a table, trade union meetings facing often hostile critics, meetings with industrialists, with statesmen – and on every occasion it was quite clear that he was master of the situation. He said that he hated politics, yet in making politics or in running a political department few could match him. He had a natural dignity which offset his endowment of determination and ruthlessness.

I suppose there was no more evident example of the latter than the Brighton Conference of 1935 when, having become very sure of the way Fascism was developing in Europe and where our response to this was likely to lead, he became determined to put a stop to the evolving pacifist atmosphere in the Labour Party which, of course, was very much manifested by George Lansbury. In what many people would regard as one of the cruellest acts – and yet, as he regarded it, absolutely essential for the future of the Labour movement and for Britain – he demolished that very loved old man, finished him for all time really, with that one devastating remark from the rostrum. 'It is placing the Executive and the Movement,' he told Lansbury, sitting behind him on the platform, 'in an absolutely wrong position to be taking your conscience round from body to body asking to be told what you ought to do with it.' Powerful stuff, ruthless stuff, determined stuff, but not done out of spite or malice.

The tragedy of Ernest Bevin was that his real opportunities came to him so late in life. To those who knew him, above all in the trade union movement, he was a great man long before the general public knew much about him. One of the formative influences on his life was the General Strike of 1926. Until then he had been very much a left-wing trade union leader, but his experiences in the conduct of the strike, during which he became contemptuous of many of the colleagues he was dealing with, had a marked impact on him. It was following this that he began to broaden his horizons. His appointment in 1929 to the Macmillan (Lord Macmillan, the judge) Committee on Finance and Industry continued this development and gave him a new understanding of industry, the City and financial matters. A few years later he was advised to rest which characteristically he did by taking up a Chatham House invitation which enabled him to make what was virtually a world trip and to attend in Australia a Commonwealth conference. He was of course already very much an internationalist from his deep involvement in the international trade union movement, but all these things, which occurred subsequent to 1926, produced the very much more rounded and complete man that we all think of him as having been now. But it is instructive to remember that in 1929 he was nearly fifty years of age.

From then on he grew in stature, but it wasn't until the war that he got his real chance to make a major impact on national history. His work as Minister of Labour during the war contributed as much to victory as that of any of the generals and, as Foreign Secretary in the Labour Government after the war, there were times when he seemed to hold the Western world itself on his great shoulders.

Given his beginnings, he was probably the greatest self-developed man that Britain has produced in the past century. If one could think of a Bevin with Churchill's inbuilt advantages, one can conceive of a very different history for this country in my lifetime.

Bevin was the man I knew best in the post-war Labour Government and Bevin was the man who had most influence on me. But not far below him in my memory comes Herbert Morrison. I shared his London background and this helps me to pay tribute to his enormous contribution to the Labour movement. Like Bevin, he started with no social advantages and damned little schooling, yet he had a wonderful capacity for grasping essentials and he was a first-class organizer in the best sense of that word.

Where Bevin was essentially a man of imaginative inventiveness himself, Morrison was much more the assimilator and developer of other people's ideas. I don't imply by any means that he didn't have great ideas of his own. Indeed he did. And the creation of the London Passenger Transport Board in the 1929 Government, for example, was very much his idea and involved him, of course, in bringing about a very significant change in much of the thinking on industrial matters of the Labour movement at that time. There was still – even as late as that – a very considerable hangover from what was essentially the earlier syndicalist thinking, and the idea of 'workers' control' was uppermost in many people's outlook. What Morrison did was to lead to the conception of a different kind of public corporation, administered not on behalf primarily of those in that particular industry, but while treating properly with them, run essentially in the name of and on behalf of the people of the country as a whole.

Many would, I know, even now quarrel with this approach. Many would say it has led to greater anonymity than is good for industrial relations and, far from increasing responsibility to the nation, has tended to produce something akin to irresponsibility, certainly to non-effective accountability.

My view is that Morrison was right in his approach. We ought to be able to improve the weaknesses, but I feel sure we would not achieve any good purpose by going back to the ideas which he succeeded in demolishing at that time. The one or two examples I can recall, where workers in the industry itself have been represented from among themselves at the decision-making level, do not seem to me to be very encouraging.

He also had tremendous courage, and courage of a different order from Bevin's, for whereas Bevin could be bold with the knowledge that he had hundreds of thousands of votes on his card, Herbert

Morrison was simply Secretary of the London Labour Party and his card vote at Party Conferences was trivial. But Herbert took on all who came at him: the mob, the Communists, the snobbish intelligentsia, powerful trade union leaders, even at times Bevin himself. But for his personal courage in staying on as candidate for Hackney in the 1931 election, Herbert Morrison could have moved to safer territory as Ramsay MacDonald had moved before him, and if so, Morrison would have stayed in the House in 1931. If that had happened, I think it is pretty certain that he would have become Leader of the Labour Party, and not George Lansbury, and in that case Morrison would almost certainly have been Prime Minister after the war. One cannot be absolutely sure about this, if for no other reason than that his personal relations with Bevin and Churchill were so dicey. But even so, I think it would have happened and history would again have been different.

In the end Herbert Morrison went down, partly because he grew old like all of us and partly because he fell victim to the politicians' disease of insisting upon having the best job going in terms of prestige. When Bevin retired, the best job going, next to the Prime Ministership, was that of Foreign Secretary, which he wanted partly for this reason and partly because of the possibility of it going to Aneurin Bevan whom he simply could not abide. This, alas, was the one job that Herbert Morrison was not fitted to do. He had bad luck of course – among other things he had the miserable business of Dr Mussadeq and the Persian nationalization of the Anglo-Iranian Oil Company where, to put it mildly, neither he nor Britain were outstandingly helped by the Americans. However, everybody has varying kinds of luck, but I think it must be accounted here, even by one as indebted to him as I am, that Herbert Morrison simply was not cut out for foreign affairs, and his period at the Foreign Office was a disaster that clouded everything that had gone before. Looking back beyond these clouds that fell on Morrison at the end of his long political life, one can see him in his true stature. Of all those in the Labour movement whom I have known, I rate him as second only to Bevin in terms of political and human greatness.

Attlee I did not know well (I worked with him closely only for the few months when I served in the Shadow Cabinet under his chairmanship in 1955). He ceased to be the Leader in December 1955. Unlike Bevin and Morrison, with whom I had common links through trade unionism or London, there was nothing very much to bring me in close touch with him. I do not think anybody was ever very close to Attlee. He was a man of great integrity, but he came to leadership of the Labour Party wholly by accident, succeeding Lansbury in circumstances that nobody could have foreseen. But when the accidents happened and he finally came to be the Prime Minister, he had the tremendous advantage of having very big men immediately below him, none of whom liked any of the others and one of whom, Bevin, carried personal loyalty to a degree hardly heard of either before or since. He also brought that very quiet incisive mind, enabling him so quickly to grasp the heart of a matter, and this qualified him so superbly to sum up even the most confused meeting. On a number of the occasions when I sat under his chairmanship, I must confess to a naughty feeling that I was not quite sure whether he was summing up for the committee or despite it.

One of his charms, although it could be very disconcerting, was that he never used three words where one would do. Many stories have been told about this part of him, one of which I can tell at first hand. When I was a very young, very new and very excited Minister of Works in 1951, the issue which was then bothering my department more than most other things (except the price and supply of bricks and cement) was where to place the statue of Field-Marshal Smuts. There were those who wanted him where he now is in Parliament Square, and there were those (they could make a good case) who wanted him in the gardens outside of what is now the Ministry of Defence. The arguments went on and on and the files reached enormous size. One day the newly installed Minister of Works (me) received a call to No. 10. It was understood that the Prime Minister wished to see me, and the usual feverish debate went on in the department. What could all this be about? Why did the Prime Minister want to summon the Minister of Works? Secretary got in touch with Secretary in the way that they still do, and finally we found out through some black-market grapevine that the Prime Minister wished to see me about the statue of Field-Marshal Smuts.

The official then running this side of the department was Sir Eric de Normann. He was a great character, wore an enormous stock and every time I saw him I thought he looked every inch 'de Normann'. It was quite easy to persuade oneself that he came over with the Conqueror and had been running the Office of Works ever since. Be that as it may, he came to my room, armed with immense files and rolls of artists' designs, and dispatched me fully briefed to No. 10. I was received by the Prime Minister in the Cabinet Room. He was doodling, as he almost continuously did, and puffing smoke.

Barely looking up from his doodling, he opened the conversation laconically in his very flat voice: 'About this statue of Smuts, Minister. Who is going to do it? I do hope not that fellow' – mentioning a sculptor whose name was on everybody's lips – 'all holes and triangles'; and that was it. My papers never got opened, the roll stayed folded, the interview was over. He said, 'Thank you for coming, Minister', and out I went. Actually, when I look at that statue today I always think the eventual sculptor managed to make that scholar and soldier look exactly like a dancer at an ice-rink. I rather regret that it wasn't done by the other gentleman.

Another I think quite beautiful story which, although I can only tell it at second hand I have every reason to believe is true, occurred when one of our colleagues, having served on a very important – even critical – international commission, couldn't get seen by the Foreign Secretary on his return so that he could make to him a personal report. Eventually, on the intercession of Herbert Morrison, Attlee was prevailed upon to give him 'ten minutes'. Our colleague had a lot to tell and it took a good deal more than ten minutes. At the end there was a silence and then Attlee, still without looking up from his doodling, said, 'Oh, by the way, saw your mother yesterday. She did look well.' End of interview. As I say, I cannot vouch for it – I was not there – but it sounds to me very likely to be true.

Attlee managed things in this way with everybody and about everything. He was certainly a considerable man, but in my view it would have been very much better if the Labour Party had been differently led – certainly in the period after the fall of the 1945–51 Labour Government.

My association with Hugh Gaitskell came later in my life and I have recorded elsewhere in this book some of the events which we shared together. He was one of the most remarkable men I have ever met, yet he was a man who never had a chance really to show what he was capable of. We met, oddly enough, when I was if anything better known in the movement than he was. I well remember the decision he made to speak on the subject of 'the abolition of the public schools' at one of the conferences before he became a national figure and when he was hoping to be elected. He only had five minutes, being an ordinary delegate, and it seemed to me a most improbable subject to choose. But he was determined to say his piece on this – he felt strongly on the subject – and so he did.

But then he travelled fast and, as I have said elsewhere, I think in a sense too fast. He became too much the product of other people and the manœuvring of other powerful figures and too little himself. Yet his capacity to inspire other people with his ideals was extraordinary. Had he lived he would have been a tremendous leader of young people and an enormous bulwark against the machine politicians, the bureaucrats and everything else which has tended to debase the currency of modern life. He didn't live, I think, because he wore himself out in fights, many of which, while important in themselves, could really have been left to other people. But Hugh was too high-minded to let other people do the graft. He was a delicate man, delicate in spirit as well as in health, easily cast down and hurt, and all this savage in-fighting took its toll. I have a feeling that he died simply of exhaustion. What kind of Prime Minister he would have made, I must confess, I am unsure.

When I think now about Hugh Gaitskell I am curiously reminded of that other great man on the far side of the Atlantic, Jack Kennedy. Both of them were made to be inspirers, leaders and prophets, but perhaps neither was really meant to be a natural decision-taker. This quality must not be confused with another quality which sometimes goes with natural decision-making but by no means always or exclusively: that of rock-like determination once the decision has been taken. There is no doubt that he had that quality. This also applied to Kennedy, who was the only other man I have ever met with a capacity to inspire others with his own idealism similar to Hugh's. We never had a chance to find out to what heights either of them could really rise, but humanity owes a great debt to both. The Labour Party owes an enormous debt to Hugh for the courage with which he fought those who would have led us down very bad paths after the Labour Government fell in 1951. Looking back with hindsight I doubt whether he was wise to fight what came to be called the 'teeth and specs' issue when he did. But if he were looking over my shoulder now I think he would say, 'George, you can't pick the moment for starting to fight, you must take it when it arises.' Who am I with my record to say that he was wrong?

Jack Kennedy was one of the two Presidents of the United States whom it has been my privilege to know well. I came to love and admire him in the sense that I did Gaitskell. He was generous, very warm-hearted and a great humanitarian. As I came to know him better, I got to feel less and less that he was a doer. A thinker, a man of imagination, a man of inspiration, a man of feeling – yes. But even though I be in a minority, here again I think he was not what I regard as a great doer. I know that in writing this I shall be reminded of Cuba, where Kennedy seemed to act with the utmost decisiveness. Yet I have a nagging feeling that Cuba was in a way a decision made for him. But he charmed Khrushchev as he charmed me and as he charmed everybody else. All I can say here is that there has been no politician, Gaitskell apart, in whose presence I have felt more fascinated, charmed and excited about the possibilities of power.

Few of those I have ever met at this level could be quite so engaging in quite such ordinary ways as Jack Kennedy. One of my visits to him coincided with a very crowded schedule which meant that I failed to see my daughter, Pat, who was then working in New York. My stay in the United States had been extended by one day so that I could meet the President. And the best I could do about seeing Pat was to telephone to her to suggest that she took the shuttle service which operated from New York to Washington so that I could get the Embassy to fetch her by car to the White House in order that she and I could have the 'joy' of flying back to New York before I took the evening plane to London. This was duly done, and while I was talking with the President an aide came in to give me a note which said that Pat was outside. The President at once asked whether I had some news, meaning political news. I said, 'No', and told him this rather sad little family story. At once he insisted that she should be brought in. Arrangements were made to show her round, she was introduced to Mrs Kennedy and given the freedom of the White House while the President and I went on with what we were talking about. This was a simple gesture perhaps, but it was a gesture which in my experience is not made by very many men right at the top.

I worked more closely with President Johnson than I did with Kennedy. L.B.J. was a very different man, yet although he lacked the charm of Kennedy he had a quality of his own which was appealing. In my view he is one of the most underrated politicians the world has seen in recent times. When things obstinately refuse to go right, although all the reasons and the arguments for taking the decisions seem so obviously right, you get a chance to see the real man behind the façade. It is then, I think, you can tell a big man from the rest. By my method of calculating, L.B.J. unquestionably comes in the ranks of the really big men. I could identify his weaknesses as easily as he could identify mine, but given all his weaknesses he was the stuff of which great men are made. If he hadn't had the misery of having to deal with intractable problems at a time when every kind of little man was trying to bring him down, he would stand out as one of America's greatest Presidents. In retrospect I think he will.

He inherited Vietnam – too often this is forgotten. Men who like to forget their previous involvement, shuffle the buck on to him, and some of these men had great involvement themselves. In many cases it was they who were responsible for much, if not all, of the basic information on which the President had to make his decisions. These men can, and do, hold up their hands in horror and affect to believe that they were never in favour of the decisions which President Johnson took. (In my own way, I have suffered from the same sort of thing.) But I know something of L.B.J.'s predicament because I know the advice he was getting. I have walked so many times round his garden with him and shared in his personal agony. Yet how could he ignore what he was so authoritatively told? It would be wonderful if every top politician had some inbuilt sixth sense which told him when the advice he was getting was wrong and could be ignored, and when the advice was right and must be followed. Alas, mortals don't have such a sixth sense. He took the decisions he felt he had to take and he took the consequences. His only real faults were, perhaps, that he was too emotional – but then so am I – and apt to be over his long political life a little inconsiderate of the feelings of others and certainly apt to forget that, while these incidents disappeared from his mind, they tended to stay a long time in the hearts and minds of those who felt themselves thus affronted. I know something of this too.

I saw much of Dean Rusk, the then Secretary of State, and had a lot to do with him over a long period of time both before and while I was Foreign Secretary. I regard him as the great workhorse of the American political machine. He was honest to the last cog. He refused to make anything out of being a leading public official to the point that he was almost on his beam-end when his official life came to an end. He refused to truckle to any popular wind, he was always master of his trade and he was loyal to his President to the nth degree. We got on well together, for each of us instinctively understood the attitude the other was likely to take in almost any circumstances. Dean Rusk is entitled in American terms to the title 'a Southern Gentleman'. A gentleman he certainly is, but he is not Southern in the sense that the phrase is often used. He was a truly great public servant who deserved better breaks than he got.

Coming back to Europe, certain men stand out and nobody quite so much in a way as General de Gaulle. My talks with him were always fascinating, and remain among my most treasured memories of the short period when I was Foreign Secretary. Whether you agreed with him or not, in his presence you felt that you were in the presence of a really great man. He had tremendous authority and power, which you sensed as you talked to him.

He had been deeply affected by the treatment he had received from the Allies during the war – mistreatment, as he felt it – and he was determined to show that France must be the leader of Europe. He was actually determined to show that he was the leader of France. Indeed, he saw himself as a great world leader, and, in his way, he was. As time went on, his greatness slipped into a kind of narrow French nationalism which one could not but deplore, but he certainly rescued France and restored French self-respect after the war. I regard him as among the most outstanding human beings I have ever been privileged to meet.

However, I think my favourite European politician must be Willy Brandt. Give or take a few years, he is about my own age and we seem to share emotions and outlook on practically everything. We were both conditioned by the years from the Spanish Civil War to Hitler in 1939. Fate has delivered many ill-favours to Willy Brandt, although one has rejoiced of course in his opportunities since he became Chancellor.

He represents all that I think of as best in that prophetic cartoon of Will Dyson that once appeared in the old *Daily Herald* in 1919 and captioned '1914 Class'. As I remember it, it showed the peace negotiators at Versailles – the great Lloyd George, the great Clemenceau and so on – haggling over the terms, and the '1914 class' was the little child who was destined to be the cannon fodder in the wars which Will Dyson so clearly saw would emerge from the Versailles haggle.

Brandt has done things which require physical, mental and moral courage to an extent which few men could sustain. He inherited a German Social Democratic Party with very out-dated traditional thinking and requiring super-human energy and understanding to reform and revive. Like others, he had little in the way of natural advantages with which to do it. He was of course lucky in his colleagues – Fritz Erler and Herbert Wehner outstanding among them – but even so it was Brandt who saw the way through, not only to leading the Social Democratic Party to victory but towards uniting Europe. He is a man of shining courage – doing things which to everybody else it seemed impossible to ask a German politician to undertake. Thanks to Willy's courage and imagination, Germany may yet bring about the beginnings of a genuine *détente* between East and West.

I have talked about some – but only some – of the many great men I have met in Europe and in America. The others that come to mind now are the Russians.

Because my first and in a way most dramatic confrontation with the Russian Communist leadership was with Khrushchev, I ought to say a word about him. This confrontation occurred at the famous – or notorious – dinner session between the National Executive of the Labour Party and the Russian leaders in the House of Commons in April 1956. This led to the rather bitter exchanges I have described, but it gave me a picture of the man which I have never seen any occasion to change.

He was, I would say, not a man of great intellect or any real stature. He was a natural bully, really insensitive (in a sense I don't think I have ever detected in anybody else) to the feelings, the needs, the proper ambitions of others. Thinking back over my own associations one way and another with Communists over the last forty years or more, I would say nobody embodied in his own person the whole outlook, attitude of the Communist machine bureaucrat as did Khrushchev.

Of course, one of the tragedies of modern politics is that no Western statesman ever seems able to get to know the Russian leaders in any personal way – I mean in a way in which one met and got to know Kennedy, Johnson, Brandt, de Gaulle, Nenni, or indeed almost any other Western leader. Brezhnev in particular I never saw on any of my visits to Russia. He was always somewhere else or too busy. Kosygin I saw quite a lot of, both in London and in Moscow, and I would place him as an able, hard, hard-working but unimaginative official. When I was in office we never really knew who was the Russian leader. Perhaps we had been brought up to believe too much that there had to be an individual Russian leader – that may have been one of our mistakes. I think that Brezhnev was probably first among equals, as it were, but by how much first it is even now impossible to say.

I was always tremendously impressed in our meetings by the complete extent of Kosygin's briefing, even about events that had taken place in the last hour or so. One thing also that impressed me about him and Gromyko was the little extent to which they referred to written briefs. We British rather tended to go into the room armed with vast compendious files all flagged and ticketted so that one could find the right subject at the right time and use it for reference. I never saw either of them do that, and yet they always seemed fully briefed. Of course in a way it was easier for them since I cannot ever remember either of them moving from the stance he adopted on first entering the room. That is not to say we did not on occasion change their minds or get something done which they didn't in the beginning want done. But the change took place behind the scenes and before the next meeting. No doubt a good deal of line-clearing had to go on with Mr Brezhnev or others before they could do this.

Kosygin, despite the almost gloomy look which he habitually wears, does in fact have a sense of humour, but the side of him that showed most was the suspicious side. He was always a total Communist Party official, and I think always suspicious not so much of other people as of what people in his own country might think of his gullibility if he really set out to indulge in the kind of discussion which might lead to a change of view. He was very much afraid of his own inadequacies if he went outside his brief. He was not, I would say, a big man, but a more than adequately tough party official.

Gromyko was no politician and I always thought really just another exceedingly able party official. He, of course, did know the outside world and did not mind letting his sense of humour show or letting his hair down on occasion. His capacity to discuss and argue was to me very impressive, but, again, getting much out of him was a very tough business indeed and in my time certainly never happened again without the interval and the obvious line-clearing elsewhere. While I was at the Foreign Office it seemed to me that Gromyko was growing in importance. His influence seemed to be becoming stronger and he probably was playing a much bigger role than before in the apparatus by which decisions were made, and was becoming much less simply the machine for carrying them out.

The final thought in my mind, as I let my memories roam on people like those I have had room to mention, is the extent to which the rational solution to the world's problems and the creation of a climate in which people can expect to live in a reasonable manner depends so very much on the knowledge that the leaders at any given moment of time have not only of the issues involved and their own national requirements but also of each other. I saw so many things go wrong which could just as easily have gone right. But they went wrong simply because of the lack of social and other contact which we all had with each other. One often reads criticisms of statesmen 'jetting' about the world. My view was that we did not 'jet' about nearly enough, and we certainly did not stay – this is very true of the British – sufficiently long enough in any one place when we arrived. In saying this, I am contradicting something I made a great fuss about when I arrived in the Foreign Office. I then said I proposed to be the first Foreign Secretary who stayed at home, sat at the desk and made his decisions there. On this, as on a number of other things, I was talking without the 'book'. I now think we were all much too conscious of being criticized for being out of the country, when so much needed to be done at home. And so we tended to play down much too much the intangible yet essential benefit that comes from sitting with your 'friend' long enough to have a chance of actually making him your friend.

14

General Election
1970

And so I come to the General Election of June 1970, which ended six years of Labour Government, and which also brought to an end my own quarter of a century in the House of Commons.

This election was in many ways the most unplanned one that any Government can ever have chosen deliberately to fight, and had it been chosen by Labour's most unscrupulous opponent in power, it could not have come at a moment which found the Party less prepared. The extraordinary thing is that everybody knew this to be so, but nobody seemed to be either able or willing to do anything about it. Not being in the Cabinet I have no way of knowing to what extent Cabinet Ministers were consulted, or the advice they gave, and one must assume that it is true that the Prime Minister did ask his colleagues, and that unanimously they encouraged him to go to the country.

My own part in the decision can be very quickly put on record. On Thursday, 14 May, I went to my constituency in Belper together with my brother-in-law, Maurice Hackett, who was going to organize my own constituency campaign whenever the election, which was then much in the air, might come. A set of opinion polls had been published showing Labour well ahead of the Tories, and this gave rise to many rumours that an election was probably imminent. I myself could scarcely credit them, for I could see no justification for a midsummer election with much important legislation still unfinished.

On the evening of 14 May the Prime Minister telephoned me in Derbyshire asking me to come back to London, so I cut short my visit and returned to London on the morning of Friday, 15 May. Although I still didn't want to believe in a June election, I felt pretty sure that the Prime Minister's message meant that a decision had been taken, and I started to put in train all the necessary work in my constituency. I ordered my election addresses, window bills and the rest before setting off for London.

I met the Prime Minister at No. 10 Downing Street and he made himself very agreeable. I asked him whether he had invited me to London to discuss the question of an election, or merely to tell me as Deputy Leader of the Labour Party what had been decided. He made it clear that he had in fact taken the decision the day before. I told him that in that case there was really nothing for me to be consulted about. I didn't quite say, 'Was my journey really necessary?' but I left him in no doubt that had I been invited for a consultation I should have argued very strongly against a June election. I gave my reasons: first, by going to the country so precipitately, it would be difficult to avoid the charge that we were running away from a possible economic crisis in the autumn; and secondly that we should find the current round of price increases an absolutely unhandleable issue. I did not believe that merely saying that the Tories would put up prices even more would get us anywhere. The Prime Minister told me that he had the now famous certificate about the economy from Mr Jenkins, and all I could say to this was, 'Well, I hope everybody regards Mr Jenkins as a completely unbiased adviser on the subject.' I also pointed out the Party's unpreparedness for an election.

However, since the decision had already been made, none of these arguments mattered any longer. We had a drink and I said that of course I would do the best I could.

When it came to discussing the election programme, I urged that we *must* try to put forward some new ideas, promising new kinds of action on our various fronts. I said that elections were not won by staying put – Herbert Morrison had been blamed (in my view somewhat unfairly) for Labour's defeat in 1951 because the theme of that election had been 'consolidation', and Mr Baldwin had not done well with the slogan 'Safety First'. My arguments evoked little enthusiasm. It seemed that 'Trust Harold' as an election theme was in some way quite different from 'Consolidation' or 'Safety First'.

But it would be quite unfair to blame Harold Wilson alone for the decision to fight the election on the theme of 'Trusting Harold'. The National Executive of the Party and the Cabinet had a day-long meeting to discuss what should go in our Manifesto. I argued the need for putting in some of the new ideas which had been worked out by our advisory committees, among them the restructuring of the taxation system to include a Wealth Tax. No decisions were taken at that meeting, and we broke up in the atmosphere of comfortable, complacent euphoria which was to dog us throughout the election campaign. Everybody was polite to everybody else – it was as if no one had ever heard of conflicts between the Government and the trade unions, and there wasn't a single boulder in our path.

Then came the writing of the Manifesto, and here we had the difficulties that I suppose we always shall have of jockeying for position when the Party is in power. We had a Drafting Committee for the Manifesto, partly nominated by the Prime Minister, partly set up from the National Executive, who were supposed to oversee the work. The actual writing was to be done in Transport House, but gradually it got shifted to No. 10. Any things that were not well-regarded there got dropped on the way, and what emerged in the end was a pretty colourless and almost totally irrelevant document.

The Manifesto was to be issued to the Press at 2 o'clock one afternoon. The meeting of the National Executive, at which it was to be approved, was called at 10 o'clock on the same day. In the interests of secrecy, no one outside the Campaign Committee had seen the document, and it had to be studied at top speed in half an hour before the meeting. Naturally people wanted to redraft the whole thing. Any Minister who felt that his or her Department had not enjoyed a sufficiently good write-up wanted to put in bits explaining all that it had been doing. Any suggestion either that something new should be done, or that something might be better done differently, was resisted on the grounds that it implied that the Minister concerned had not been doing as well as he should. All potential criticism of Ministers had to be removed, and what had been a Wealth Tax became an unexceptionable statement that those possessing greater wealth should contribute more than the poorer to the national finances. Even this, however, was considered tactically dangerous, for the Prime Minister argued that the word 'wealth' could be misconstrued, that it would be seized on by the Press and might cost us the election. So out went 'wealth' and we ended with a pious exhortation that the richer should pay more than the poorer!

The election campaign itself, like the weather of that lovely summer, was too good to be true. The opinion polls continued to give Labour a lead, and the atmosphere at meetings was extraordinarily good, seeming to promise that we were assured of victory.

Yet if only we had read the figures rightly, those very polls showing Labour's lead should have conveyed a warning. It seems astonishing now that so many mathematicians, statisticians, economists and financial wizards in the Party couldn't see the difference between figures showing Labour in front and figures showing an actual swing in Labour's favour. True, we were in front of where we had been in the past two disastrous years, but the electorate was a good deal bigger than it had been in 1966, and it was perfectly possible for us to have a national lead and still lose seats. The questions we should have been asking was how many seats were at risk, and what should we be doing to save them?

Moreover, the optimistic forecasts of the opinion polls were not borne out by the returns of our canvassers. Practically everywhere I went on my national tour the Party organizers would warn me when we sat down to tea that the canvass returns were not agreeing with the polls. This became a sort of theme-song, and although as the campaign went on I was myself misled by the general air of optimism, I took care to convey to Transport House what the Party organizers were saying. As things turned out the canvassers in the constituencies were right and the rest of us were wrong.

We misled ourselves. The decision had been taken to fight a cool, low-keyed campaign, and we did nothing to show that we had fire in our bellies. The stating of issues was kept rigidly to the leader himself, supported by Mr Callaghan, Mr Healey and Mr Jenkins at Press conferences in London. Official policy was to let the Tories run themselves into the ground.

By the end of the second week of the campaign it looked as if the Tories had just about done this and that we had succeeded in doing what we set out to do. In spite of Lord Cromer's intervention, had Polling Day come a week before it did, I believe that we should have won. We should have lost seats, but we should have been returned to power.

It was in the third week that things went decisively against us. We should have sensed this, but we didn't. It should have been clear that certain difficulties were obstinately refusing to go away. One was the question of prices – there was no doubt about the effect that rising prices were having on women. And we had very little way of finding out what women, as distinct from voters in general, were going to do. The other cloud that wouldn't go away was the vague shadow of an impending economic crisis. However much we tried to explain that we had put the economy in good shape, we couldn't overcome the doubts raised in people's minds by the very fact that we were holding an election a year before we need. It looked as if we just might have something to hide, and however unfounded such doubts may have been we did not dispel them. The trade and unemployment figures published in the last week certainly did not help. One month's figures may be irrelevant in indicating the true state of the economy, but those figures, coming when they did, were psychologically bad.

Newspapers and television on the whole treated us badly. The *Daily Mail* was easily the worst example in respect of the so-called economic crisis. A good many television interviewers seemed to make Tory propaganda considerably more effectively than the official party-political broadcasts.

After one of these 'factual' programmes I felt so incensed that I rang up the BBC to complain, but although the programme containing the interview had not quite come to an end, it seemed that all the people responsible for it had left the building. I asked if I could speak to the head man in charge of programmes and I was told that he had gone home. So I asked if I could have his telephone number so that I could ring him at home. This produced a shocked response that home telephone numbers could never be disclosed like that, but that if I would give my number they would ring up the man concerned and that he would telephone me.

I gave the duty-officer the number of the hotel where I and my party were staying and waited. Nothing happened. After a time a girl from Transport House who was acting as my secretary on my election tour suggested that she should telephone the BBC as Mr Maudling's secretary. She had an absolutely beautiful private-school accent and she spoke to the same duty-officer, saying that Mr Maudling had been most impressed by the programme and would like to speak to the head man about it. The duty-officer again demurred about giving a home telephone number, but she said that Mr Maudling really did want to speak personally about such an interesting programme. Whereupon the home telephone number was duly given. The point about this little anecdote is that you don't have to be Mr Maudling himself but merely his secretary to get what you want out of the BBC, whereas if you are Labour's Mr George Brown they stick to the rules.

Having got the telephone number I rang up and spoke to the man, but of course nothing else happened.

I lost my own seat at Belper to my Conservative opponent Mr G. Stewart-Smith by 2,124 votes. I had held Belper since 1945, but I did not think that it could be held in 1970. This was not because

of the suddenness of the June election, nor because I spent the first
two weeks of the campaign away from the constituency, making my
national tour for the Labour Party. The decision to lose Belper was
taken in 1969, when the Government, for a variety of specious reasons
which I opposed at the time, decided not to carry out the recommendations of its own Boundary Commission for the redistribution of
seats.

Populations change, and under the Representation of the People
Act, an earlier Labour measure, a Commission was established to
keep the size of constituencies under review and periodically to
redraw the boundaries of those that had become too big or too small,
to bring them back within the tolerances laid down in the Act.
Belper, with an electorate of 87,100, was one of the constituencies
due for revision. The electorate had increased by over 10,000 since
1966, mainly from the growth of middle-class housing estates, so
that most of the new electors could be expected to vote Tory. Since
my majority in 1966 was 4,274, an influx of 10,000 new voters,
mainly Tory, obviously imperilled the seat.

If the Boundary Commission's recommendations had been carried
out, some 26,000 voters, mainly in the Tory areas around Derby,
would have been transferred to neighbouring divisions. But somebody had calculated that the Commission's recommendations, taken
as a whole, would mean the loss of from twelve to twenty Labour
seats. This was disputed by our organizers at Transport House, and
there's no way of knowing whether the calculations were right or
wrong. Somehow they became accepted doctrine, with the result
that the Government decided to defer carrying out the recommendations. This led to rather damaging charges of gerrymandering, and
as in the end we lost sixty seats, it was not a very successful gerry-
mander. The irony of the situation is that the new Conservative
Government is putting the recommendations into effect, so that when
the next election comes Belper will almost certainly become a safe
Labour seat.

Between 1 and 14 June 1970 my wife and I travelled over 2,000
miles and I addressed 102 meetings, not counting the dozens of
impromptu gatherings that took place as well. The tour was a really
wonderful piece of planning organization, mainly done by Neil
Vann, Labour Party National Youth Officer who was seconded for
the job, and Peter Ward, a Labour Party regional publicity officer in
Newcastle who acted as my press officer. Colette Rumball, also from
Transport House, came along as my secretary. She did not in fact

have much secretarying to do, but worked as one of the team sharing out the administrative duties. She was the girl who enacted Mr Maudling's secretary in the contretemps with the BBC. We were in a different hotel practically every night, and every meal had to be arranged in advance so that we didn't waste a minute. Our meetings varied from seven in a day to about fifteen, depending on how much travelling we had to do. We'd leave our hotel every morning sharp at half-past nine, and carrying on until five, with a brief interlude for lunch. Then in the evening there would be other meetings, as many as three.

It was a tremendous job of organization. Quite apart from the political task of addressing over 100 meetings, there were all the mechanical things to see to – making sure that cars were there at the right time, that bills were paid or signed and arrangements made to pay them.

We suffered from some of our traditional ways of going about things. In this second half of the twentieth century, when practically every teenager has a good modern radio and tape recorder, it is extraordinary to meet some of the antiquated loud-speaking equipment that one comes across at election-times. The things we were offered varied from the tiniest of hand-held loud-hailers non-mechanically assisted to ancient pieces of horned equipment that had been kept going with string and adhesive tape from the time when, with great daring, they had been acquired for the election of 1945.

Warned by my experiences in 1964 and 1966, I had arranged with the National Agent to have first-class equipment of our own secreted in the back of our car. This worked admirably for the first week of the campaign, but one night in Manchester the car, with all our Labour Party posters on it, was parked in the open instead of being locked up. It was promptly stolen. It was recovered about a week later – minus our beautiful loudspeaking equipment.

So for the second week we had to rely on what we could get locally; sometimes it was up to date, sometimes not. This is one of the small things that really do make a difference at election times, and I wish all local Labour Party organizers would take note of it.

The Times tells me that 'the marathon George Brown election tour' may be the last of its kind in British elections. I think *The Times* is probably wrong. Contrary to what the professionals say, I don't think that elections will ever be wholly won on television or by London

Press conferences. What the Americans call 'flesh pumping' has to be done – people want physical contact with political activity, to feel that they are part of it. All parties have people who are good drawing-cards at elections, and I think they must continue to be used if there is to be enthusiasm at the grass roots of our democracy.

My tour was quite different from the Prime Minister's 'Meet the People' visitations. That sort of activity has its merits and its place in an election campaign, but it is not the same as an election tour. For one thing the visits are not announced in advance – that may have an advantage in avoiding eggs, but it has the disadvantage of avoiding other things too – sometimes the very people who would most like to meet you because they don't know that you are there!

My stops were all known in advance and they provided opportunities for local candidates and party workers to address people both before and after my own performance. I found the tour a most moving and inspiring experience: people seemed to want to come to meetings – even at 10 o'clock in the morning you could find several hundreds, or even a couple of thousand, assembled outside a town hall.

One of the outstanding memories from my tour is of a day when we were driving back from Wales. We had stopped at various places *en route* and I was due to lunch in Welshpool. Welshpool is a town of about 5,000 or 6,000, and the organizers hadn't thought it worth while to push another meeting into my crowded day because the Montgomery division, in which Welshpool is, is such bad country for us. In the 1966 election Labour only just escaped being bottom of the poll. It's one of the few Liberal seats left, with the Tories taking second place and Labour struggling with the Welsh Nationalists in Plaid Cymru to come third. But we had a gallant young candidate (D. W. Thomas) fighting in Montgomery, and although there wasn't time for a public meeting in Welshpool, I'd arranged for him to join us for lunch so that we could at least say 'hello'. We got to Welshpool a little after 1 o'clock and met the young candidate and his agent, who was the local official of the Transport Workers Union. These two chaps, who between them formed the main Labour fighting force for the whole county of Montgomery, were not content with just having a drink and being photographed with me – at once they began twisting my arm about holding a meeting. I said, 'Well, I've got to leave here at half-past two. We've got to have lunch, and nobody knows I'm here, anyway.'

The candidate said, 'It's a small town, and people will know soon enough. If you leave without doing a meeting it will look as if you're just saying that you've written us off.'

Liking his attitude (and being perhaps a bit soft) I said, 'Now look, I'll tell you what I'll do. We'll cut lunch short, and if you can get round the town with loudspeakers to tell people that I'm here, I'll be on the Town Hall steps at 2.15. But I *can* only spend ten minutes, because I really do have to get on to Shrewsbury.'

He went off with his union official friend, dashed round the town with his one loudspeaker, and when I got to the Town Hall steps at a quarter past two there were over 2,000 people assembled for me to talk to. It had to be a short meeting, but it was a very exciting one – a splendid little political occasion. This is what I mean when I say that television just can't replace the flesh-and-blood meeting in an election campaign. For all that it's in poor country for Labour, people in Welshpool wanted that meeting; it gave them a chance to feel that they really were participating in the election, and it gave the candidate, fighting for a pretty hopeless seat, a chance to go on talking to the meeting and answering questions after I'd gone. It's just this kind of activity that transforms a 'hopeless' seat into a victory for one's own party an election or two ahead.

So I would hope that when Labour has seriously debated the election campaign of 1970, it will work out the kind of planning that needs to be done for future elections. First, I think, the Party must consider how the decision to hold the 1970 election was arrived at. The Party has got to be the Government again before that point has any direct relevance to events, but it is just as well that it should be discussed. The whole conduct of it, the way the election decision was taken and the way in which the campaign was then conducted, reinforces my feeling of unhappiness about the mechanics of Government since 1964 and the method by which decisions are made. The election decision seemed almost a replica of the pattern of decision-making which led me to resign from the Government in 1968. There was no planning about it, it was a rush decision based, as far as I can see (and I must repeat that I was not then in the Cabinet), on the optimistic arithmetic of the opinion polls. To my knowledge – and although not in the Cabinet I was still Deputy Leader of the Labour Party – no serious consideration was ever given to what the situation would be in October if we waited until the summer was past. Nobody worked out the effects of people on holiday not having votes. It was just assumed that it would cancel out, but nobody *knew*, and no attempt was made to find out – there wasn't time. When I raised the matter I was told that the Wakes Weeks and so on following would make any month in the summer worse than June, and therefore we should go in June. But why did it have to be the summer? October was not considered, apparently because it was thought that it would be too great a risk to wait; and if we were to go in October and lose, everybody would accuse the poor leader of having misjudged the situation in June. Why nobody should accuse the poor leader of having misjudged the situation in June if we went in June and lost left me as puzzled then as it does now. But nobody has accused the leader of misjudgement, so I can only conclude that all the colleagues who were closest to him were involved and that it was a collective calamitous mistake.

Some of our old-time election procedures are pretty out of date. I don't think that there is any longer much point in going round laboriously writing up canvass cards as Labour, Tory or Doubtful and then transferring them to elaborate records in the constituency office. There *is* a lot to be said for going round canvassing to find out what people are saying – in other words, conducting your own opinion poll in your own constituency. But the idea that people are necessarily going to tell you the truth when you ask them how they are going to vote, or that they won't change their minds before Polling Day, obviously has no longer much validity.

Labour should do much better in getting out the postal vote. It is by no means an unimportant vote, particularly in marginal con- stituencies. The Tories are exceedingly well organized on the ground and one of the things they do really well is getting out this postal vote. With the majority of doctors being openly on their side, they have no difficulty in knowing who is sick or who is going to be confined. We ought to have that kind of organization, but we don't have it. It is not as difficult as people sometimes try to make out to discover who is likely to need a postal vote. All it needs is making somebody responsible for each street, or group of streets, in towns, and having one man or woman in every village to send in a return on who needs postal votes. I had 121 villages in my constituency and I'd arranged for a team of half a dozen students to go round them in the summer of 1970 to make a survey of the need for postal votes. I don't think that they could have made any difference to the result – as I have explained, Belper was lost to Labour when it was decided not to act on the recommendations of the Boundary Commission – but it would have given me at least several hundred more votes. More important, it would have given the bed-ridden a chance to feel that they could still play a personal part in the election.

In another generation I doubt if 'traditional' Labour areas will exist in an electoral sense. They are declining now, and being re-placed by new housing estates like those in the 'difficult' belt of Belper, and at every election Labour will have to fight for the loyalties of the people who live there. They will never become permanent Labour voters – it's our job to prevent them from becoming Tory voters. We've got to learn to understand these people. They are the working-class sons and daughters who have become office workers, draughtsmen and the like, and they feel that they have emancipated themselves from working-class backgrounds, that they have come up in the world. It's easy to be irritated by this sort of snobbism, but it's better to try to understand it. In terms of physical amenity they *have* come up in the world, mainly as a result of Labour policies and political pressure since the end of the First World War. But their lives can be dreadfully drab. They live in great blocks of little rabbit hutches put up by mass-building firms, with next to no social facilities at all. If they have a place that calls itself a 'shopping centre', it's likely to be a place with a few shops to which women push their prams; it has no community meaning. Thus they are difficult to organize; it's difficult to get at them, to get them to talk frankly about their problems, even to understand their own problems. But because it's difficult, it's all the more important to tackle the job of trying to make them feel that the Labour Party is just as much for them as it is for any coalminer or steelworker.

In a real sense, the Labour Party is suffering now from its own achievement. The outstanding achievement is to have brought about a degree of prosperity reflected in the standard of living of the bulk of the people in Britain far beyond what we thought possible in 1945, and infinitely far beyond anything we ever dreamed of in the 1930s. And this prosperity is spread pretty well across the nation. We've still got miserable places in the cities, miserable slums and dreary urban centres, but outside of these pretty well everybody now is well fed, well dressed, well looked after, and, for the most part, has a regular job at earnings which enable him or her to live a life that is utterly different from the sort of life that most people had even one generation ago.

This struck me sharply at several places on my election tour. One was at Connah's Quay, which is part of the great steel complex of Shotton. We drew up there in the forecourt of an absolutely magnificent Labour Club. It had cost about £50,000 (all or most of it borrowed from the brewers and being paid back out of the profits that were being made), and it provided a really wonderful place for people to spend their leisure hours, drinking, playing bingo, or whatever they wanted. There were delightful facilities for families to go there with their children – compared with anything we knew in the 1930s, everybody there was living the life of Riley.

I stood in that forecourt to address a meeting of 200 or 300 people, and inevitably somebody raised the question of high prices. I said, 'Oh, come off it. However high prices are, with the earnings you've got nowadays you're enjoying a life you could never have had before.' The heckler wasn't satisfied with this, so I went on, 'You know, only a couple of years ago at the Labour Club in my constituency you'd have seen a poster advertising the annual outing. It used to be a day at Blackpool or New Brighton or Skegness. Where do you think people go now?'

At this the secretary of the club broke in and said, 'If you want to know the answer to that, have a look at the bill inside this club advertising our annual outing.'

I asked, 'Where is it?'

He said, 'We're going for a week to the Mediterranean.'

This is evidence of Labour's achievement, but of course once you've achieved that degree of emancipation you have also changed people's habits of thinking. Part – and a big part – of the endless complaint about prices is not that things cost more but that people want to buy more expensive things. If you want wine instead of beer, television instead of sound radio, a car instead of a motor-bike, well, it just does cost more.

And I'm afraid that with the changed habits of thinking among those who now have access to all these good things of life, there has come a decline of interest in those who are less well off. I discovered on my election tour, for example, that the most unpopular thing the Labour Government ever did was to arrange to 'claw back' family allowances from the better off. Where a husband and wife are both working, they may often have a joint income nowadays of over £2,000 a year. If they have young children, they will get family allowances, but a good deal of the allowance will be taken back in tax. It infuriates such people to see a neighbour whose wife doesn't go out to work (it is always assumed that this is just because she won't) pay less tax on family allowances. Selfishness creeps in as one gets better off.

Another example of this is the common attitude to taxation on high earnings. A Labour Government wants to do a lot of things. It wants to rebuild the country, it wants improved facilities for education, health, housing, roads and so on – all the things that people themselves want. But to do these things you have to raise very large sums of money. That means that a Labour Government is bound to be a Government of high taxation. Yet I found on my tour that the very people who were demanding most vociferously better schools, better housing and all the rest were the ones who were most angry about paying taxes.

One young man came up and showed me a wage ticket which showed him to be earning well over £30 a week. He was a single man, and he had to pay tax of £6 or £7. That made him exceedingly angry. He wasn't pleased to be earning thirty quid – he was just bloody angry at the amount of tax he had to pay.

There were similar instances all over the place. Sometimes people would say to me, 'I'm not such a fool as you take me for, so every now and again I don't work for a bit, and then I get my tax back again.' The idea that you may be hurting the community by not working in order to recover tax is something that never crosses many people's minds.

This, then, seems to me to be our biggest failure in the Labour movement. We've raised people's standards, we've raised earning capacity, we've enabled men and women to enjoy a vast new range of life, but somehow we haven't persuaded people that all this has to be paid for. We haven't managed to convince enough of those who live in contemporary Britain that they are much better off in the sort of society that Labour has created than they would be in a society where taxes might be lower but where earnings would be lower, too; where there would be fewer social benefits and the needs of others would be less well taken care of. Society in Britain nowadays is largely a selfish society. Maybe this is an inevitable phase – first, you make people physically and financially better off, and then you have to wait for human understanding and compassion to catch up.

Old Tom Williams used to say in the 1945 Labour Government that the farmers could never afford to pay their entrance fee to the Conservative Club until they had Labour agricultural policy – and then they all went off and joined the Conservatives. That, I am afraid, is true not only of farmers but of a great many of our own people. You can only afford to be a Conservative after Labour has been in power for a few years! Perhaps the corollary of this is that you've *got* to have a Labour Government whenever the Conservatives have been in power for a few years!

But one must not make too much of this: not everybody is selfish, not every vote is cast for miserable and cynical reasons. We lost sixty seats in 1970, but although we lost power we didn't suffer any great electoral disaster. Our defeat was not, I think, because a lot of former Labour voters turned round and voted against us, but because about a million people who would have voted Labour if they'd gone to the polls stayed away and didn't vote at all. Those abstentions may have been brought about partly by the euphoria of the public opinion polls, but there was nothing in our own presentation of ourselves to strike any note of idealism to make people *want* to vote for us. Any left-wing Party, any radical Party, has got to be a Party of idealism and change. Our failure in 1970 was that we didn't offer enough idealism. I think, perhaps, we wanted too much to stay in power. If we'd been less anxious to go on *being* the Government, even to the extent of saying, 'We don't particularly want you to put us back unless you really want us to do these things we offer', then I think we might, paradoxically enough, have stood a better chance of winning the election.

It may seem contradictory to say that a selfish person can also be swayed by idealism, but it's true. I found over and over again that when one did break away from the bread-and-butter issues of prices and taxation to talk about the conflicts in the world and the opportunities for practical idealism, there was always an instant response. The teenagers, the new voters, were, I think, very much on our side. They've known television and motor-cars and holidays abroad all their lives: in a sense they've been inoculated against materialism. They are looking for ideals, and I'm convinced that if Labour can retain its idealism it can rely on the loyalties of the youngsters who are growing up now. It's the young marrieds whom we've failed to hold, the people in their mid-twenties to the mid-thirties, who have in many ways had the worst of the squeeze. They're the ones who've really felt high mortgage rates and all the other things that Labour, as the Government in power, was bound to be blamed for. And we didn't offer enough idealism to counteract their frustrations and personal discontents. If we could have shifted the argument on to other planes and got people talking about all the things we ought to be doing in the next five years instead of the unfulfilled ambitions of the past, then the outcome of the election might have been very different.

As I look at things with the detachment that comes with the closing of one long chapter in my political life, I see two other problems, both of which are rather frightening. One is the growth of *something* that produces hysterical, brainwashed groups. Whether it's Vietnam or South Africa or anything you like, *something* produces groups of people who are just not interested in reason, or argument, or even old-fashioned heckling, but who are ready to stampede into violence at the drop of a hat. From what I saw on my election tour, there are no spontaneous eruptions – there is something organized. In the old days, if you'd talked like this people would have said that you were the kind of fellow who sees a Communist under every bed. Well, Communism, in the sense in which we used to use the term, is no longer a very relevant factor – and in the days when Communists used to do battle with Ernest Bevin and Arthur Deakin they fought in ways quite different from those of the violent, instant 'demo'. It is not Communist organization that I mean. There's a whole collection of things, Maoist, Trotskyist, Anarchist, heaven knows what – and the titles haven't got much meaning – which nowadays seems able to call on some central direction to organize instant protest about anything. These groups I'm talking about seem to know exactly where to go in any given area, and they can put on quite an act.

There aren't very many of them at any time. The rowdiest meeting I had was at Colchester, where we had physically to fight our way out of the hall. The violent ones were, I suppose, students of some sort, and they may have come from Essex University, though I have no means of knowing. I left one long-haired young man who had been shoving me about in no uncertain fashion very surprised indeed when he found himself lying on the floor as a result of the accidental collision of his chin with my fist. He promptly ran out of the hall and held an impromptu Press Conference to announce that George Brown had hit him. The important thing about this incident was that the violence shown by a few alienated practically everybody. For the first time in my life, the Press men covering my trip earned my whole-hearted admiration – all of them, without a moment's pause, went into physical combat on our behalf.

This organization of instant violence is one phenomenon. The other, which is related to it, although often not directly, is a terrifying

s

willingness among ordinary people to let who will, lead. People just don't bother their heads about the kind of leaders they are getting, or the kind of policies that are put forward in their name. This is quite new to me in the trade union and Labour movement.

People seem willing to allow anybody to say or do anything, provided that it doesn't create too much of a headache or a nuisance for themselves. With earnings as high as they are, and with plenty of opportunities to make good any shortfall, too many people just don't seem to bother if the leadership in an industrial dispute is extreme, or contrary to their own real wishes. If you are called out on strike now, it's not like the old days – you don't have to worry about the rent or mortgage because they'll be suspended, you don't have to worry about your wife and children because they'll be taken care of by social security. You don't even have to bother much about whether your union is going to give you strike pay or not, because there are various sources of income open to you, like a bit of window-cleaning, and you don't necessarily have to tell the Tax Inspector exactly what you earn. And if you stay out a couple of weeks, the Chancellor starts paying back the tax money which – in your view – he quite improperly took away from you in the first instance.

Of course, there are still people who suffer severely in a strike, but for quite a lot of people a strike nowadays is just another form of paid holiday. As long as people are not kept out too long, it is all too easy for irresponsible leaders, or leadership which does not really represent its members' views, to call a strike. And if going back to work is likely to involve physical violence with an extremist minority, it is all too easy to decide to keep out of the way.

These are two particular problems which seem to me already serious in themselves and likely to become more serious. I do not know an answer for either. I suppose that if the pendulum of violence swings too far, then one day it will swing back again; but the repression that may come about before that happens is not good to contemplate.

The best hope seems to be in the young, the sixteen- and seventeen-year-olds. In my own election campaign I found that it was the boys and girls in this age-group who were keenest to participate, who really wanted to know what it was all about and who were ready to work and to help. When these become young marrieds, I think that in many subtle ways they will be different from the young marrieds of our present generation. They will want to read more for themselves, to listen more, to make up their own minds and not be content to accept whatever is offered to them in the name of leadership. I have immense confidence in these youngsters. When they become the pacemakers of society, I think that we shall have the beginnings of a new and much healthier society – unless the Tories, blast their hides, succeed over the next five years in cutting back standards and putting us all back where we started from.

But, my God, there are dreadful influences to fight against. Press and television, all the mass media, have reached a lower level than I have known in my whole life so far. They can hardly ever be persuaded to present an issue in a clear and rational way. Their paymaster is the advertiser, and there is a constant fight for the lowest possible standard of entertainment to secure the largest amount of passive viewing or readership. I sometimes think that the level of supporting entertainment is deliberately brought down to make the commercial advertisement seem worth looking at. If I were asked to put a date on when the rot in our society set in, I'd say without hesitation that it began with the introduction of commercial television. And the BBC, which is supposed to be immune to commercial pressures, is as bad as the rest, because if it doesn't reduce its own standards to the level of the others it won't get its precious audience-ratings. And now the Tories want to bring in commercial radio for no better reason than to let a few people make fortunes out of it. It's a terrifying prospect.

All this helps to promote a society which genuinely prefers mediocrity. There is less and less room for what people call (for want of a better word) 'characters' in Parliament, in the Press, in every walk of life. And yet . . . and yet . . . if my own life proves anything, it proves that people still respond to convictions passionately held. I've done a good many quite ridiculous things in my life, and yet as I go about the country I find that my standing – and I say this without self-satisfaction or conceit – remains pretty high. Why? Well, I think more than anything else it is because people say, 'Well, you know, he didn't mind leaving the bloody Government, he doesn't mind getting kicked out of Parliament, just surviving isn't for him, the be-all and end-all of existence.'

APPENDICES, NOTES
AND INDEX

APPENDIX I

Text of the United Nations Security Council Resolution 242,
adopted by the Security Council on 22 November 1967

The Security Council

EXPRESSING its continuing concern with the grave situation in the Middle East.

EMPHASIZING the inadmissibility of the acquisition of territory by war and the need to work for a just and lasting peace in which every State in the area can live in security.

EMPHASIZING further that all Member States in their acceptance of the Charter of the United Nations have undertaken a commitment to act in accordance with Article 2 of the Charter.

1. AFFIRMS that the fulfilment of Charter principles requires the establishment of a just and lasting peace in the Middle East which should include the application of both the following principles:

  (i) Withdrawal of Israeli armed forces from territories occupied in the recent conflict;

  (ii) Termination of all claims or states of belligerency and respect for and acknowledgement of the sovereignty, territorial integrity and political independence of every State in the area and their right to live in peace within secure and recognized boundaries free from threats or acts of force;

2. AFFIRMS further the necessity

  (a) For guaranteeing freedom of navigation through international waterways in the area;

  (b) For achieving a just settlement of the refugee problem;

  (c) For guaranteeing the territorial inviolability and political independence of every State in the area, through measures including the establishment of demilitarized zones;

3. REQUESTS the Secretary-General to designate a Special Representative to proceed to the Middle East to establish and maintain contacts with the States concerned in order to promote agreement and assist efforts to achieve a peaceful and accepted settlement in accordance with the provisions and principles in this resolution;

4. REQUESTS the Secretary-General to report to the Security Council on the progress of the efforts of the Special Representative as soon as possible.

APPENDIX II

Letter from The Hon. Henry Kissinger, Special Assistant to the President for National Security Affairs

The White House,
Washington.
November 7, 1970.

Dear George:

I have been reading with pleasure excerpts from your unsurprisingly refreshing memoirs in the London *Sunday Times*. In them you make one statement, however, that has happily proven unfounded – your view that appointing John Freeman as Ambassador here was one of your rare mistakes as Foreign Secretary.

I can tell you that just the opposite is true, that indeed you can consider this appointment one of the wisest decisions you made. Starting out his assignment under somewhat of a cloud, John has moved with great skill and charm to gain the admiration of all of us here. He is not only a highly able and effective representative of your country – we have come to expect that of British Ambassadors – he is a man with very fine human qualities. I count him a close friend as well as respected colleague.

Warm regards,
(Sgd.) HENRY A. KISSINGER

The Rt. Hon. Lord George-Brown,
House of Lords,
London, S.W.1.

BIOGRAPHICAL NOTES

These notes make no attempt to be comprehensive. They are intended as a brief biographical guide where full explanations are not given in the text.

ATTLEE, The Rt. Hon. Earl, Clement Richard
1883–1967.
Secretary Toynbee Hall 1910. 1st Labour Mayor of Stepney 1919–20. M.P. (Lab) Limehouse Div. of Stepney 1922–50 and West Walthamstow 1950–55. P.P.S. to Leader of Opposition (Ramsay MacDonald) 1922–24. Posts held included Deputy Leader Labour Party 1931–35. Leader of Opposition 1935–40. Deputy Prime Minister 1942–45. Prime Minister 1945–51. Minister of Defence 1945–46. Leader of Opposition 1951–55.

BACON, The Rt. Hon. Alice Martha. Baroness
M.P. (Lab) N.E. Leeds 1945–55 and S.E. Leeds 1955–70. Minister of State Home Office 1964–67. Joint Minister of State Dept. of Education and Science 1967–70. Member of Labour Party National Executive Committee from 1941 and its Chairman 1950–51.

BEAVAN, John Cowburn. Now Lord Ardwick
1910–.
Journalist. London Editor *Manchester Guardian* 1946. Asst. Director Nuffield Foundation 1955. Editor *Daily Herald* 1960–62. Political Adviser to Daily Mirror Group since 1962.

BEVAN, The Rt. Hon. Aneurin
1897–1960.
Miner. M.P. (Lab) Ebbw Vale 1929–60. Treasurer of Labour

Party from 1956. Minister of Health 1945–51. Minister of Labour and National Service 1951. Resigned 1951.

BEVIN, The Rt. Hon. Ernest
1881–1951.
National Organiser of Dockers' Union 1910–21. General Secretary T.G.W.U. 1921–40. Member of T.U.C. General Council 1925–40 and its Chairman 1937. M.P. (Lab) Central Wandsworth 1940–50 and E. Woolwich 1950–51. Minister of Labour and National Service 1940–45. Foreign Secretary 1945–51.

BUTLER OF SAFFRON WALDEN, Lord, Richard Austen
1902–.
Now Master of Trinity College, Cambridge. M.P. (C) Saffron Walden 1929–65. Many Ministerial appointments including Chancellor of the Exchequer 1951–55, Home Secretary 1957–62, Deputy Prime Minister 1962–63 and Foreign Secretary 1963–64.

CLAY, Harold Ewart
1886–1961.
President of Workers' Educational Association for 15 years. Chairman of London Labour Party 1933–48. Asst. General Secretary T.G.W.U. Member of Labour Party National Executive Committee 1941–48. Member of British Transport Commission 1948–53.

COLLICK, Percy Henry
General Purposes Committee T.U.C. 1930–34. Asst. General Secretary Associated Society of Locomotive Engineers 1940–57. Member of Labour Party Executive Committee 1944. M.P. (Lab) West Birkenhead 1945–50 and Birkenhead 1950–64. Joint Parl. Secretary Ministry of Agriculture, 1945–47.

CRIPPS, The Rt. Hon. Sir (Richard) Stafford
1889–1952.
Barrister. M.P. (Lab) E. Bristol 1931–50 and S.E. Bristol 1950. Solicitor-General 1930–31. H.M. Ambassador in Moscow 1940–42. Lord Privy Seal and Leader of House of Commons 1942. Minister of Aircraft Production 1942–45. President Board of Trade 1945. Minister of Economic Affairs 1947. Chancellor of the Exchequer 1947–50.

COUSINS, The Rt. Hon. Frank
1904–.
General Secretary T.G.W.U. 1956–69. Seconded as Minister of Technology 1964–66. M.P. (Lab) Nuneaton 1965–66. Resigned

over Prices and Incomes Bill. Member of T.U.C. General Council 1956–69. Chairman Community Relations Commission 1968–70.

CROOKSHANK, The Rt. Hon. Viscount, Harry Frederick Comfort 1893–1961.
Member of Foreign Service 1919–1924. M.P. (U) Gainsborough 1924–56. Parl. Under-Secretary Home Office 1934–35. Secretary of Mines 1935–39. Financial Secretary 1939–43. Postmaster-General 1943–45. Minister of Health 1951–52. Leader of House of Commons 1951–55. Lord Privy Seal 1952–55.

CUDLIPP, Hugh 1910–.
Journalist. Chairman Odhams Press Ltd. 1961–63. Chairman Daily Mirror Newspapers Ltd 1963–68. Chairman International Publishing Corporation since 1968.

DALTON, The Rt. Hon. Lord, Edward Hugh John Neale 1887–1962.
Barrister and University lecturer. M.P. (Lab) Camberwell (Peckham Div.) 1924–29 and Bishop Auckland Div. 1929–31 and 1935–59. Parl. Under-Secretary Foreign Office 1929–31. Chairman of Labour Party Executive Committee 1936–37. Minister of Economic Warfare 1940–42. President Board of Trade 1942–45. Chancellor of the Exchequer 1945–47. Chancellor of the Duchy of Lancaster 1948–50. Minister of Town and Country Planning 1950–51. Minister of Local Government and Planning 1951.

DEAKIN, The Rt. Hon. Arthur 1890–1955.
Acting General Secretary T.G.W.U. 1940–46, General Secretary 1946–55. President T.U.C. 1951–52.

DOUGLAS-HOME, The Rt. Hon. Sir Alec 1903–.
Disclaimed peerage in 1963. M.P. (U) South Lanark 1931–45, M.P. (C) Lanark 1950–51 and Kinross and West Perthshire 1963–. Ministerial appointments held include Commonwealth Secretary 1955–60, Foreign Secretary 1960–63 and Prime Minister, 1963–64. Leader of Opposition 1964–65. Foreign Secretary since 1970.

EDEN, The Rt. Hon. Anthony Robert. Now 1st Earl of Avon 1897–.
M.P. (C) Warwick and Leamington 1923–57. Ministerial

appointments held include Foreign Secretary 1935–38, 1940–45 and 1951–55, and Prime Minister 1955–57.

EVANS, Sir Trevor

1902–,

Boy from South Wales mining village who became leader of the corps of industrial correspondents writing for the national press. Industrial correspondent of the *Daily Express* for many years. Outstanding figure of the industrial correspondents' group recording affairs of the Labour and trade union movement. His distinction recognised by way of a Knighthood and Directorship of Beaverbrook Newspapers Ltd.

FOLLICK, Dr Mont

1887–1958.

Professor of English. Advocate of English spelling reform and decimal currency. M.P. (Lab) Loughborough 1945–55. Secretary to Aga Khan, Sir Robert Philip (Prime Minister of Queensland) and Muley Hafid (Emperor of Morocco).

GAITSKELL, The Rt. Hon. Hugh Todd Naylor

1906–1963.

M.P. (Lab) S. Leeds 1945–63. Principal Private Secretary to Minister of Economic Warfare 1940–42. Principal Assistant Secretary Board of Trade 1942–45. Parl. Secretary Ministry of Fuel and Power 1946–47. Minister of Fuel and Power 1947–50. Minister of State for Economic Affairs 1950. Chancellor of the Exchequer 1950–51. Leader of the Labour Party 1955–63.

GOOCH, Alderman Edwin George

1889–1964.

President of National Union of Agricultural Workers from 1928. M.P. (Lab) Northern Norfolk from 1945.

GORDON WALKER, The Rt. Hon. Patrick Chrestien

1907–.

M.P. (Lab) Smethwick 1945–64 and Leyton from 1966. P.P.S. to Herbert Morrison 1946. Commonwealth Secretary 1950–51. Foreign Secretary 1964–65. Secretary of State for Education and Science 1967–68.

GREENWOOD, The Rt. Hon. Anthony. Now Lord Greenwood of Rossendale

1911–.

M.P. (Lab) Heywood and Radcliffe 1946–50, Rossendale 1950–70. Colonial Secretary 1964–65. Minister of Overseas Development 1965–66. Minister of Housing and Local Government 1966–70. Member of Labour Party Executive Committee 1954–70, Vice-Chairman 1962–63, Chairman 1963–64.

GRIFFITHS, The Rt. Hon. James
1890–.
M.P. (Lab) Llanelly Div. of Co. of Carmarthen 1936–70. Member of Executive Committee of Miners' Federation 1934–36. Minister of National Insurance 1945–50. Colonial Secretary 1950–51. Secretary of State for Wales 1964–66. Member of Labour Party Executive Committee 1939–59 and its Chairman 1948–49. Deputy Leader and Vice-Chairman of Parl. Labour Party 1955–59.

GRIFFITHS, William
1912–.
Consulting Ophthalmic Optician. M.P. (Lab) Moss Side Div of Manchester 1945–50 and Exchange Div. of Manchester since 1950. P.P.S. to Minister of Health 1950–51 and to Minister of Labour 1951.

HACKETT, Sir Maurice (Frederick)
1905–.
Brother-in-law of author; married Deborah Levene who died 1969. 1st National Chairman Labour Party League of Youth. Chairman: Southgate, South Kensington, Barnet and Herts Labour Parties, Barnet Group Hospital Management Committee 1960–62, S.W. Middx. Hospital Management Committee 1962–65, S.E. Region Economic Planning Council since 1966, N.W. Metropolitan Regional Hospital Board since 1965 (member since 1949).

HERBISON, The Rt. Hon. Margaret McCrorie
1907–.
M.P. (Lab) North Lanark 1945–70. Minister of Pensions and National Insurance 1964–66 and Minister of Social Security 1966–67. Member of Labour Party Executive Committee and its Chairman in 1957.

ISAACS, The Rt. Hon. George Alfred
1883–.
Secretary of National Society of Operative Printers and Assistants 1909–49. Former President Printing and Kindred Trades Federation. M.P. (Lab) Gravesend 1923–24, N. Southwark 1929–31 and 1939–50, Southwark 1950–59. Ministerial appointments held

include Minister of Labour and National Service 1945–51 and Minister of Pensions 1951. Chairman T.U.C. 1945. President World Trade Union Conference 1945.

JAY, The Rt. Hon. Douglas Patrick Thomas
1907–.
Journalist. M.P. (Lab) North Battersea since 1946. Economic Secretary to Treasury 1947–50. Financial Secretary 1950–51. President of Board of Trade 1964–67.

KING, Cecil Harmsworth
1901–.
Chairman: Daily Mirror Newspapers Ltd and Sunday Pictorial Newspapers Ltd 1951–63, and International Publishing Corporation 1963–68.

LANSBURY, The Rt. Hon. George
1859–1940.
M.P. (Lab) Bow and Bromley Div. of Poplar 1910–12 and from 1922. Formerly Editor of *Daily Herald*. First Commissioner of Works 1929–31. Leader of Labour Party 1931–35.

LASKI, Harold J.
1893–1950.
Writer and University lecturer. Long association with Labour Party. Member of Labour Party Executive Committee 1936–49 and its Chairman 1945–46.

LAWTHER, Sir William
1889–.
Former President National Union of Miners and T.U.C. Former Secretary of Miners International. M.P. (Lab) Barnard Castle 1929–31. Member National Labour Party Executive Committee 1923–26. Member of T.U.C. General Council 1935–54.

LEE, The Rt. Hon. Frederick
1906–.
M.P. (Lab) Hulme Div. of Manchester 1945–50 and Newton Div. of Lancs from 1950. Minister of Power 1964–66, Colonial Secretary 1966–67 and Chancellor of the Duchy of Lancaster 1967–69.

MACDONALD, The Rt. Hon. James Ramsay
1866–1937.
M.P. (Lab) Leicester 1906–18, Aberavon Div. of Glamorganshire 1922–29, Seaham Div. of Co. Durham 1929–31, and (Nat. Lab) 1931–45. Chairman Independent Labour Party 1906–9.

Leader of Labour Party 1911–14. Chairman Parl. Labour Party and Leader of Opposition 1922. Prime Minister and Foreign Secretary 1924. Prime Minister 1929–35. Lord President of the Council 1935–37.

MACKAY, Ian
1898–1952.
Journalist who was confidante and friend of many leaders of the Labour Movement. Industrial correspondent of the *News Chronicle* for many years.

MACLEOD, The Rt. Hon. Iain Norman
1913–1970.
M.P. (C) Enfield West 1950–70. Minister of Health 1952–55. Minister of Labour and National Service 1955–59. Colonial Secretary 1959–61. Chancellor of the Duchy of Lancaster and Leader of the House of Commons 1961–63. Editor of the *Spectator* 1963–65. Chancellor of the Exchequer 1970.

MACMILLAN, The Rt. Hon. Harold
1894–.
M.P. (U) Stockton-on-Tees 1924–29 and 1931–45, and M.P. (C) Bromley 1945–64. Ministerial appointments held include Minister of Defence 1954–55, Foreign Secretary 1955, Chancellor of the Exchequer 1955–57 and Prime Minister 1957–63.

McNEIL, The Rt. Hon. Hector
1907–1951.
Journalist. M.P. (Lab) Burgh of Greenock from 1941. Held junior Ministerial posts at Ministry of War Transport and Foreign Office. Secretary of State for Scotland 1950–51.

MAUDLING, The Rt. Hon. Reginald
1917–.
M.P. (C) Barnet Div. of Herts since 1950. Ministerial appointments held include President of Board of Trade 1959–61, Colonial Secretary 1961–62 and Chancellor of the Exchequer 1962–64. Deputy Prime Minister and Home Secretary from 1970.

MEANY, George
1894–.
American labour leader. Since 1955 President American Federation of Labor and Congress of Industrial Organizations (AFL/CIO).

MORRISON OF LAMBETH, Lord, Herbert Stanley
1888–1965.
Secretary of London Labour Party 1915–47, Treasurer 1948–62.

Mayor of Hackney 1920–21. M.P. (Lab) South Hackney 1923–24, 1929–31 and 1935–45, East Lewisham 1945–51 and South Lewisham 1951–59. Minister of Transport 1929–31. Minister of Supply 1940. Home Secretary 1940–45. Deputy Prime Minister 1945–51. Lord President of the Council and Leader of the House of Commons 1945–51. Foreign Secretary Mar.–Oct. 1951. Deputy Leader of Opposition 1951–55.

NENNI, Senator Pietro
1891–.
Italian politician and journalist. Secretary General Italian Socialist Party 1944–63. Foreign Minister 1946–47 and 1968–69. Deputy Prime Minister 1963–68. Former President Partito Socialista Italiano. Life Senator.

PHILLIPS, Morgan Walter
1902–1963.
Served Labour Party throughout his life. Secretary/Agent to many Local Labour Parties. Joined Labour Party Headquarters 1937. General Secretary of Labour Party 1944–62. Chairman Socialist International 1948–57.

REUTHER, Victor G.
1912–.
Brother of Walter Reuther. American labour union executive. Administrative Assistant to President of United Automobile Workers (UAW) and Director of its International Affairs Department.

REUTHER, Walter Philip
1907–1970.
Brother of Victor Reuther. American labour leader. President United Automobile Workers (UAW) since 1946. President of parent union Congress of Industrial Organizations (CIO) 1952. Led UAW split in 1968; allied his 1,300,000 members with Teamsters Union in 1969.

REYNOLDS, The Rt. Hon. Gerald William
1927–1969.
M.P. (Lab) Islington North 1958–69. Minister of Defence for the Army 1965–67 and Minister of Defence for Administration 1967–69.

ROBENS OF WOLDINGHAM, The Rt. Hon. Lord, Alfred
1910–.
Chairman National Coal Board since 1961. Officer of Union of

Distributive and Allied Workers 1935–45. M.P. (Lab) Wansbeck Div. of Northumberland 1945–50 and Blyth 1950–60. P.P.S. to Minister of Transport 1945–47. Parl. Secretary Ministry of Fuel and Power 1947–51. Minister of Labour and National Service 1951.

SMUTS, Field-Marshal Jan Christiaan
1870–1950.
South African soldier and statesman. A Boer leader in the Boer War 1899–1902. Largely instrumental in effecting Union of South Africa. Its Prime Minister 1919–24 and 1939. Minister of Justice 1933–39.

SNOWDEN OF ICKORNSHAW, The Rt. Hon. Viscount, Philip
1864–1937.
Civil Service 1886–93. Retired to journalism and lecturing. M.P. (Soc) Blackburn 1906–18 and Colne Valley Div. of Yorks 1922–31. Chairmen of Independent Labour Party 1903–6 and 1917–20. Chancellor of the Exchequer 1924 and 1929–31.

STANLEY, The Rt. Hon. Oliver Frederick George
1896–1950.
M.P. (C) Westmorland 1924–45 and Bristol West from 1945. Parl. Under Secretary Home Office 1931–33. Minister of Transport 1933–34. Minister of Labour 1934–35. President of Board of Educ. 1935–37. President of Board of Trade 1937–40. Secretary of State for War 1940. Colonial Secretary 1942–45.

STEWART, Sir Iain Maxwell
1916–.
Chairman Fairfields (Glasgow) Ltd 1966–68. Deputy Chairman Upper Clyde Shipbuilders Ltd 1967–68. Chairman Hall-Thermotank Ltd. Deputy Chairman Scottish Television Ltd. Director of many companies.

STRACHEY, The Rt. Hon. Evelyn John St Loe
1901–1963.
M.P. (Lab) Aston Div. of Birmingham 1929–31, Dundee 1945–50 and West Dundee 1950–63. Resigned from Parl. Labour Party in 1931. Parl. Under Secretary Air Ministry 1945–46. Minister of Food 1946–50. Secretary of State for War 1950–51.

STRAUSS, The Rt. Hon. George Russell
1901–.
M.P. (Lab) North Lambeth 1929–31 and 1934–50, Vauxhall Div. of Lambeth 1950. P.P.S. to Minister of Transport 1929–31 and

T

to Lord Privy Seal and later Minister of Aircraft Production 1942–45. Parl. Secretary Ministry of Transport 1945–47. Minister of Supply 1947–51.

THOMAS, The Rt. Hon. James Henry
1874–1949.
M.P. (Lab) Derby 1910–31 and (Nat Lab) 1931–36. President International Federation of Trade Unions 1920–24. General Secretary National Union of Railwaymen 1918–24 and 1925–31. Ministerial appointments held include Dominions Secretary 1930–35 and Colonial Secretary 1935–36. Vice Chairman Parl. Labour Party 1921.

THOMSON OF FLEET, Lord, Roy Herbert
1894–.
Chairman: The Thomson Organization Ltd (and subsidiaries including *The Times* and *Sunday Times*), The Scotsman Publications Ltd, Thomson Newspapers Ltd, Canada. Founder of The Thomson Foundation.

TIFFIN, Arthur Ernest [Jock]
1896–1955.
General Secretary T.G.W.U. 1955. Member of T.U.C. General Council 1955.

TILLETT, Benjamin
1860–1943.
Secretary of Dock, Wharf, Riverside and General Workers Union from its inception in 1887 to its amalgamation with the T.G.W.U. in 1922. M.P. (Lab) N. Salford 1917–24 and 1929–31. Chairman T.U.C. 1928–29.

WATSON, Samuel
1898–1967.
Secretary Durham Miners' Association 1936–63. Member: Council of Durham University, Labour Party, Durham Co. Executive Council. Part-time member: National Coal Board and Central Electricity Generating Board.

WILLIAMS OF BARNBURGH, Lord, Thomas
1888–1967.
M.P. (Lab) Don Valley Div. of Yorks 1922–59. P.P.S. to Minister of Agriculture 1924 and to Minister of Labour 1929–31. Parl. Secretary Ministry of Agriculture 1940–45. Minister of Agriculture 1945–51.

WILLIAMSON, Lord, Thomas

1897–.

M.P. (Lab) Brigg Div. of Lincoln and Rutland 1945–48. General Secretary National Union of General and Municipal Workers 1946–61. Member of Labour Party Executive Committee 1940–47. Member T.U.C. General Council 1947–62 and its Chairman 1956–57.

WILLIS, Lord, Edward Henry

1918–.

Joined Labour League of Youth in 1934, later becoming its National Chairman. Founded National Youth paper *Advance*. Has always been an active member of the Labour Party. Playwright (as Ted Willis). Was writer of War Office films and Ministry of Information documentaries. Television scriptwriter. Films. Publications. President Screenwriters' Guild 1958–68.

INDEX